BASED ON A TRUE STORY

NO ORDINARY SUNDAY

BASED ON A TRUE STORY

One Sunday, unimaginable tragedy tore our family apart… *but God was still in control*

CHERYL BATTLE-FREEMAN

No Ordinary Sunday

Editing and Interior Design by Katherine Editorials
Graphic design by Usama/IBEX Concept
Book Cover by Awan Designer

eBook ISBN: 979-8-9896929-0-3
paperback ISBN: 979-8-9896929-1-0
hardcover ISBN: 979-8-9896929-2-7

1. Main Category – Non-Fiction Memoir
2. Other Category – Inspirational
3. Other Category – Christianity

First Edition

I dedicate this book in memory of my big brother,
George Anthony Battle.

*Through your death,
I was awakened to my purpose.*

NO ORDINARY SUNDAY
BASED ON A TRUE STORY

One Sunday, unimaginable tragedy tore our family apart…
but God was still in control.

PREFACE
"Spared on Purpose"

Many fond memories are made and shared on Sundays, making it one of the most special and anticipated days of the week.

For those fortunate enough to be off from work that day, Sundays can be a welcomed day of rest, reserved for kicking back and relaxing—watching movies, reading the newspaper or a good book, or simply catching up on some much-needed sleep in preparation for the new week.

Still, for others, Sunday can turn out to be one of the busiest yet most well-spent days of the weekend as people find themselves engaging in all kinds of activities ranging from attending worship services to spending quality time with family and friends, completing projects and assignments, and so on.

As kids, my brothers and I really looked forward to Sunday because it meant 'extended' playtime, and ordinarily, we'd spend the latter part of the day, after church, running around outside, laughing, and playing with our friends until nighttime.

However, one Sunday in August 1973 proved to be anything but ordinary, as an unimaginable tragedy changed our family forever.

For years after that day, I questioned my existence.

"Why am I still here?"

I became convinced that God Himself had abandoned me and my family.

After all, He's in control of all things and could have stopped the things that tore us apart.

But since He didn't, to me, that meant that He either didn't care or just had completely forgotten about our family.

So much has transpired since August 26, 1973, including a changed mindset for me, and it is my sincere desire that the deeply personal story relayed throughout the pages of this book will encourage and inspire others.

That fateful Sunday, life as my family and I knew it was altered forever.

However, what never changed was God's Plan for us, for He was at work even then amid our greatest tragedy.

His Plan shows how very intentional and purposeful He is about what He allows.

Here is my story.

CHAPTER ONE

OUR NORMAL

DADDY HAD ALREADY LEFT FOR WORK

After serving several years in the U.S. Army, he'd accepted a position with the largest steel mill in town. Working at least five days a week, plus a lot of overtime, he earned a good enough salary so that Mama could stay at home with us kids. Daddy's shift began early in the morning and often stretched well into the late evening. Generally, we didn't see him until around dinnertime, and sometimes not even until the next day, whenever he'd signed up to work a double shift.

Although Mama didn't work outside the home, she had more than enough work to do, taking care of me, 6 at the time, and my two brothers, Chris, 5, and George, 9.

Keeping our household together was a chore, and Mama would sometimes seem so sad. At other times, she'd look upset as if someone had made her angry, though she seldom lost her temper with us. In fact, when we'd get into trouble for acting up, most times Mama would just give us a firm talking to or would tell Daddy when we'd misbehave, leaving it up to him to punish us. However, on rare occasions, Mama's chastisement was extreme, and she would pull out a belt or even an extension cord and hit us several times, using long, hard whips.

Wanting to avoid those spankings at all costs, my brothers and I did our best to behave and not upset Mama to the point of her whooping us.

George, Chris, and I mostly bickered when trying to decide what to watch on the only television in the house or when placing the blame for a big mess that one of us had made. George, however, being the voice of reason, would settle most of our arguments. I really looked up to my big brother.

I would be going to school for the first time in a couple of weeks, entering Kindergarten. I wasn't too afraid because I would be attending the same school as George, who was slated to begin fourth grade, and Chris would continue to stay at home with Mama until he was also old enough to go to school.

Along with taking care of me and my brothers, Mama, almost by herself, kept our house nice and clean. Residing on the northeast side of Houston, we lived in a modest three-bedroom, one-bath brick home. Mama did a great job decorating our entire home, with just the right mix of furniture and colors to make anyone feel right at home. Because I was the only girl, I had my own room, while my brothers shared a room, which was no big deal for them since they liked hanging out and playing together anyway.

Their bedroom had the typical boy flare, with slate blue paint adorning the walls. Even their bed linen: pillows, sheets, and comforters gave off a 'boy-town' appeal, as did the assortment of hot wheel cars and action figures often strewn all over the wood floor during playtime.

My room was decorated just right for me, and I loved it! The walls, the furniture, and even the bed linen were a vibrant pastel pink color. A nightstand was situated right beside my bed, with a little pink and white lamp resting on top of it. Just the perfect size for me, my twin bed was so comfortable and was layered near the headboard with several small, solid-colored pink pillows.

Our home was neat and tidy but was also still kid-friendly because Mama allowed us to have fun and spread our toys out and play if we agreed to clean up afterward. Whenever the weather was too bad for us to go outside, we'd enjoy playing in my room or in my brothers' room, and regardless of what we played with, whether it was cars, dolls, or a mix, the three of us would sit and play together for hours.

However, even after some of the fiercest thunderstorms had passed, we'd, without hesitation, when Mama would allow it, that is, head outdoors to splash around in the rainwater. Usually, our goal after it had rained was twofold: first, to stomp around in as much standing rainwater as we could before it disappeared, and second, to make mud pies while the dirt was still moist and saturated with water, making it easy to dig in.

The best days were during summertime because there was no school for George, and we could play outside up until nightfall. At dusk, on Saturdays especially, we would wait for the bats to come out so we could throw rocks at them. You could hear the commotion of kids running and screaming, getting such a thrill out of seeing small, black bats swoop down and then back up out of sight. Admittedly, throwing rocks at bats was not the smartest thing to do, but no one ever got hurt or bitten, so it became almost like a weekend tradition.

Though we enjoyed playing in the front yard and in the street, our favorite place to play was in our enormous backyard! I believe we had the largest backyard on the block, which was perfect for kids because there was more than enough room for all of us to run and play.

Fenced in on all sides, our backyard was covered with green grass from one end to the other. Just how Daddy was able to keep most of the grass growing so well was a mystery to me because we were always trampling all over it, especially during summer.

Near the back wall of our home were a couple of fig trees, which stood nearly twice our height. There was also a plum tree not far away. When the fruit on the trees were in season, we'd pick them right off the branches and eat them, following a quick wash-off with the water hose, of course. Those green plums and soft figs did a good job satisfying our appetites in between meals.

Adding to our selection of treats was a tall pecan tree in our next-door neighbor's yard. Several of its long branches hung over the fence into our backyard. When the pecans fell to the ground, we'd have a grand time cracking them open, tossing the pecans into the air, and trying to catch them with wide-open mouths.

To the left corner of the backyard sat our awesome playground set. Leading up to a winding slide on one side were metal stairs, and to the right of the slide were three chain-linked swings with leather seats: the perfect number for me and my brothers. Our play set brought a lot of our friends on our block over to our house for hours of fun most days of the week during the summer.

To help us cool off, Mama would bring us tall, ice-filled glasses of Kool-Aid (grape and cherry were my favorite flavors) to drink, and it would always be welcomed with huge smiles!

Nobody could make Kool-Aid like Mama because she knew how to perfectly sweeten it to taste! On any given weekend afternoon, you could hear kids laughing and screaming with excitement from our backyard.

I remember the afternoon Daddy came home early from work and surprised us and our friends when he walked through the back gate holding a little, adorable black and brown German Shepherd puppy.

We, with very little deliberation, named him *Shep*.

With big black eyes that sparkled in the sunlight, Shep seemed to grow larger and larger by the day, and in no time, he transformed from a little puppy to a full-grown dog!

It was as if Shep was a kid just like us. Whenever we played in the backyard, Shep was right there, running, jumping, and licking us all over our faces. Even though we'd grimace from the wet, slobbery mess he'd leave on us, we giggled and wanted more of his 'doggy' kisses.

Waking up early on Saturday mornings was no problem for us because the sooner we got up, the more time we'd have to play. On church Sunday mornings, however, Mama often remarked that trying to wake us up was like 'trying to wake the dead.'

Still, on weekends when we didn't have to run errands with Mama or after we'd made it home from church, we'd hurry and get dressed, most of the time throwing on the nearest shorts, t-shirts, and tennis shoes. We had mastered the art of brushing our teeth in record time, barely a minute or less. Eating breakfast was also done quickly as we would gulp down our food, typically consuming either cereal and milk or oatmeal, before we would head outdoors to see which kids were already outside.

Sometimes, I ate a little slower than my brothers, and oh my goodness, how upset they would become!

This Saturday morning was one such time:

"Come on, Cheryl, *man*…finish your food so we can go outside and play!" George said anxiously. That was about the only time George would get impatient with me.

We weren't allowed to go outside until all three of us had finished eating.

"Yeah, hurry up, you eat too slow!" said Chris, then deeply sighing.

"I'm chewing as fast as I can!" I snapped back, with food muffling my speech.

"You don't even have to chew…it's oatmeal! Just swallow it!" Chris stated very matter-of-factly.

He was really starting to irritate me.

As I shoved my spoon into my bowl of oatmeal, I squinted and then rolled my eyes at Chris for rushing me.

"I'm almost finished, Chris… just wait a second!"

Chris grunted and then frowned, folding his arms while he continued to stare at me.

The truth is, I wanted to get outside just as badly as my brothers did, so after gobbling down the last of my oatmeal, I jumped up from my seat, ran over to the kitchen sink and tossed my bowl and spoon into it.

Barely washing my hands and mouth, I made a mad dash for the living room. My brothers and I tried to outrun each other as we all bolted out the front door, pushing the front screen door open so widely that it banged against the bricks on the side wall of the front porch.

It was funny how quickly we could get over the little spats we'd have because, in the end, we just wanted to have fun.

On the weekends, the agenda was to 'PLAY, PLAY, PLAY!' outside for hours with our friends, only breaking to use the restroom and eat lunch.

It was early Saturday morning, and we had the entire day ahead of us to mill around with our friends.

Our community was a mix of Black and White people, with there being considerably more African Americans. We loved that there were quite a few families on our block that had kids around our age.

The grownups watched out for all of us kids as if we were one big family. There were also older kids around, and they, too, would keep their eyes on us. Our neighborhood street felt like having a lot of big brothers and sisters you weren't really related to.

"Let's go see if Caren and James can come outside and play," I said, following my brothers into the street.

Caren and James were siblings who lived diagonally across the street from us.

We ran across the street and knocked on their front door to ask if our friends could come out and play. After just one knock, they opened the door, laughing.

"Can you come outside?" George asked with a smile of anticipation.

"Yeah, let me put my shoes on," said James, running towards the back of his house to his room to grab a pair of sneakers while Caren stepped out onto their front porch where we were standing.

James was the oldest, about ten years of age, and Caren was six years old, about to turn 7 in a couple of months.

James burst through the door, and we all headed out to the street.

"What do you want to do?" George asked.

"Hey, I have a bat and a ball. We can play with that," said Caren.

"Ok, go get it!" George eagerly responded. "Where is it?"

"It's in my garage. I'll be right back," Caren said, turning and running back towards her house.

The rest of us stood there talking and laughing, waiting near the edge of the driveway for Caren to come back.

It was another typical August afternoon, with the temperature warming quickly.

The sun was beaming down on us, causing sweat to form on our brow. We didn't care about the heat, though. We'd been outdoors in hot weather practically all summer.

A few minutes later, Caren came jogging back towards us with a bat and ball in hand.

"Okay, let's play," she said, tossing the ball high up in the air, causing all of us to giggle and scramble for it.

In the middle of the street, the five of us played ball, taking turns throwing the ball and swinging the bat.

A little while later, two more of our friends, Kyla and Andrew, came out, and there was now a group of seven of us playing ball, racing up and down the street.

"You want to go and play in our backyard?" Chris asked.

"Yes!" "Yeah!" exclaimed all of us, almost simultaneously.

We all ran to our house and then along the concrete sidewalk that ran along the side of our house, leading to the back gate, which opened to our backyard.

Chris, detouring, ran inside our house to get some more toys for us.

We stood on the back porch and could hear Mama talking to Chris.

"What are you doing? Why are you not outside playing with the other kids?" asked Mama as Chris hurried past her, headed towards his and George's bedroom.

"I'm just getting some stuff for us!" Chris replied excitedly, barely stopping to answer her.

"Don't you take a lot of toys outside, Chris!" Mama yelled back.

"Yes ma'am!" Chris said, just glad Mama didn't make him stop and turn around.

In the past, some of our toys had been broken by our friends or even 'borrowed' and never returned.

Chris brought out all kinds of games, little trinkets, toy trucks, etc., dropping it all to the ground because his little arms could no longer carry it all.

Kyla picked up the ball and jacks and began playing with them. There were more than enough toys for all the kids to play with, and those who weren't playing with the toys were busy swinging and sliding on our play set.

At least 3 hours had passed, and it was now getting close to lunchtime.

Mama opened the back door, stuck her head out and called for us to come inside so we could eat. Sometimes Mama would invite the other kids to eat with us, but I guess there wasn't enough food to go around that day because she didn't offer them anything.

"George, you all need to come in and eat. Tell your friends to come back later."

"Yes, ma'am," George replied.

"Hi, Miss Faye!" the kids said, waving at Mama.

"Hi," Mama responded back, barely glancing at the kids before closing the door.

I thought Mama must not have been feeling well. She was usually much friendlier to the kids.

"Hey, you guys," George said to all of us, "It's time for us to eat lunch. Can y'all come back in a little while when we're finished?"

"Yeah, I'm hungry too," said Caren, heading towards the back gate.

"Me too," said Andrew, chiming in, dropping the ball he'd been playing with and walking behind Caren, followed by Kyla.

"Ok, we'll be back later after we eat something too. Y'all should be finished around then too," said James.

"It won't take us long, okay, so you'll go and hurry up and eat too and come back so we can play some more," George said.

He didn't want our friends to find something else to do and not come back and play with us.

The kids left to go home and eat, and Chris, George, and I went inside to wash up and have lunch.

Mama made chilidogs!

"All right, chili dogs!" I said with a huge smile on my face.

"Thank you, Mama!" said George, showing all his teeth, so happy too that Mama had fixed one of his favorite meals.

"Thank you," said Chris, reaching for his chili dog on his plate.

Mama was busy wiping up some water that had spilled onto the kitchen counter. Looking up briefly, Mama glanced in our direction but didn't say anything.

She'd usually smile or say, "You are welcome, baby," or *something*, but today, nothing. Turning back around, she continued to soak up the water with a towel.

'Mama must really have a lot on her mind,' I thought to myself.

This Saturday, except for passing by Mama during the occasional trip to the bathroom, we didn't see much of her at all. Normally, she would peak her head outside the door every so often just to check on us, but I hadn't noticed her doing that at all.

Saturday was Mama's time for cleaning the entire house, so she probably just had so much to do. Meanwhile, we'd returned playing outside.

Waiting until the very last minute, I ran into the house and headed for the bathroom, trying not to pee on myself. Inhaling the fresh smell of Pine O' Pine, I quickly washed my hands after I was done and ran back through the house, heading outdoors.

As I was making my way back to the back door, I noticed Mama standing in the kitchen, staring out of the window situated just above the sink. I guess she had been keeping her eyes on us after all. I could tell she still had to clean the kitchen.

Anyway, it was generally the last area she would tackle. This Saturday was no different in that respect because the kitchen was a bit cluttered as usual, with pots and pans strewn here and there, as if Mama wasn't sure which ones she was going to use.

There were also carrots and celery on the cutting board and a knife nearby, so I thought maybe we were going to have homemade stew for supper.

Daddy really liked Mama's homemade stew, though most times, she would cook that during the winter months when it was cold outside.

Whatever Mama was going to cook for supper, I was sure we would like it because she was a good cook.

It was late Saturday afternoon, and although Mama didn't have much makeup on, she was still beautiful to me. Dressed in a long, emerald green lounge dress, Mama had her shoulder-length hair brushed back so that it rested just below the collar of her gown.

Still looking tired, she opened the back door and called for my brothers and me to come inside. It was nearly dark now, and our friends had just gone home.

We'd had so much fun playing in our backyard that we hadn't

ventured to the front at all that evening.

After a hard day of playing, the three of us gathered the toys Chris had brought out and headed for the back door. Besides Mama calling us in, we knew it was time to retreat inside because from our backyard, we could tell the streetlight in the front of our house was on.

That streetlight was always our signal to call it a day and go indoors, even if Mama or Daddy had forgotten to call us in.

Mama had dinner prepared, and just as I had supposed, we were having beef stew, Daddy's favorite! We were all getting our favorites that day!

What an appetite we'd worked up from all of that running and playing! After washing our hands and faces, we sat there at the table and waited for Mama to bring our plates.

We dug right in!

You could tell that we were very hungry because we hardly said a word at the table. The only sounds we made were those coming from chewing our food and gulping our water.

The stew tasted just as good in the summer as it did in the winter! I cleaned my plate, even being tempted to lick it, but immediately had second thoughts, not wanting Mama to catch me and scold me for doing so. She'd let me know that was not 'proper' to do.

After finishing dinner, my brothers and I took turns taking our baths.

Mama let us watch an hour or so of TV so that our food could digest, and then off to bed we went.

As I settled in under my covers, I thought to myself, 'This is another night that we are going to bed without saying our prayers with Daddy.' He hadn't made it home from work yet.

Mama rarely went to bed at the same time as us, generally having this or that to do. She'd already reminded us that we would be going to church the next morning, so she was no doubt busy getting our clothes and shoes ready.

Sometime during the night, Daddy did make it home, but by then, we were fast asleep and wouldn't see him until the next morning.

CHAPTER TWO

UNRAVELED

SUNDAY, AUGUST 26, 1973, 7:30 A.M.

"Wake up, go wash your faces and brush your teeth. We need to get ready for church," Mama's voice came echoing in a *couple* of times.

Struggling to wake up, we rolled out of our beds, rubbed our eyes, and headed for the bathroom.

Daddy was just leaving for work.

Glad to at least be able to say goodbye, we each took turns hugging him for a moment before he disappeared behind the door, with Mama following closely behind him. I was really hoping he would be able to come home early from work today.

Climbing onto the sofa, I waved at him one more time from behind the open blinds of the front window. It made me feel good when my daddy turned and looked at me, almost as if he'd heard my hands waving.

He smiled back and waved to me.

I missed seeing Daddy; we all did.

Because of his work schedule, we saw him more during the week than on weekends. He tended to work longer shifts on Saturdays and Sundays because then he got more overtime covering the shift of someone who couldn't make it in to work. I guess that's why Daddy hardly ever went to church with us.

We only had one car, and since Daddy used it to get back and forth to work, most times, we'd have to catch a ride to church with one of Mama's friends.

Like clockwork, Mama's friend picked us up at the same time she always did, and we headed to church. Once inside, we sat close to the front of the sanctuary.

When the pastor did an altar call, Mama went up front for prayer while we stayed seated with one of the sisters in the church.

Looking at Mama's eyes, I could tell that she'd been crying.

After being prayed over by the pastor, Mama came back and sat down. Reaching for Chris, she sat him on her lap and fixed her eyes on the front podium.

Several times during the service, with a bowed head and closed eyes, Mama prayed softly and cried to herself. I couldn't understand what she was muttering, but I did spot the tears streaming down her cheek. It made me want to cry too.

I turned away and stared down at my hands.

The service was going on and on, and so I did as my brother Chris had done—I closed my eyes, leaned against Mama's shoulder, and took a nap.

When I woke up, church was over, and it was time to go.

Noticing that George had also fallen asleep, I woke him up by nudging him with my elbow. Looking at each other and stretching, George and I were both glad the church service had finally ended.

We arrived home early enough to still have plenty of time to play outside.

After quickly changing into our play clothes and eating peanut butter and jelly sandwiches for lunch, my brothers and I headed outdoors.

It was another hot August day. The sun was shining brightly, and there wasn't a cloud in the sky.

Mama, after changing out of her church dress and back into the same long green lounge dress she had worn yesterday, went into the kitchen to start preparing for dinner.

It seemed to be kind of early for her to be working on dinner already, but maybe she was planning to cook a big meal to surprise Daddy, so she needed to get an early start. Maybe she was hoping, like I was, that he'd come home early today.

Typically, on Sundays, Mama would play loud church music on the radio, loud enough to be heard outdoors. Sometimes, she would even put one of her favorite church albums on the record player and *CRANK UP the* volume, but this Sunday, it was strangely quiet inside.

Mama was very religious and would read her bible a lot. A couple of times a year, Mama would even attend these church conventions downtown.

Generally, she didn't take us with her and would instead lock us up in the house with our dog, Shep. While she was away, we'd play or watch TV until she got back home, which was always before Daddy returned from work.

He didn't find out until years later that Mama would leave us at home alone like that. I never felt scared, though, because my brothers and I were together.

Mama always seemed to come back home happy after attending one of those conventions. However, she hadn't gone to one of those meetings in a while. My guess was that's probably why she'd been so sad lately; she just needed to go to one of those meetings, and then she'd be happy again.

The entire afternoon after church, Mama remained in the house. Meanwhile, we were busy playing outdoors, in the backyard, with our friends.

Shep had been tied to the big oak tree near the center of our yard since we'd come home from church. A large hole with dirt scattered all around it was near where he'd been sitting in the shade. Sometimes, while watching us play, he'd take a break from digging and would bark and wag his tail, wanting to join in on the fun.

However, Mama, like today, would tie him up because he'd play too rough, causing some of the younger kids to be afraid to play in our backyard.

My brothers and I had just finished making some awesome mud pies by pouring water from the outside faucet on the very dry dirt. We were now hunting for beetles and doodle bugs.

Our friends, who'd played with us most of the afternoon, had already gone home. Their mom sent their big sister to get them.

It was close to 5:00 o'clock.

On most Fridays and Saturdays, Mama would allow us to play outside until the streetlights came on, but rarely on Sundays, so we knew there were only a few more minutes to play.

My brother George unexpectedly stood up, dropping his shovel of dirt and placing his hand on his forehead.

"What's wrong?" I asked as both Chris and I looked up at him, being a little startled by his sudden movement.

He then knocked the dirt off his hands and pants.

"Where are you going?" I asked him, surprised he was getting ready to stop and go inside before Mama had even told us to.

Placing his palm on his forehead again, he replied, "My head all of a sudden just started hurting. I'm going to get something for it from Mama".

"You are coming back, right?" I asked, concerned.

"Yeah, I'll be right back," he said as he headed for the back door.

Satisfied with his answer, I went back to digging in the dirt, searching for more bugs. We weren't ready to go inside just yet, and I hoped George would come right back outside and play with us before it was time for us all to go in and clean up for dinner.

George grabbed the knob to the back door, opened it, stepped inside, and then disappeared out of sight as he closed the door behind him.

I expected to hear George talking to Mama as soon as he walked inside, but she must have been in another part of the house. She wouldn't have seen him walk in but certainly would have heard the door open and shut, knowing that at least one of us was in the house.

Our kitchen opened to the living room. Towards the rear of our home were the remaining two bedrooms, separated by a hallway closet and our only bathroom. The boys' room was to the left of the bathroom, and our parents' room sat on the right side.

I kept digging in the dirt, expecting George to come back outside at any moment.

Some minutes passed after George entered the house, and then I heard a terrible, high-pitched, gut-wrenching scream! It was such a gut-wrenching cry that it caused me to jump to my feet in panic immediately. My heart began racing, feeling like it was beating twice as fast as normal.

"Who in the world was screaming like that!?" I thought.

After standing up, I dropped my shovel and dirt, looking down at Chris. Chris also heard the scream, stopped digging in the dirt and looked up at me. We both were shaken and didn't say one word to each other.

Quickly knocking the dirt off my hands, I instinctively jumped the back fence and took off running on top of the concrete sidewalk, which ran along the side of our house, while Chris stood up and followed me over to the gate, too short to jump it, however. He couldn't open it either because the handle was too hard to move, pressing against the pole.

Just as I turned the corner to my right, I saw my mother running out of our house, crying uncontrollably! My eyes got even bigger, and I became even more terrified just seeing the look on her face.

Still wearing the same dark green lounge dress she'd put on after we'd come home from church, Mama now looked much different than before, as her hair was no longer neatly pulled back but was instead all over her head as if she'd been in a fight. Her face was wet, and she was crying hysterically.

She looked at me and, without stopping, passed right by me, carrying something in her hand, as she continued to run across the street towards our neighbors' house.

I couldn't understand why Mama didn't stop to tell me what was going on, and though I was terrified, for some reason, I didn't run after her. George wasn't with her either, which meant he had to still be in the house.

I ran to the front porch of our house, grabbed the handle to the front screen door and rushed inside. Stopping and standing in the middle of our living room, I leaned over onto my knees with my hands, barely able to catch my breath. It wasn't the short run that had taken my breath; it was the fear of thinking something bad had happened.

Standing back up straight, I called out for my brother,

"George!"

I didn't get a response back.

"George, George…where are you!? Are you okay!?"

"Where are you, George!?" I shouted again, with my voice trembling.

Scared, I looked around at the walls for a moment. My eyes felt like they were bulging out of their sockets. Sweat was collecting on my brow.

As I slowly walked through the living room towards the hallway, I looked to the right into my room and didn't see anything or anyone. Continuing towards the hallway, looking for George, I took deeper breaths to try to calm myself down so that my panting would ease up. It seemed to be working… until I reached my brothers' room.

Nothing in life could have prepared me for what I was about to see.

As soon as I turned to the left and had just barely stepped into my brothers' room, I spotted him—George. My nine-year-old brother lay on the floor in a large pool of blood. His mouth was closed, his head was leaning to the side, and his eyes were wide open, staring straight ahead as if he were looking directly at me. He wasn't moving at all.

The white t-shirt and green khaki shorts he'd put on after church were now saturated with his blood, and there was blood still slowly oozing from his neck area near his chin.

There was blood everywhere—on the walls, on the comforter draped over my brothers' bed, on the floor—EVERYWHERE! Even the toy cars on the floor near where George lay were speckled with blood.

With my eyes continuing to bulge, I stared at George, with my eyes fixed on him, completely unable to move.

THIS CAN'T BE REAL!! I wanted to convince myself.

I wanted to run, but my feet were stuck and wouldn't budge; fear *completely* seized me. My chest felt like it had stopped up, and it became hard to breathe.

Suddenly, for a split second, I was distracted by a noise just outside the window, and that was all I needed to get my feet going! Turning away from George, I ran back towards the bedroom doorway as fast as I could! On my way out, I saw blood on the door and on the doorknob. I hadn't noticed any of that when I'd first entered the room because my eyes immediately became fixed on George.

As I ran through the living room, the walls seemed to be spinning. I was so afraid, but I dared not stop! Bursting through the front door to the outside at full speed, I flung the screen door against the outside brick wall, causing a loud bang! Remembering that Mama had run towards our neighbor's house across the street, I ran in that direction too, hoping to find someone who could help my brother.

So many questions were *swirling* around in my head.

What had just happened to my brother!!!?

Where was Mama!!!?

Why wasn't she trying to help George!!!?

Why didn't Mama protect George from whoever had done that to him???

Why did she leave me and Chris behind???

My neighbor's garage door was up, so I raced directly inside it and headed for the door which opened to the inside of their house. Literally running into the door, I grabbed the doorknob to turn it, but it was locked.

By then, I was crying so hard that it was difficult for me to see through my tears.

"Help! HELP ME!" I yelled as loud as I could as I banged on the door with my fists.

Someone was in the house because there was a lot of commotion, and I could also hear loud voices coming from inside. I was sure I'd even heard Mama's voice, so I hollered again, "Mama, Mama!"

I cried, "Somebody help! My brother… HELP US PLEASE!!"

No one seemed to have heard me. Then I heard Mama sobbing so loudly, and I knew for sure this time it was her! I couldn't understand a word she was saying, it all sounded like babble. Though she was drowning out my knocking, I banged even harder, hoping I would get someone's attention.

There was a small opening in the curtains, and I leaned up against the door, though unable to keep my head steady, and tried to look inside.

An old man was seated near a table, trying to hold Mama down across his knees. It looked like he was whipping her with his hand! Mama was just wailing her hands and arms erratically, screaming and babbling, while other people were trying to calm her down.

Shaking with fear, I continued to bang on the door and window, calling out to Mama, but my knocks and calls went unanswered.

Finally, after what seemed like an eternity, a lady named Ms. Sue spotted me at the door. Running to open it, she pushed me back at the same time and shut the door behind her. She picked me up and ran through the garage, quickly whisking me away from the house.

With tears in her eyes, she held on to me as we got further and further away from the house, further away from Mama.

"Ms. Sue, please go help my brother George! Something bad happened to him, and he's on the floor in his room…and there's blood and…," I cried, begging for her to help George.

"Oh my God!" Ms. Sue said, crying, finally coming to a stop at the edge of the driveway and just holding me tight. I could feel the wetness of her face from the tears rolling down her face.

"Please help us," I cried and just buried my face in Ms. Sue's dress, sobbing on her shoulder.

"Oh, precious," she said as she rocked my entire body from side to side, still clinging to me tightly.

I thought maybe she was crying because she'd seen what happened to George, too.

"I want to see my mama. Can I please see my mama?" I asked, continuing to sob as I fixed my eyes on Ms. Sue's face.

Ms. Sue pushed my head gently back down on her shoulder, and sniffling, she just continued to rock me.

"I want to see my Mama!" I demanded, with tears and snot accumulating under my nose.

"You can't see her right now, baby," said Ms. Sue, with tears streaming down her cheeks.

Wiping my face with her hand, she just kept apologizing repeatedly to me, saying, "I'm so sorry baby, I'm so sorry!" as if she'd done something wrong.

"But my brother, please go help my brother!" I insisted.

By that time, our neighbor who lived directly across the street from us ran out into the street and began yelling and crying, "Oh my God, she killed her baby! She killed her baby! Oh Lord, *no!*"

Her words echoed down the street, causing a stir as people who were outside began to run towards our house, towards us. Before long, people from our street and from other streets in the neighborhood were coming, some running to see if the story was true.

My heart sank because I realized the person who killed her baby was Mama, and the baby was my brother, George.

I couldn't believe it. It made absolutely NO sense to me! Our mama wouldn't hurt us! She was our *mama*—she loved us. You only get rid of things you don't love, don't need, or don't want.

Getting down from her arms and now standing next to Ms. Sue, I continued to sob and then buried part of my face in her house dress.

The people continued to come.

Ms. Sue just held me close and started praying.

Amid all of the chaos, I suddenly remembered that I hadn't gone back to get Chris!

As soon as I remembered, I started panicking and looking across the street to see if I could see him. Just as I began patting Ms. Sue on her hip, getting ready to tell her that I'd left my little brother in our backyard, I saw him standing off to the side with a couple of our other neighbors.

Pointing to him, I said to Ms. Sue, "That's my little brother! I have to go get my little brother!"

"What, what did you say?" Ms. Sue asked, bending down and looking at me in my face, wiping my tears with her fingers. She had a hard time hearing me because so many people around us were talking loudly and causing all kinds of commotion.

"I need to get my little brother! He's over there. He's right there!" I exclaimed, pointing to him again, trying to get Ms. Sue to see him too.

"Oh God help me," she said, panicking now too, because she still didn't see Chris. I don't see him, Cheryl. What's he wearing?" Ms. Sue asked anxiously, scanning the crowd.

"Some blue shorts and a red T-shirt," I said irritably, "He's right there!" I said, still pointing. Then, grabbing her hand, I tried to pull Ms. Sue as I began to rush toward Chris.

There were so many questions being tossed at Ms. Sue. However, moving towards Chris, as I led her by the hand, she refused to answer anyone, only saying, "I don't know anything. Please let me get to this child!"

I felt horrible thinking Chris had probably been standing there at our back gate waiting for me, or somebody, to come back and get him. He looked as confused and scared as I was, and he ran to me when he saw me and Ms. Sue headed his way.

My little brother hadn't seen what I'd seen, and I wasn't sure if, at that point, he even knew that something bad had happened to George.

As soon as I put my arms around Chris, Ms. Sue quickly grabbed both of our hands and led us back through the crowd and back across the street near the edge of Ms. Diane's driveway where we had been standing before.

Not knowing what else to do, she told us we were just going to wait there because help was on the way.

"What's going on, Sue?" "What happened to little George?" "Is it true...did Mrs. Battle really do that?"

The questions kept coming.

Very shaken up, she just told everyone that she didn't know what had happened. Ms. Sue knew what had happened because she was there in the house when Mama was crying.

"Where's their daddy?" "Where's Mr. Rudy?"

There was no response.

Off in the distance, we could hear the sirens of emergency vehicles blaring. They were getting closer, and soon after, the ambulance and police entered our street.

A man in the crowd yelled, "Everybody move out of the way and let them get to that little boy!"

The people scattered, running this way and that way, as the police and ambulance pulled up in front of our house with brakes screeching. The police and paramedics flung open their doors, jumped out of their vehicles, and immediately ran towards our front door.

A couple of the dads on our street had already positioned themselves at our front door to keep people from going in.

With medical bags in hand, the medics, led by police, hurried inside our home. Other officers positioned themselves outside of our house and began controlling the crowd and moving back the people who'd gathered in our front yard. About three officers hurried into Ms. Diane's house, where Mama was.

Chris and I continued to stand still with Ms. Sue, just staring across the street at our house.

It was all so unbelievable, almost as if we were on the set of a movie being filmed. Only this was no movie; it was real life. It was our family.

Once again, I demanded to see Mama.

"I want to see my mama!"

There must have been a mistake.

Starting to cry, Chris covered his eyes with his hands.

"Baby, we have to wait here for right now," stated Ms. Sue, with her voice cracking. She stood there almost motionless.

I protested yet again to see our mother, "I want my mama! Why won't you let me talk to her?"

"No, I'm sorry baby, you can't see her right now," Ms. Sue said, looking down at me and hugging both me and Chris, keeping us close by her side.

Other neighbors came over to help Ms. Sue with us.

"Cheryl…No!" Ms. Sue shouted, grabbing me by the waist as I attempted to run off.

"Let me go! I want to see my mama!" I wiggled, and twisted, and even started throwing my fists with all my might, trying to break Ms. Sue's hold.

Chris' eyes got really big, and he became even more upset watching me fight Ms. Sue and the other grownups who'd stepped in to help.

Struggling hard to get free, I soon realized their hold was too much for me and only continued to get tighter and tighter. I finally gave up, tired from all the tussling, and just stood there mad and crying, wiping my face with the back of my hand.

"Come on, baby, it's going to be alright! Listen to me, Cheryl," Ms. Sue said, hugging me and trying to comfort me, "Daddy's on the way, okay baby? You're going to be alright."

Someone called our daddy at work and let him know there was an emergency at home and that he needed to get there right away.

Meanwhile, the police and EMTs who'd gone into our house hadn't come out yet, and that was causing me even more anxiety.

What were they doing in there!?

We never heard from Ms. Sue that Mama killed George, but we could hear what was being shouted and said about Mama and George by the people standing near us in the street. Some of the people were even cursing, calling Mama bad names.

"How could she do such an evil thing…to her own son!?"

"You know there's something so wrong with a mother who kills her own kid."

"Oh yeah, she'll burn in hell…she deserves to!"

"I know you're right. I hope she suffers for killing that little boy. Her own baby?!"

"He didn't deserve to die like that. No child does!"

"God help those kids…I just can't believe she would do that; how could she do that? My God, that poor little boy."

So many kept saying that Mama had done this terrible, unforgivable thing. I listened, I heard what they were saying and started to feel ashamed because that was my mama they were talking about.

It hurt so much, and I didn't want to believe the story, but I kept playing over and over in my head how Mama came running out of our house. She was running from something, and I kept seeing George's eyes looking at me while he lay on that floor in all that blood.

Our close friends Caren, James, Andrew, and Kyla, were all standing off at a distance with their parents looking at all the confusion and, like everyone else, were overwhelmed by it all. They looked our way but didn't come over right away to where we were standing.

Eventually, Caren and James' mom walked over and gave us a big hug.

With tears in her eyes, she said, "We love you, Cheryl and Chris."

That was all she said.

What else could she say?

We'd all been so close, but now, because of what had happened, I felt like I was standing amongst a bunch of strangers. Nothing I was looking at—my friends, my house, or my street—looked normal.

Once in a blue moon, someone on our street would do something not so good or get into some kind of trouble, and word would spread quickly among the neighbors.

At that moment, I got such a pain in my gut, as I thought to myself, 'Now people will talk about our family…they'll say how *bad* our family is, saying Mama killed George.'

What could be worse than that?

Looking towards our house again, I saw two policemen exiting the front door. They stopped and talked briefly with a couple of our neighbors, one of whom pointed at us. I sort of hid my face again in Ms. Sue's dress.

When I peeked out a few seconds later, the officers were standing right in front of us. Only wanting to talk to Mama, I had no desire to talk to any policemen. One of the officers just looked at me and Chris, while the other one began talking, almost in a whisper, to Ms. Sue.

"Hi, ma'am, what's your name?" the officer asked, taking a notepad out of his shirt pocket, holding it in his hand and preparing to write on it.

"Uh, my name is Sue Johnson."

"Are these the mother's kids also? The little boy's brother and sister?"

"Yes, sir." Ms. Sue said, wiping her nose with a tissue as she spoke with the officer.

"This is Cheryl and her little brother, Chris."

"Is it ok if we try to talk to them?"

Ms. Sue nodded to the officer. She looked down at us, still stuck to her side and clinging to her dress.

"Cheryl, Chris... these officers are here to help us. It's okay, babies," Ms. Sue said, trying to reassure us.

I don't know what Chris did, but I buried my face in Ms. Sue's dress. My guess is that Chris did the same thing.

"It's ok, babies. They won't hurt you. They are here to help, okay?" she said.

I clung to Ms. Sue even tighter and looked down at the ground as the officer got closer to me.

The officer placed his hand on Chris' head, and almost simultaneously, Chris backed away, nearly lifting Ms. Sue's dress up.

"That's okay, I know he's scared. He has every reason to be," the officer said, sighing and looking at Chris.

Chris and I had such a fear of the police from hearing what the big kids would say about them. They'd sometimes threaten to call the police on us because they said we 'were being bad.' Chris and I hadn't done anything bad, but I still didn't want to talk to them.

Turning to me, the police officer asked in a very soft voice, "Cheryl? Is that your name, sweetheart?"

Shyly, I gave him a nod.

He knelt, looking at me in my eyes. Most of the white people in my neighborhood had black, brown, or even blue eyes, but this officer had grey eyes. They were calming.

Chris, peeking his face out from behind Ms. Sue's dress, looked at me and then at the officer.

The officer gently took my hand and lightly rubbed it as he began to talk, "I know you are afraid, honey, and probably very confused."

I just stared at him.

"Cheryl, we're here to help you and your family, okay?"

"Where's my mama?" I asked softly, wiping my eyes because the tears were starting up again.

Regardless of what the people continued to say, I still wanted to know what happened from my mama.

"Your mama is being helped," he said, grabbing both my and Chris' hands. "We've called for your daddy, and he'll be here soon."

He'd gained some confidence with Chris after Chris saw how nice he was to me. There was no need for us to be afraid of him.

Letting go of both of our hands, the officer stood back up.

Once again, speaking softly to Ms. Sue, the officer said something about George but was talking too low for me to really make out what he was saying.

His voice then got louder as he said to Ms. Sue, "...so since we haven't heard from the daddy yet, I really need to see if she can identify the little boy so we can go ahead and have him removed from the house."

The coroner was there waiting to take George. The fact that George was still in the house caused the people not to want to go away. The situation was as tense as it was sad.

Several police were walking the crowd, trying to calm everyone down.

"Ok," Ms. Sue said, continuing to hold me and Chris tightly at her side, "but I don't know if she can do that. She's just a baby, you know," Ms. Sue said, sounding a bit surprised at the request.

"Yes, ma'am, and I assure you that she'll only see his face. Since they are the next of kin, and since she's the oldest, uh, maybe she can do it? We just need for her to look at his face if she can. If the dad were here, we wouldn't need her to do it, but as it is, he hasn't arrived yet, and we really want to get the little boy's body out and away from here."

Ms. Sue, sighing, looked at the officer and nodded, noticeably uncomfortable with his request but not saying anything else.

No one knew I'd already seen my brother lying on the floor. They didn't even know that I'd seen my mama run out of the house afterward.

They and the reporters who later reported the story thought Chris and I had been in our neighbor's backyard when everything happened, but we were, in fact, in our own backyard playing up until everything happened.

However, no one had asked us anything about what we'd seen or heard. If they had, I would have let them know that I'd heard and seen more than I'd be able to ever forget.

Taking his hat off, the officer wiped the sweat that began beading all over his face with his shirt sleeve.

The officer, kneeling, then began speaking directly to me again.

"Cheryl, now what I'm getting ready to ask you is not something you have to do if you don't want to. I want you to understand that."

"Where is my daddy?" I asked, interrupting him.

"Uh, yes, honey, we're still waiting for him, and I'm sure he's coming. I think it's just taking a little time to get the message to him that he needs to come home, but I'm sure he is on the way," he said, squeezing my hand to comfort me.

"Right now, because your daddy isn't here, I want to ask if you think you can go over with me into your home and tell me who the little boy inside is?"

Ms. Sue interrupted, "Baby, I'll be right there with you, and only if you think you can, you can go in there. Otherwise, we'll just have to wait for your daddy to come."

She was a nice lady, and I trusted her because she seemed to care about what was going on with us.

"Yes, sir," I nodded, looking towards the ground.

The officer seemed taken aback that I'd said 'Yes' without hesitating. "Yes?" He asked.

"Yes, sir," I said again, speaking very softly and looking up at the officer.

Taking me by the hand, he said, "Ok, Cheryl, we'll only be in there long enough for you to tell me who he is if you can, and then we'll leave right away. I promise you that. He's covered up, so you won't see anything but his face, okay, sweetheart?"

"Okay," I replied.

Ms. Sue softly kissed me on top of my head.

"Okay," he said, standing to his feet, "so we'll all walk over there together. Ms. Sue, I'll hold on to Cheryl, and you just continue to hold on to her little brother, and you'll walk directly behind us. The quicker we move through the crowd, the quicker we can get this over with," said the officer to Ms. Sue.

"Okay," Ms. Sue replied, making sure she had a good grip on Chris' hand.

The officer led me by the hand as we began walking back across the street and toward our house. Honestly, I was afraid to go back in there, but I was willing to go and tell the officer who George was, knowing that the police, Ms. Sue, and Chris would all be in there with me.

We started walking, and as we got closer to our house, there were some people I recognized and others that I didn't. Some of them were leaning up against the police cars parked outside our home, while others simply sat or stood in and near the street or in the grass of our front yard.

They were fanning themselves, wiping sweat off their faces, and, I guess, waiting to see what was going to happen next.

I didn't know what to expect.

"Step back folks…please move to the side!" the officer ordered in a loud voice.

The crowd of people began to move to the side, making room as we moved through.

There was like a hush as we passed by, with all eyes on us. A few tried to reach out for our hand or tried to touch us in some way, but the officer told them, while shielding us from them with his arm, "No, please don't get in the way…just let us pass, folks. Let us pass, please!"

Beginning to lose his patience because the people were moving too slowly, he shouted, "Come on, move back now!" startling a couple of people who were standing directly in our path, so engaged in their conversation that they were unaware that we were right behind them.

The people obliged and quickly moved out of the way. Many of the same people who just minutes earlier were talking loudly amongst themselves now stood whispering, some of them even praying and staring as we neared the front door, no doubt wondering why we were going back inside our home.

About three officers were standing watch at the front screen door, making sure no one entered. They opened the door for us as we stepped onto the front porch.

The officer and I were the first to walk through the door, and as I stepped inside our house, I looked back to make sure Chris and Ms. Sue were still walking behind us, and they were. When we entered the living room of our house, I noticed policemen roaming all over our home. They appeared to be looking for something, but for what, I didn't know.

Our home felt like a strange place. The atmosphere was tense and very solemn. You could tell something terrible had happened.

We headed towards the back of our house with the officer leading us. I saw two officers standing, talking in the doorway. They were all standing near George's body, talking amongst themselves.

Ms. Sue at first stopped at the door but then stepped inside, still holding Chris' hand. Picking him up, she made him rest his chin on her shoulder, looking behind her so that Chris wouldn't see George.

My brother was covered from head to toe with a white sheet.

Still holding my hand, the officer allowed me to go at my own pace and walked me over to the covered body on the floor. We stood there in front of my brother.

Kneeling, he looked up at me and asked, "Are you ok, honey?"

I nodded 'yes'.

There were still blood stains on the wall, but the toys had all been moved off the floor and placed in a bag. I felt slightly dizzy again and was ready to leave.

"It's okay," the officer said, seeing the uneasiness in my face. "As soon as you see his face and tell me his name, if you can, we'll leave," he said, still holding on to my hand as he knelt.

My eyes were focused once again, just as they had been earlier, on the spot where George lay. I braced myself as one of the officers in the room removed the sheet from George's face, down to just beneath his chin, as the officer instructed him.

"That's my brother, George," I said, looking just long enough to identify him and then immediately turning away, beginning to sob again.

"Thank you, baby," the officer said, clenching my hand and quickly covering George's face back up.

The officer nodded at the other officer, who then, along with the coroner, walked near George's body.

Just as he had promised, and while never letting go of my hand, he quickly led me, Ms. Sue, and Chris out of the house.

It's alright, babies," Ms. Sue said, kissing both Chris and me on the forehead, and then, taking both of our hands, held us close as the officer walked in front of us and escorted us back across the street to Ms. Diane's house.

As we were crossing the street, we overheard someone in the crowd say, "They just took that crazy ole '#*%' away!"

"Good!" said someone else, "I really hope she gets what she deserves!"

Finally realizing we were present, someone tried to whisper, "*Shhhhh*...those are her other two babies".

It was too late, however, because we'd already heard them. Ms. Sue gave them a look as we passed by.

The officer stopped just near the driveway and thanked us again, and then Ms. Sue, Chris, and I kept walking.

Minutes later, the coroner brought our brother's body out of the house, loaded up on a stretcher. It was still covered, only now with a black zip-up cover. Wide straps near the top, middle, and bottom of his body kept him tied down, preventing him from slipping off the stretcher.

Many of the kids, including my little brother, were told to turn their heads and look away as the stretcher was rolled out of the house.

It was the quietest moment since everything had begun.

Some of the grown-ups even looked away while covering the faces of the younger kids, not wanting to even get a glimpse of George's now lifeless body beneath the black drape.

I'd already seen so much and again found myself being drawn to George's body. I couldn't help but stare at the black cover, looking for any kind of movement—*anything*.

The stretcher was loaded into a white van, and the police had to again make the people move so that the van could leave.

George was being taken to the morgue.

That's when it really sunk in: George was dead. He wasn't coming back to talk to us, to play with us, to eat dinner with us, to watch TV with us, to stomp around in the rainwater. None of it. He was gone.

The pain in my throat returned, feeling like something had swollen up in there, and it was hard for me to swallow. My chest started hurting again, and my eyes began watering up again. I wanted to cry, but it hurt to even breathe.

We stood there, watching the van slowly move down the street, turn the corner, and disappear out of sight. As for me and my family, in a matter of hours, our lives had completely unraveled.

CHAPTER THREE

IN DADDY'S ARMS

No sooner than the coroner left our street, Aunt Doris and Grandmother Wilma, Mama's sister and mother, turned onto our street.

Right behind them was Daddy!

Spotting our car, Chris and I bolted out of Ms. Sue's arms. Nothing could keep us from our daddy, and recognizing our car, she didn't even try to stop us. Swiftly walking behind us, Ms. Sue was heading over to talk to Daddy when she was stopped by one of the police officers asking her more questions.

Daddy, unable to get to our driveway, parked just a couple of houses down and jumped out of the car as it barely came to a stop.

People were rushing over to him to tell him what was going on, but the only thing he asked was where Chris and I were. The police also started making their way to Daddy.

"Where are my kids?" Daddy asked, with a look of panic, wiping the sweat out of his eyes.

One of the neighbors standing near him pointed in our direction, and Daddy, spotting us running towards him, started running towards us.

Aunt Doris and Grandmother followed suit.

It was obvious that Daddy had left work in a hurry. His Armco Steel uniform shirt was hanging outside his pants, his steel toe boots were covered in some kind of soot, and his face was drenched with sweat, as were his arms, but when he got to us, he grabbed us, lifting both of us off the ground at the same time, hugging us as if he hadn't seen us in a long time. Daddy held us tightly against his sweat-soaked shirt, and that was fine with us.

We were just so happy that he was finally there with us. Chris and I clung to him and cried. Overcome with emotions, we couldn't even talk and tell him what had happened. I just wanted Daddy to hug us and never ever let us go.

"Everything's going to be alright," Daddy said. Holding us even tighter, he reassured us, "I'm here. Daddy's here," softly kissing both of us, with tears streaming down his face.

Grandmother Wilma and Aunt Doris stood there, and we all cried together.

Later, Grandmother Wilma shared that she sensed that something wasn't right but never would have imagined that her daughter would have done such a thing. It was that strange feeling in her spirit that led her to ask Aunt Doris to drive her by our home to check on us. Without warning, she found out that her grandson had been murdered and her daughter had allegedly done it.

We were all numb. It simply didn't seem real.

Aunt Doris and Grandmother cried, hugging each other.

Daddy buried his face between me and Chris as he continued, over and over again, telling us how everything was going to be alright.

After allowing us to console each other for a few minutes, one of the police officers who'd walked up when Daddy arrived lightly placed his hand on Daddy's shoulder to get his attention.

"Mr. Battle?" he said.

Daddy lifted his head and looked at him.

"Mr. Battle, I'm Officer Monroe, and this here is Office Kleen."

"Sir, we are so very sorry for your loss."

Daddy nodded his head while still holding on to us.

"I know this is a very difficult time, Mr. Battle, for you and your family, sir, and I can't even begin to imagine what you are going through, but we do need to ask you some questions and get some information. Can we walk over to your house and talk?"

"Ok," Daddy responded, with tears steadily streaming down his cheeks.

"You just got here, I know, and have only bits and pieces about what happened, so we want to fill you in, Mr. Battle, with what we know so far."

"Ok, yes," Daddy said, looking down at the ground while Officer Munroe struggled to get his words out, with Officer Kleen standing close by, sadly staring at Daddy.

With weary, bloodshot eyes, Daddy said, "I know my wife killed our son," looking somberly at Officer Munroe.

The policeman continued, "Yes...and I want to let you know, Mr. Battle, that your wife, Alice, has been taken downtown to be processed at the county jail. Your son George's body has also already been removed from the home and is en route to the morgue."

Daddy stared at the ground again as he wiped sweat and tears from his face.

"Uhm, Mr. Battle, your daughter, Cheryl, um, she was very brave in identifying George for us," the officer explained.

"My daughter saw...!" Daddy started but couldn't finish his sentence and just looked angrily at the officer in dismay and disgust.

"Yes sir, we thought it was best, uh, given the extremely sensitive situation, to go ahead and remove your son's body as soon as we could. Our understanding was that there was some difficulty finding you at work, so we asked your daughter to just look at his face to identify him. You have my word, Mr. Battle, that she only saw his face," the officer said, seeing Daddy's disapproval.

Daddy was angry. He grinded his teeth and shook his head in disbelief.

The officer then said, "I know this is such a huge tragedy, Mr. Battle, for you and your family, and again, you have our condolences."

Daddy just stared past the officer with disgust and said, "I was on the way...they, …my kids didn't have to go in there! I was coming. I left as soon as I got word."

"Yes sir…we only did what we thought was best for everyone."

"Best for my daughter?" Daddy asked, staring at the officer, "They shouldn't have been allowed to go in there!"

Daddy didn't know that I'd already been in there. I'd already seen George on the floor.

Chris and I were getting heavy in Daddy's arms, but he wouldn't put us down and instead, just kept repositioning us in his arms.

"Sir, would you like me to hold one of your kids for you? I don't mind helping you carry them. We're here to help you and your family however we can," Officer Kleen offered, reaching out for one of us.

"No, I'll carry my own kids," Daddy said, holding us even tighter, refusing the officer's help.

"Ok, uh, we'll have to get that information from you, Mr. Battle, to help us with the investigation, so if you don't mind, I'd like to go ahead and walk across the street over to your house. There are officers there who really need to speak with you and get a statement."

"That's fine," Daddy responded to the officer, not making eye contact with him.

By that time, a couple of the officers, including the one who asked me to identify George, walked up to us, and Daddy, with bloodshot eyes, remained composed as he spoke briefly with them, only answering a few basic questions. The deeper questions would come once Daddy was alone with the officers.

Visibly distraught and weary, Daddy let out a deep sigh as he held on to us, and we all listened to the police officer.

"Ok, Mr. Battle, if you'll follow me," Officer Munroe said, beginning to walk back towards our house.

Aunt Doris and Grandmother followed us as we walked back to our house with the police. Neighbors hugged us as we walked through the crowd.

"Rudy, we're praying for you and the kids."

"We love you guys."

"We're here for you all, Rudy. I'm so sorry for you and the kids."

"God keep you and your family. He'll see you through this, Rudy."

One after the other, now, instead of talking bad about our mama or about the horrible thing she'd done, people were offering words of comfort to Daddy.

Daddy would say 'Thank you' or just nod his head as we walked slowly to our house because we kept being stopped by so many neighbors and friends.

Daddy needed to leave us with Grandmother Wilma and Aunt Doris while he talked to the officers, discussing things that he didn't want us to hear and that we shouldn't hear.

"It's okay, Rudy," Aunt Doris said, stepping in and placing her hand on his arm, "They'll be alright. We'll be right over there. You'll be able to see them, and they'll see you. You go ahead and talk to the police so they can get the information they need from you."

During the conversation with Daddy, one of the officers mentioned that Mama had left a note that provided some explanation as to why she did what she did. I guess that's what those officers were looking for in our kitchen drawers and cabinets.

Soon, our other grandparents, Daddy's parents, arrived, as well as other relatives and close friends of our family.

Our grandparents had gone to run errands and were not home when Daddy called, so he called their next-door neighbor, Ms. Mandy, and she gave them the message. As soon as they heard, they rushed from the other side of town to be with us.

Like all of our relatives, they were grief-stricken. Hugs, kisses, and tears was the theme for the rest of the evening.

The evening hours passed, and night finally fell.

After a chaotic, turbulent evening, the night was still, and our street looked the way it had much earlier in the day, absent of police cars and ambulances. Most of the neighbors had gone in by now, and we finally had a quiet moment with no reporters or police officers, just us.

So much of the rest of that night is a blur for me, but I do remember the sound of the wooden broom straws brushing against the hard-wood floors as my aunt swept up George's blood, a lot of which had pooled in the corner of the wall, into a metal dustpan. I don't know what she did with it after that.

For the rest of that evening, I didn't utter Mama's name. In fact, I didn't say too much about anything. I was just glad Daddy was with us. At that point, that's all that mattered to me because I trusted him to keep us safe. I still couldn't get that image of George's wide-open eyes out of my mind, however.

Aunt Doris and Grandmother Wilma said goodbye to each of us, taking turns to hug us before walking away. They both still looked in disbelief as they turned to give us a final wave. Daddy spent a few minutes alone with them outside, talking as he walked them to their car still parked down the street. They left after letting Daddy know they'd come out to see us tomorrow.

Temporary plans were put in place for us and Daddy for the night. We were going to stay with our daddy's parents, Grandmother Hilda and Granddaddy Walter.

"Can I do anything for you, Rudy?" Aunt Della, Daddy's only sister, asked, calling Daddy by his nickname as he walked back into the house.

She and her husband, Irving, were going to follow us to our grandparents' house.

"No, I'm just going to grab a few things so we can go," Daddy said, walking towards the back of the house.

"We've already taken care of that. Come on, let's get the kids and go," Aunt Doris said to Daddy. Our Aunt Doris and Aunt Della had already packed some things for the three of us, enough for several days.

I didn't know how long we were going to stay at Grandmother's. I just knew that I didn't want to be at our house anymore. I didn't know when we'd come back, but anytime soon would be way too soon.

"Are the kids asleep?" Daddy asked Aunt Della, not being able to tell whether our eyes were open or closed because of how we were lying on the sofa.

"Almost," she replied, walking over, rubbing our backs, and sitting with us on the sofa.

Grandmother and Granddaddy had already left to go to their house to prepare a place for us all to sleep and make other arrangements since we'd be bunking in with them for at least several days. I heard Grandmother making plans for the next day's meals and saying that she needed to make groceries first thing in the morning. She wanted to be sure she had everything she needed to cook for us.

Daddy quietly walked to the boys' room, stood there for a moment, and then grabbed the door to lock it shut. No one would be allowed back in there for some time.

Walking into his and Mama's room and looking around, Daddy paused for a moment again and then walked out, also closing that door behind him. He grabbed our stuff, which was packed in a large duffle bag and a couple of small bags, and went outside to load everything into the trunk of our car.

He came back inside the house and, looking at us, asked, "Are you all ready?"

"Yes," Aunt Della replied, speaking for all of us.

"Ok, let's go," Daddy said, reaching down towards our aunt's lap to help us to our feet. Chris and I had both laid our heads in Aunt Della's lap and fallen back asleep.

"Here, let me have him, Rudy," Uncle Irving said, reaching for and taking Chris from Daddy.

"I got Cheryl," Aunt Della said.

"You go ahead and lock up. Me and Della will load the kids into the car," Uncle Irving said.

Aunt Della and her husband carried us to the car, which had been moved to our driveway, while Daddy made sure the back door was secure and then came through the front door, locking it behind him. Aunt Della waited with us at the car for Daddy while Uncle Irving went to their car, which was parked on the opposite side of the street.

I stared at the porch area, waiting for Daddy to appear. When I saw him, I sat back in the seat, and Aunt Della buckled me and Chris in.

At about that time, we were all distracted by the mosquito spray truck coming down our street spraying for mosquitoes. It had been so quiet that the sound of the truck kind of scared me. Daddy stepped onto the porch, watching as the truck passed by.

Seeing Daddy walk off the porch, Aunt Della said, "OK Rudy, we'll be right behind you. We'll see you all at Mother's," as she began walking to her car, where Uncle Irving was waiting with the engine idling.

"Della...," Daddy said, stopping Aunt Della in her tracks.

With his voice cracking, I heard Daddy say, "I should have done more. I thought I was doing the right thing, you know. I thought she was ok. I never believed she could do anything like this. Della, if I'd thought for one second...,"

"Rudy, don't you for one second blame yourself for what Alice did!" Aunt Della said, grabbing and hugging Daddy tightly.

"Who saw that coming? None of us." Aunt Della said, continuing to try to comfort Daddy.

"We all know that you didn't leave her with those kids, believing she'd harm them. No one thinks that, and if anyone does, they don't know what the hell they are talking about!"

Realizing how angry she was becoming, Aunt Della paused a second and let out a big sigh to calm down.

"Rudy…we all thought she was okay, or at least on her way back to being okay, and who would have thought she'd hurt her own kids? I mean, what mother does that? Only a very sick one. It's not your fault. Do you hear me, Rudy? It's not your fault."

"It just really hurts. I can't believe he's gone or that any of this happened," Daddy said, staring off into the night.

"I know," Aunt Della said, hugging him again as he hugged her back, almost clinging to her.

"You know he was my boy, my firstborn, and now he's gone…just like that, Della. I just saw him and hugged him this morning before I left for work. I didn't think that would be the last time I'd see my son alive. She took him away from me." Daddy said, breaking down and bending over as he cried in his hands.

Uncle Irving, seeing Daddy and Aunt Della standing there still talking, got out of his car and walked back over to them.

"It's going to be alright, Rudy," Uncle Irving said, bending down and putting his arm on Daddy's back to console him. Aunt Della passed a tissue to Daddy and took one for herself, wiping her face and blowing her nose.

Sobbing, Daddy stood up and began saying, "I'm so glad she didn't do the same thing to Cheryl or Chris because the police said she was actually planning to kill all of our children. She was planning to kill all three of our kids."

"My God, my God…she's out of her mind. Alice really snapped this time, Rudy." Aunt Della said, shaking her head, with tears trailing down her face and falling onto her shirt.

"Well, I can tell you this: where she's going now, Rudy, she won't be able to hurt anyone else anymore. That's it. No more."

At that moment, after hearing Daddy and Aunt Della's conversation suddenly go silent, I moved closer to the car window to look and saw Aunt Della bending over, sobbing. She started crying louder and louder, so loudly that my eyes started to well up with tears again.

Other than having light from our porch light and the streetlights, we were surrounded by pitch darkness. So shaken by the events of the day, Chris and I were sitting very close to each other, holding hands.

Daddy saw me looking at them through the window and just stared back at me with a very gloomy look on his face as he patted Aunt Della on her back to comfort her.

Standing back upright and wiping away the tears with her hands, Aunt Della said, "At least we know he is in Heaven with the Lord."

Daddy, with his hand resting on her shoulder, nodded his head and looked at the ground.

As heartfelt as Aunt Della's words were at the time, it seemed of little consolation to say that George was with the Lord because Daddy, like all of us, wanted George to still be with us.

Our daddy wasn't much of a religious man, but he did believe in God. Work often prevented him from going to church, but I know he prayed to God because Daddy taught me, Chris, and George how to pray before we could barely form sentences. He believed in God and, like many people, wondered why God would allow this to happen.

Why didn't God step in and stop it?

Once I got older, I questioned that for many years.

If God is such a good God, why didn't he keep Mama from killing George? Why didn't He just heal Mama and allow us to be a 'normal' family?

After wiping her eyes with the now worn-out piece of tissue, Aunt Della said, "I know the Lord will get us through this. We must draw on His strength and trust Him," she said, trying to muster up a reassuring smile.

As witty and full of laughter as Aunt Della normally was, that was the first time I'd noticed her trying to be hopeful the entire evening.

"As hard as all of this is, God allowed it to happen for a reason. We don't understand it; it doesn't make sense to us, but I do still believe that God is in control, Rudy. Even now, He's still in control."

"Yeah, well, right now, my biggest concern is Chris and Cheryl. They're so young; they don't know what's going on, and I don't know how to tell them. Their brother is gone because of their mother, and I don't know how to explain that to them," Daddy said, looking at the ground.

Aunt Della responded, "Well, Rudy, what you tell them is that their mother is *very, very* sick and that what happened to George wouldn't have happened if she had been well. What else can you say other than that? And Rudy, that is the absolute truth".

"I'm just so sorry that Cheryl and Chris had to witness all of this. But you know what? We still have them. *Thank* God, Rudy, we still have them. We could have lost them all. That was her plan, but God did say 'No' to that."

"That's right," Uncle Irving said.

He'd been standing there, not saying much.

"Yeah, I am grateful for that," Daddy said, wiping his eyes and then swatting away mosquitoes.

"Well, we'd better go. These mosquitoes are pretty bad tonight," Daddy said.

"Yeah, Della, Rudy...we need to go," Uncle Irving said. "It's late, and you know Mr. and Mrs. Battle are waiting."

Daddy kept all the windows rolled up to keep the mosquitoes out.

Gazing at us for a second, Aunt Della said, "Auntie will see you in a little bit, okay?"

I nodded at her with heavy eyes, fighting sleep. Chris had already fallen asleep again, laying his head on my shoulder.

Daddy got into our car, started it up, and we all left with Aunt Della and Uncle Irving following us.

The ride to Grandmother's was a quiet one. It was just us and our daddy.

Daddy drove without ever turning on the radio, only clearing his throat a few times but not saying a word all the way to our grandparents' house. Daddy looked straight ahead, almost as if in a daze.

I closed my eyes, wishing the day could start all over again but be completely different—just be normal, ordinary. I could only wish because I knew and was finally accepting the truth that:

Mama was gone.

George was gone.

The way our family had been was gone.

Just hours earlier, my brothers and I had been outside playing together, doing what we normally did, and now life had changed for our family, and it would never be the same.

We made it to our grandparents' home. They were already dressed for bed and sitting up, waiting for us. It was pitch dark outside, and our car's headlights lit up the driveway, followed by our uncle's car, as they pulled in behind us. Our grandparents' front door opened and out came Grandmother, trailed by Granddaddy. She walked over to the car to open the back door while Granddaddy walked over to give Daddy a hand with our things.

"Hey, Son," Granddaddy said, "Let me help you with those," while opening the front passenger side door and grabbing a couple of the bags from the seat.

"Don't worry about the bags," Daddy said, gently taking the bags from Granddaddy, "I'll get them. We only have a couple."

"Alright, Son," Granddaddy said, letting the bags go.

Granddaddy and Daddy hadn't always had the best relationship, but after Daddy got married and had us, things between them did improve.

"Well, okay, you'll come on. We have the backroom ready for you," Granddaddy said, lightly patting Daddy on his back as he carried our bags into the house.

Grandmother and Aunt Della had already gotten us out of the car, and we were standing just inside the doorway, waiting for Daddy to come in.

We'd been over to our grandparents many times before and felt at home, but now very clingy, Chris and I wanted to stay as close to Daddy as possible.

Grandmother hugged us and kept her arms around us.

Granddaddy and Aunt Della had taken a seat at the dining room table while Uncle Irving sat in the recliner. Uncle Irving had been at work the entire day like Daddy and was tired.

We were very close to our aunt and uncle because they stayed just around the block from our grandparents, and most times when we went to visit our grandparents, we'd also visit them. Aunt Della and Uncle Irving had been married for what seemed like forever, but they didn't have any kids of their own.

Uncle Irving reclined back and closed his eyes.

Daddy went back out to the car just to lock it, and it took him more than a few minutes to return.

Finally walking through the door, he leaned over and gave Grandmother a hug as she stood nearby, waiting for him to reappear. Daddy wasn't a very tall man, but because Grandmother stood only about 5'4, he seemed to tower over her. Daddy's eyes were very red, and his eyelashes were wet, so we could tell he had been crying some more.

That's why it was taking him so long to come inside. I think Grandmother probably knew that.

Looking at us, she said, "It's late, but I did come home and fix you a little something if you're hungry. Anybody want to eat?"

"No, Mother, thank you, we're fine," Daddy replied.

"Yeah, Mother, some of Rudy's neighbors brought over food after you all left, and the kids had some of that," Aunt Della added.

"Well, what about you, Rudy? Did you get a chance to eat something?"

"No, ma'am, I didn't eat...but I'm not hungry," Daddy said.

"I understand, Son, but you need to eat Rudy," Grandmother said to Daddy.

"I'm alright, Mother. I just need to sleep, get some rest," Daddy respectfully said.

Not pushing the issue, Grandmother said, "Ok, Son, but if you change your mind, I've left you a plate covered up on top of the stove."

"Ok, Mother. Thanks."

"I know these babies need a bath, right?" Grandmother asked.

"Yes ma'am, they do. We all do," Daddy responded.

"OK, I'll help them. I'll draw you two some bath water. Cheryl, you come with me, baby. You can go first," Grandmother said, taking me by the hand and leading me off to the bathroom.

"Daddy, can you come with me?" I stopped and asked.

Before Daddy could answer, "Come on, sugar, Grandmother will be in there with you. Let Daddy stay here with Chris. You'll be back soon." Grandmother said.

I looked back at Daddy as Grandmother put her hand around my shoulder, continuing to take me to the bathroom.

"I'll be right here, baby, when you get out. I'm not going anywhere," Daddy said, taking a seat on the sofa with Chris in his arms.

Assured by what Daddy said, I didn't put up a fight and just went on along with Grandmother. Grandmother made sure I cleaned myself well. I got out of the tub, dried off, got into my pajamas, and headed back to the living room.

"Ok, Chris, your turn," Grandmother said, walking over to Daddy and taking Chris from his arms, where he'd fallen asleep.

We weren't used to being up so late. We'd normally go to bed around 8:30 pm, and now it was almost 11 pm.

Uncle Irving got up, took Chris from Grandmother, and carried him into the bathroom, with Grandmother walking behind them. I took Chris' place in Daddy's arms.

Out of the blue, there was a knock at the door.

"Wonder who that is this time of night?" Granddaddy asked, starting to stand to his feet.

Aunt Della quickly rose to her feet from the sofa where she'd moved to to be with Daddy and Chris.

"You sit back down, Daddy, I'll get it...that's probably Mandy," Aunt Della said, walking over to the front door.

Granddaddy, as tired as he was, sat back down and let Aunt Della answer the door.

"Hey girl," Aunt Della said, opening the door to Ms. Mandy, our grandparents' next-door neighbor. Aunt Della was right. If anyone would come over at that late hour to check on us, it would be Ms. Mandy.

"Hi everyone," Ms. Mandy said, greeting everyone and stepping inside the house.

"I didn't want to go to bed without knowing Rudy and the kids had made it in. I came over earlier, Della, to help Ms. Battle get the back room ready."

"Oh, that's so sweet of you," Aunt Della said to her, reaching to give her a hug.

Ms. Mandy was one of the nicest neighbors on our grandparents' street. They could call on her for just about anything, and she'd be there.

"Well, I'm here to help however I can. Bless your hearts," she said, with her voice cracking. Speaking to Daddy, she said, "I'm praying for you guys, Rudy. You know I'm here for you."

Ms. Mandy was from Louisiana, and though she'd lived in Houston for many years, she still had a Louisiana 'draw' when she spoke.

"Thanks, Mandy, we appreciate that," Daddy said, attempting to get up with me still in his arms.

"Oh no, you sit. The baby is asleep, and I don't want to wake her up. I'll come to you," Ms. Mandy said, making her way over to Daddy to hug him.

Continuing, she said, "I know it's late, but I wanted to just make sure you had everything you needed before I went to bed, and I just needed to see you guys myself, Rudy, see my babies...make sure you'll are okay."

"Thank you, Mandy," Daddy said.

Sound asleep, I never moved.

"Well, thank you, we really appreciate you. Mother is in the bathroom bathing Chris, but I'll let her know you came by," Aunt Della said, turning toward the door to lead Ms. Mandy out.

"Oh...ok, so y'all are fine. You don't need anything right now?" Ms. Mandy asked, realizing Aunt Della was cutting her visit short. It seemed a little rude, but it was very late, and Aunt Della, like all of us, was worn out. The day had been so emotionally draining.

"No, thank you, Mandy, we are fine, but thank you for coming over and checking on us," Aunt Della said, smiling slightly while opening the door.

"Okay, well, just let Mrs. Battle know that I'll drop in tomorrow to check on you guys. I'll talk to her then," Ms. Mandy said, not appearing at all offended.

Ms. Mandy said "Good Night" to everyone and exited back out of the door.

A second later, Grandmother walked back into the living room after Chris was dressed and said, "I thought I heard Mandy's voice?"

"Yes, ma'am. Mother, she was here for just a minute and said to tell you that she'd dropped by and will talk to you tomorrow," replied Aunt Della, as Daddy, Uncle Irving, and Granddaddy remained quiet.

"Oh, ok, yeah. I'll talk to her tomorrow. She came over earlier and helped me get the room together for Rudy and the kids. That Mandy really is such a nice neighbor," Grandmother said, looking at Aunt Della.

"Yeah, that's what she told us, that she'd come over to help you. Mother, you know I would have done it if I had been here," said Aunt Della, taking all of the balled-up tissue out of her pocket and walking over to the trash can to throw it away.

"Oh, Della, I know that, but you needed to stay with Rudy and the kids, and I didn't have that much to do. She just helped me get the bed linens out of the closet so that we could make the bed. That's all," Grandmother said, not wanting Aunt Della to feel bad for not being there to help.

"Where's De'Walter? Already sleep?"

"Yes, Mandy kept him for us this evening, and after helping me with the room, she put him to bed in your daddy's room.

Uncle De'Walter was Grandmother's and Granddaddy's firstborn. He was born with some kind of developmental problem. He didn't grow right and was challenged with his thinking and speech. He'd been with Grandmother and Granddaddy his entire life, never able to live on his own. Uncle De'Walter was in his late 40s.

Grandmother woke me and Chris up and said, "Ok, little ones, let's get you all into bed."

Daddy stood to his feet, and Uncle Irving grabbed me as Daddy grabbed Chris and carried us to the back room, where we'd all be sleeping.

Grandmother tucked us in while Daddy and Aunt Della began talking about plans for the next day.

After kissing us good night, Grandmother walked over to Daddy and gave him another hug, saying, "It's going to be ok, Son. God will see us through."

She knew how much agony Daddy was in, and like any good mother would, she tried to comfort him as much as she could.

"Yes, ma'am. It's just been some kind of day. We all need to get some rest."

As Grandmother stayed with us in the room, Daddy walked back into the living room to say good night to Granddaddy.

"Goodnight, Daddy. We'll see you in the morning."

"Ok, you'll get some sleep, Son. See you tomorrow," Granddaddy replied.

Aunt Della and Uncle Irving also said, "Good Night," and left.

After Daddy walked back into our room, Grandmother looked up from the bed and said, "Rudy, you can sleep in the bed if you'd like, and the kids can sleep on the pallet on the floor."

"I took a lot of my old quilts and blankets and made it so they should be comfortable on it."

Daddy started talking, "Oh, I'll just sleep on the pallet and give them the …".

"Daddy, can we all sleep in the bed together?" I blurted out before he was able to finish his sentence. I was asleep but woke up at that very moment to make sure Daddy would be sleeping in the bed with me and Chris.

"Okay, sure, baby. We can do that," Daddy said, sensing my uneasiness.

Just the thought of Daddy lying on the floor, or us lying on the floor, made me immediately think of George lying in that pool of blood, and I became terrified again.

I sat up in the bed and waited for Daddy to come out of the bathroom from taking his shower. Grandmother sat there with us, reading us a story from one of our books we'd accidentally left there the last time we visited. That worked out well for us.

As hard as it was to fight sleep, I was too afraid to go to bed without Daddy.

As soon as Daddy lay down in the bed between me and Chris, I fell fast asleep. My eyes were so heavy, and I couldn't keep them open any longer.

Unfortunately, though, my sleep was short-lived from having a terrible nightmare about George and waking up crying.

Chris was fast asleep, and even my crying didn't wake him up. It did, however, wake up Daddy and our grandparents, who immediately got up and came into our room.

Grandmother began praying for me as she lay her hands on my forehead for the nightmares to stop. Daddy then held me in his arms and rocked me back to sleep. He quietly thanked her and Granddaddy as they returned to their rooms. Daddy moved me closer to him and held me tightly in his arms.

His presence was my protection.

In my Daddy's arms was the safest place for me to be.

Sunday, August 26, 1973, ended very differently than the way it began. Our brother George was dead, and our mother had been taken away, accused of killing him.

For weeks beyond that Sunday afternoon, our community reeled from the story of the mother who had taken her own child's life.

As for me and my family, our lives completely unraveled that day. It would take much more than a few weeks for us to adjust to not having Mama or George anymore and to fully come to terms with what had happened.

CHAPTER FOUR

THE BREAK

"...FELT GOD HAD FORSAKEN HER, MOTHER KILLS SON"
(Houston Chronicle Newspaper)

A spokesperson at the county jail made the following statement:

> *"A bewildered, frightened and frequently hysterical Alice Faye Battle sat in the visitor's room of the county jail. Her head was lying on the folded arms which she had placed on her drawn-up legs. It was obvious she was crying and that the tears were those of remorse, regret, and a way of asking for forgiveness."*

WITHDRAWAL AND NEGLECT

In the beginning, Mama was excited about being pregnant and having children. She went to the doctor for prenatal checkups and avoided the typical things that could cause harm to an unborn child, such as smoking and drinking. My brothers and I were all carried to full term and born healthy.

Mama was a very good mother early on, taking care of us, bathing, feeding, and clothing us, and making sure we had what we needed.

When we were sick, she would rub our chests and temples down with vapor rub and wipe our runny noses. Bandaging our 'boo-boos' when we'd fallen and scraped our skin, Mama knew how to make us feel better. In so many ways, Mama did what mothers do, and we depended on her for everything since Daddy worked so much.

That's why, following the tragedy, it was so hard for me to accept, with any kind of understanding, what happened because I remembered the countless hugs and kisses we'd get for no reason just because she loved us. Even the things that stood out once they were exposed seemed at the time to be normal because I was used to things being that way.

HOME ALONE

One thing that did stand out later on was how Mama would leave my brothers and me home alone, locked inside the house with our dog, Shep, while she attended the church conventions previously mentioned. Not only did Mama leave us alone, but most of the time, she left us without anything to eat; we didn't even have access to food in the pantry.

At the time, Daddy smoked Kool cigarettes, which he usually lit using long, wooded kitchen matches. Because he smoked in the house, we had ashtrays on just about every table throughout our home. Whenever we were left home alone and became hungry, we'd search every ashtray in the house for burned matches and would eat the tips of the charred matches.

I don't know why, in the world of all things, we'd eat those burned match tips; it had less to do with how they tasted and more to do with the fact that we were just that hungry. I watched George do it one time, after which Chris and I began doing the same thing. Soon, we were all scavenging the house in search of ashtrays with burnt matches. Daddy didn't find out until many years later, to which he responded with a look of dismay and teary eyes.

Over time, Mama was becoming more and more withdrawn as her behavior became more erratic.

The Breaking Point

The newspaper reported that Mama believed the only way to deal with life was to end it, hers and ours.

She poisoned Daddy's lunch that day, and when the police searched our home, they found a large bottle of poison, which she later told them during an interview that she'd intended to drink after she carried out her plan to end our lives.

Her exact words were, *"I had planned to kill them one at a time when they came in from playing, and then I was going to drink the poison."*

Mama was convinced that this life only offered suffering and pain.

She lamented, *"Everything looked dim. We were running out of food. And…there didn't seem to be any kind of help we could get. Poor people don't have nothing in this world, and I just kinda figured things would be better for all of us if we went to heaven."* 1 (The Forward Times Newspaper, August 1973)

The three-page handwritten letter left by Mama the day she killed George revealed the deep depression she'd been battling for some time, emotional issues that caused her to snap eventually.

Mama told the authorities that during that morning at Church, she'd prayed a long time.

Grandmother Wilma said Mama was seeking some kind of 'message' from God that would condone what she was about to do. The message never came. Mama stated she thought God would be displeased with her actions, but at least her children would not be blamed, and they would go to Heaven.

Our local newspaper, the **Forward Times Newspaper,** reported the following events of that day:

'It was about 5 p.m. when nine-year-old George Anthony came into the house after playing all afternoon. Dressed in a white T-shirt and some short green pants, George meandered into the bedroom where his mother was waiting to carry out her diabolical plan. In Mrs. Battle's hand was a 12-inch long butcher knife and as the innocent child walked into the bedroom, his mother plunged the knife into his throat. ***AS BLOOD SPURTED FROM*** *the little boy's throat, Mrs. Battle said she knew she had done the wrong thing. She grabbed the butcher knife from George's throat and ran down the street to the home of her neighbor, Diane Guillory, an 18-year-old Weyburn Street resident. "I told Diane that I needed some help because I had just killed my boy," this distraught mother cried. When we got back to the house, George was still there on the floor. He was jumping. His eyes were open. Blood was all over the place. I knew he was dead". The young Guillory Woman ran out of the house to call an ambulance and Mrs. Battle fell to her knees. Again she prayed, but the answer to that prayer—just like the other—did not come." (The Forward Times Newspaper, August 1973)*

Initially, after discovering my brother's body on the floor, I thought that the scream I'd heard must have come from him, but after discovering this article some years later containing a portion of Mama's statement, it became apparent to me that the screaming I heard had to have come from Ms. Diane. The object Mama was holding in her hand when she and I came face to face was the knife with which she'd just killed George.

During an interview, Grandmother Wilma said, *"My Daughter must have been… well…there's no nice word for it…insane, totally insane when she did that"*.

"She worshipped George. Why, just last school year, the teachers were telling us she was overprotective of George- you know, she didn't want him falling and skinning his knees like other children. Things like that." (The Forward Times Newspaper, August 1973)

Grandmother said she didn't want Mama to go to prison for what she did because she believed Mama was sick, very sick, and needed to be in a mental hospital where she could receive therapy and psychiatric treatment.

Her words were*:*

"We don't want her to get out of jail where she would be out and in a position to hurt or…kill…somebody else. We want her put in a hospital where she can get some help. You see, her mind comes and goes," she went on to say. *"This minute she's got just as much sense as the next person. The next minute, her mind's gone. We wouldn't take that chance by getting her out of there."* (The Forward Times Newspaper, August 1973)

THE WARNING SIGNS

Mama said she prayed to God for relief, but the answer she sought never came. Deeply troubled, she felt she had run out of time *waiting* to hear from God. There seemed to be no hope for her.

Our family also ran out of time, unable to see just how serious Mama's mental health issues were and how quickly she was emotionally declining.

"The real problems—bordering on schizophrenia—started when

Alice married…" the reporter writes as Grandmother Wilma shares Mama's mental history, trying to make some sense out of what she did. (The Forward Times Newspaper, August 1973)

Because I was a kid, I didn't understand what she was going through, but it's evident to me now that Mama was *crying* out for help…help that didn't come in time.

ACTING OUT

There were occasions when Mama's behavior was so bizarre and even turbulent that it should have been evident that something was not right.

One evening, Daddy drove Mama, my brothers, and me to his job to pick up his paycheck. While my brothers rode in the back seat of our late model blue Chevrolet, I sat in the front seat between Mama and Daddy.

Out of nowhere, Mama and Daddy began arguing soon after he'd driven off from the steel mill. As we traveled down the highway and headed back home, their argument became more intense, and without warning, Mama took a pile of letters sitting on the dashboard and began throwing them up against the front windshield.

"Alice, what's wrong with you!? Stop it, I said!" Daddy yelled, "You're going to get us killed!"

"You don't care anything about us!" Mama angrily responded. "All you do, Rudy, is work. I'm at home all the time with these kids! I can't take it anymore! I told you it's too much!" Mama said, hurling more letters, but this time directly at Daddy, hitting him on the side of his face.

"Alice, stop! Don't start this now!" Daddy shouted, quickly scowling at her while also trying to keep his eyes on the road.

"Are you crazy?! You know we have the kids in the car, and I'm trying to drive! Wait till we get home! We'll talk about it then!" Daddy said, furious with Mama. Angrily, he stretched his hand out towards her while at the same time trying to defuse the situation.

Mama didn't listen and continued with her rant, gathering the letters she'd previously thrown, and threw them again, and hitting Daddy again in the face. She had a snub look on her face as if she was taunting him.

"I mean, you better stop it right now before I pull this car over!"

"You pull it over then, you son of a_____! Do it, and we won't go home with you!" Mama shouted back at Daddy.

"What!? You're crazy! And you'd better watch your mouth in front of these kids." Daddy said sternly, looking at Mama and then trying to focus back on the road.

My brothers and I began crying, looking at both Mama and Daddy, not knowing what would happen next.

I nervously tried to listen to the radio and tune them out. For a brief, very brief moment, things quieted down, but then Mama started up again, scooping up the same letters that were near her and throwing them at Daddy once more.

"Ok, that's it!" Daddy said, slowing down our car and pulling over to the side of the road.

Suddenly, without warning and while the car was still moving, Mama opened her door, causing Daddy to panic and temporarily lose control of the steering. Our car began to swerve on the gravel roadside!

Managing to regain control of the car somehow, Daddy shouted at Mama again while stepping on the brakes, preventing us from running back into traffic.

Our car had just barely come to a rolling stop when Mama abruptly grabbed me, dragging me across the seat as she jumped out of the front passenger door, attempting to pull me out of the car with her.

"Alice, stop it! You've lost your mind!" Daddy shouted, reaching for me but unable to take hold of me because Mama was fighting him off with her hands, with me in between the two of them.

With his foot still on the brake, Daddy, for the first time that I'd ever witnessed, leaned over and struck Mama in the face with his hand as he was finally able to grab me in an effort to keep me in the car with him.

Mama went into an all-out rage, unlike I'd ever seen her do, and came back for me, refusing to let Daddy win the tug-of-war over me.

"No, Alice, don't do this! Let her go!" Daddy screamed at Mama, tussling with her over me, dragging me back and forth across the front seat.

I screamed, cried, and hollered for them to stop!

Daddy, with a look of anger and panic on his face, wouldn't give up, and Mama, determined to snatch me away from Daddy, held on tightly too! George and Chris continued to scream in the back seat of the car. It was pure chaos!

Mama, crying even more hysterically because Daddy hit her, let me go but then opened the back door and grabbed Chris, who was sitting next to the door on the passenger side.

"Alice, my God, please stop it! You are scaring the kids!" Daddy said, pleading with Mama, but it was as if she didn't hear him.

Mama was in a fit of rage, out of control, and nothing Daddy said was calming her down. She only continued to escalate.

Pulling Chris out of the car and causing him to fall on the ground, she then came back for me. By this time, Daddy had let me go and was on his way out of the car, headed around to the other side, where Mama was with Chris. As Mama reached for me again, this time yanking me out of the car, our car began moving, with no one at the wheel and George stuck in the backseat! In all the commotion, Daddy had forgotten to put the car in park!

"Oh my God…George!" Daddy said, terrified and running back around to the driver's side, jumping in and applying the brakes to stop the car.

George was shaking and crying uncontrollably.

Daddy running to save George meant leaving me and Chris alone with Mama. By the time he put the car in park and jumped out again, Mama had run off with Chris and me so quickly that Daddy lost sight of us, not knowing the direction in which we'd run. Chris and I didn't know what to do but to run with Mama as fast as we could, as she screamed at us, "Run!" leaving George behind with Daddy.

"Come on, run!"

She continued to shout at us, almost dragging our little legs because we were having a hard time keeping up with her pace. My brother and I held on to her for dear life as we ran, breathing hard, too hard to cry. We ran away with Mama as if Daddy was going to do something bad to us—as if we were afraid of him. It all happened so quickly, and yet it all seemed to happen in slow motion.

Eventually, we ended up in a nearby neighborhood to the right of the highway, where we'd last seen Daddy. I was sure Daddy hadn't seen where we'd gone, or else he would have come after us.

Things hadn't ever escalated to that point that I could remember.

Chris and I were so frightened and confused because we didn't understand why Daddy would hit Mama and why Mama would run away with us, leaving George with Daddy. The three of us ended up on the doorstep of people we didn't know.

Mama, with her face now turning purplish and beginning to swell from the blow of Daddy's fist, was sobbing as she banged on their front door.

An old white-haired, burly-looking man in about his 60s, wearing dark-rimmed glasses, opened the door and had a look of bafflement on his face, wondering who we were and why we were standing on his porch crying.

Mama, beginning to break down, explained to him, "Sir, I'm so sorry to bother you. I know that you don't know me, but me and my husband just had a fight, and he hit me in my face in front of our babies!"

The man's facial expression then turned to one of concern and compassion.

"I grabbed my two kids here, but my oldest son is still with him. Oh God, I just ran as fast as I could with them to try to get away from him! Please help us…" Mama pleaded, becoming even more distraught and beginning to cry even louder.

Chris and I continued to cling to her as she begged the man to allow us to come in. She told him she feared Daddy might find us if we stayed outside.

"Okay, okay…calm down ma'am. You'll come on in. Let me get my wife. Honey…," the man called out to his wife as he opened his front door wider, allowing us inside. Just as he closed the door behind us, his wife came hurrying out of the kitchen.

"Well, I thought I heard voices," his wife said, looking bewildered.

The man, who we later found out was a pastor, walked us over to his sofa, and his wife began inquiring about what was going on. Mama, while still crying, told the lady the same story.

"Oh my gosh, well, that's just terrible. You poor things," the wife said, sympathetically shaking her head and rubbing Mama on the arm.

You could tell she genuinely felt sorry for us.

"Well, you stay right there, and I'll get some ice for your face and get y'all something to drink to help you calm down."

She immediately got up and went into the kitchen for ice and beverages.

"Thank you, ma'am," Mama responded, blotting her eyes with a tissue that the pastor had given her.

Sitting in between me and Chris, Mama hugged us both, trying to comfort us. Though we weren't audibly crying anymore, we still had tears in our eyes. Everything happened so fast that we were still trying to process it all.

The couple showed us a lot of love, and that's just what we needed at that moment. The pastor's wife, a small-framed, gray-haired woman, returned from the kitchen with coffee, ice (for Mama's swollen face), and juice and crackers for Chris and me. After turning on the television for us, she then joined Mama and the pastor on the couch, and they continued to talk.

Chris and I sat on the floor and watched cartoons, which helped us at least temporarily forget what had just happened.

Meanwhile, the pastor was talking to Mama, as his wife listened, and then grabbed a bible and began reading some scriptures to Mama. He talked to Mama for a long time, so long that the pastor's wife made us dinner. Mama was noticeably feeling much better, even smiling a little bit again. Whatever the Pastor told Mama eventually led to her calling Daddy.

We'd fallen asleep on the floor on top of a makeshift 'pallet' bed the Pastor's wife made for Chris and me. Not too long after Mama made the call, there was a knock on the door, which woke us up. When the pastor opened it, Daddy walked in.

How tired and worried he looked when he stepped into the house.

Our eyes lit up because we were so glad to see him!

I was a 'daddy's girl' to my heart, and seeing my daddy caused me to smile from ear to ear. Chris and I ran to him as he picked us up and gave us both huge hugs, holding on to us tightly, obviously relieved that we were alright. After kissing each of us on the forehead, he put us down.

George, however, was not with Daddy. He'd been dropped off at Grandmother Hilda's house.

We were very close to our grandparents, especially Daddy's mother and father, and would visit them a lot during the summer months, often spending the night with them. They'd spoil us really good and smother us with love before sending us back home to Mama and Daddy.

Daddy approached Mama, and without saying a word, the two of them just hugged. Mama began to cry, and the pastor led her and Daddy over to the sofa, where they sat down.

Chris and I were ready to go get George and go home, but we had to sit again while the pastor talked to Mama and Daddy together.

It was already late, close to 10 p.m.

When the three of them finished talking, Daddy shook the pastor's hand while Mama waited to give him a hug.

The saga for the day was over, and Daddy walked over to us and said, "Come on y'all, let's go home."

Daddy seemed relieved. We were all so exhausted. It had been a very long evening.

Our parents made up, and after picking George up from our grandparents' house, we were all together again as a family. We went home, and things returned to normal *until* about a month or so later when Mama tried to run away with us again, this time while Daddy was at work:

That day, Daddy arrived home much earlier than expected and found all of our clothes packed in trash bags and sitting on the living room floor. Mama was very surprised to see him home so early, and when he questioned her about the bags, she told him that we were leaving.

At that moment, a huge argument erupted, and Daddy called his parents for help with Mama because he said she was 'out of control again.'

Before they arrived, Daddy let Mama know in no uncertain terms that she wouldn't be taking us anywhere. Our mother, very frustrated, headed towards the kitchen. She began making a lot of noise, throwing pots and pans, taking out her anger on them.

Not being able to deal with Mama by himself, Daddy knew their argument wasn't over, so he waited for our grandparents to arrive before approaching her again, hoping that Grandmother and Granddaddy would be able to help calm Mama down.

However, when they arrived and tried to talk to Mama, things only worsened into an even more heated altercation as Mama very angrily picked up a big knife and threatened Grandmother Hilda with it.

Everyone began urging her, "Put the knife down, Alice!" "Put it down!!!"

The police were not called out that night because Mama, after attacking Grandmother verbally, did finally listen and put the knife away. After more conversation, the situation seemed to be extinguished. Mama's fit had passed.

It was apparent that Mama's outbursts were becoming more and more frequent, but no one thought she would break to the point of wanting to hurt, much less kill any of us.

During her interview with the reporter, Grandmother Wilma continued to share information about Mama's emotional state, saying that Mama 'began acting peculiar around the age of 14'.

According to Grandmother, that's when she began sensing that something was wrong with her. Up to that age, Grandmother said of Mama, "She was a beautiful child, and she behaved *almost* normally."6

Grandmother Wilma said 'almost' normally because doctors told her Mama's brain had been damaged during childbirth, as she was pulled out with forceps. Grandmother and the rest of the family didn't give it much thought until Mama began having fits of rage. Accepting that something was wrong with Mama, Grandmother Wilma said, "It became obvious to us that she was ill." Grandmother said the outbursts were short in duration and not violent enough to lead Grandmother to think that Mama needed to be placed in a mental institution.

Grandmother said, "Alice Faye grew up in the Church, along with her siblings. They were all Christians, but Alice seemed to have a deep-seated religious feeling, *one like we've never seen before*. Her religion seemed to have a lot to do with her problems." 7 (The Forward Times Newspaper, August 1973)

Grandmother intimated, "It appeared like she was unable to get God out of her feeble mind."

She said that she knew Mama was reaching the end of the 'sane road' when she started talking about Jesus 'turning His back on her.' She stated that Mama said 'she'd been so loyal to God, and yet God was allowing her to be sick.'

"She was also so disgusted with the state of affairs in the world," Grandmother said. "…she'd talk about how the rich were getting richer, and the poor were getting poorer, and that she could not see where poor people were progressing at all."

Recounting how just two weeks earlier Mama went into a violent rage and tossed around everything in our house, Grandmother stated,

"I mean, she literally tore up everything. She pulled curtains off windows, light fixtures from the ceiling, turned over chairs and tore up the furniture."[9]

Going back even further, Grandmother said, "About nine months ago was when it started. It just got to the point where it occupied her mind every minute for the past three weeks. She [Mama] didn't talk about anything but the bible and Jesus. She'd sit there and quote scriptures. When she got out of the Austin State Hospital, we thought she was alright. Then, like I said, about nine months ago, her every thought was about Jesus, God, and the Bible."

Grandmother, referring to a recent incident, said, "She was sitting here one day quoting scriptures when she went into a rage, and we wrestled all over this living room. She was near the end then." [10] (The Forward Times Newspaper, 1973)

Out of feelings of hopelessness and sheer desperation, our mother planned to end it all. She thought she had no other option, no other way out, and was fully persuaded that life wasn't worth living.

Prior to meeting and marrying Daddy, Mama had already been committed to a mental institution on one occasion following a nervous breakdown. The psychiatric treatment she received seemed to help rehabilitate her so that she could lead a normal life. About six years into her marriage to Daddy, Mama's mental issues began to surface once again. It became more and more obvious that her condition was deteriorating, and again, a move was made to send her to the hospital for therapy and treatment.

However, when she didn't seem to be getting any better, Grandmother Wilma had her committed to a State Hospital. At that time, I was only two years old and had no memory of Mama being gone, a confinement which lasted two and a half years.

When Mama was released from the hospital, the family thought she was not only better but 'well.' Sadly, however, Mama had only been home for a year and a half before she had the most severe breakdown of them all.

Grandmother told the newspaper reporter that no one knew exactly what caused the final breakdown. Speculating, she shared, "Alice was just not able to cope with married life and its problems. There was her husband and the children and everything seemed to have crashed in on her." (The Forward Times Newspaper, August 1973)

Mama had a history of mental breakdowns, and she revealed to her doctor that, prior to taking George's life, she felt herself breaking down again.

Grandmother, recognizing that all was not well, recalls, "I tried to get my son-in-law to get her committed, but he just didn't think she was that sick to send her back to Austin."

Grandmother revealed that because Daddy continued to refuse to send Mama back, she was just about to step over him and do it herself like she did in 1969. Grandmother saw the signs many others missed, flags signaling that Mama was in trouble. Daddy blamed himself for what happened because he didn't act quickly enough to protect us.

Surprisingly, Mama had even confided in several close friends, telling them of her intentions to kill our family and herself. Though she revealed her plans to more than one person, not one of them came forth with that information until it was too late.

What a difference that revelation might have made for our family.

CHAPTER FIVE

SEPARATED

The Coroner's report stated that George had suffered a fatal wound to the neck. The knife Mama stabbed him with pierced his jugular vein and caused him to bleed to death…an unimaginable death for anyone to suffer, especially a child…and so undeserved for my 9-year-old brother.

THE DAY AFTER THE TRAGEDY

I don't know what time it was when I finally woke up the next morning. I tossed and turned the entire night.

The smell of bacon frying in the skillet and Grandmother's voice as she talked to someone from inside the kitchen caused me to open my eyes and sit up in bed. Daddy had already gotten up, but Chris was still asleep next to me, wrapped up in a sheet. I tapped him on his back, and he began to move. Slowly sitting up in bed, he looked at me and then looked around the room, I guess remembering that we were at Grandmother's house and not at home.

Life had changed overnight, and I was just glad to see a new day. Still pretty tired, we were glad to wake up to Grandmother's chuckle.

Whoever she was talking to made her laugh, and what a hearty laugh she had. Her entire upper body would move, jiggling up and down, as she tilted her head backward as if she were trying to catch her breath. Whenever I saw her laugh, I would giggle, even when I didn't know what she was laughing about. It was just so entertaining to watch.

Though Grandmother was not a very large woman, she did have the typical round girth that many grandmothers have, just the right size for grandkids to wrap their arms around and cling to. She had short, gray hair, which she wore curly most of the time. Grandmother's skin was very light, and her eyes were the most peculiar shade of blue. She was African American but mixed with Indian, we were told.

Daddy resembled Granddaddy more than Grandmother because Granddaddy, like Daddy, was dark-skinned. Granddaddy was balding on top and was a very tall man, standing well over 6 feet. His husky build made him look intimidating, but he was not as mean as he looked.

Grandmother was the more jovial one of the two, while Granddaddy had the more serious demeanor.

Rubbing my eyes, I got out of bed, followed by Chris, and we headed for the living room where everyone else was.

Daddy, Grandmother, Granddaddy, and Aunt Della were sitting at the dining room table talking. I was very surprised to see Aunt Della this time of the morning. It seemed like she'd just left.

Staying just four blocks around the corner from our grandparents, Aunt Della dropped by every day and sometimes more than once a day. Though her home was well within walking distance of our grandparents, Aunt Della seldom walked to their house, usually driving her car instead.

Noticing that we were up, they all turned to look at us, with Grandmother immediately getting up from where she was sitting and walking towards us. Daddy also got up from the table and walked over to us.

"Hey, good morning Cheryl and Chris. Are you all hungry?" Grandmother asked, giving us a big hug, followed by a smile and hug from Daddy.

"Good morning, babies," said Aunt Della, also smiling.

Granddaddy greeted us, also with a grin and a wave of sorts.

Everyone seemed upbeat, a far cry from hours earlier. I believe it was for us, more than being how they actually felt.

"Y'all ready to eat?" Grandmother asked, leading us over to the dining room table and pulling out chairs for us to sit.

"Yes, ma'am, are you fixing bacon?" I asked, smiling a little as I continued to take in the overwhelming scent of bacon.

Mama didn't fix bacon that often, only for special occasions or when she felt like it. We normally either ate cereal for breakfast (Frosted Flakes was my favorite) or oatmeal.

"Yes, we're having bacon and pancakes for breakfast, babies," answered Grandmother, looking back at us as she walked into the kitchen to turn the fire under the skillet off.

"Well, come on and let's get your faces washed and your teeth brushed, and then Grandmother will fix your plates. How about that?" Grandmother said, walking back to where we were sitting.

"Yes, ma'am," Chris and I responded, getting up, turning around and walking with Grandmother to the bathroom.

"Where'd Daddy go?" I asked, looking around Grandmother's waistline, trying to spot him. I thought he was walking behind us, but I turned to see that he was not there.

"You'll see your daddy in a minute. I think he went outside to get something out of the car. He's been waiting for you all to get up so you all could eat breakfast together."

At this point, nothing could make us smile more than being able to eat breakfast with Daddy. He always left for work so early in the mornings that we rarely got the chance to eat any meal with him other than an occasional dinner.

By the time we'd finished cleaning ourselves up and getting dressed, Daddy had come into the room.

"Alright, y'all ready to eat?" Daddy asked, walking over and drawing us close to his side with his hands.

"Y'all feeling ok this morning?" he asked, looking at both of us in our eyes.

"Yes, sir," we responded at the same time.

"Ok...good. Grandmother fixed us some good stuff for breakfast."

Turning to Grandmother, Daddy said, "Smells good, Mother. I've missed your cooking."

"Well, there's plenty for everyone. Y'all come on to the table," Grandmother said, gathering the pajamas we'd slept in and setting them to the side.

She walked out of the room with us in tow.

On our way to the table to eat, I asked, "Daddy, are we going to see Mama today?" taking him by surprise with my question.

I don't even know why I asked to see Mama. He didn't answer immediately but instead looked at Grandmother, who looked a bit stunned at my question as well.

"Uh, no, Whooper...not today," Daddy replied, giving me no reason or explanation for his answer. ('Whooper' was my nickname.)

Daddy gave me that name because I liked to punch or 'whip' him when we would play fight during the few times he was actually home early. He probably also called me that because he'd heard from Mama how I would sometimes get into fights with other kids, fights often initiated by the infamous 'knock the stick off my shoulder' threat. The fights were never serious and ended almost as quickly as they began. I, however, never backed down from a good scuffle. My friends and I would fight, makeup, and then head to the street or our backyard to play.

Attempting to change the subject, Daddy said, "Come on, let's go eat. Grandmother's going to make our plates".

I did temporarily drop the matter, only because that bacon was 'calling' my name, and I couldn't wait to dig in. No matter how sad I was about anything, there was just something about Grandmother's cooking that could put a smile on my face, and today was no different.

She made the best 'made from scratch' pancakes! I loved drizzling syrup over my double-stacked pancakes topped with a teaspoon of butter until the syrup ran down the sides of the pancakes and onto the plate. Her perfectly fried bacon was fat and crunchy, but not so fat that it was rubbery, and not so crunchy that it fell apart as soon as you bit into it.

A glass of ice-cold water washed the entire meal down.

Chris and I sat there at the table, eating a lot and saying little. Daddy was quiet, too, as he chewed on his food and watched us eat.

After finishing breakfast, Daddy let us go outside and play, telling us not to leave the front yard. He opened the blinds of the window in the front room so he could keep his eyes on us as we played.

Chris and I looked around the front yard and found a few sticks to use to dig up dirt in Grandmother's flower bed, which had only a couple of dried-up flowers left in it. It had been a hot summer, and not too many of Grandmother's flowers had survived the heat. Other than playing in the dirt, there wasn't too much else to do. Unlike at our house, there wasn't a swing set at Grandmother's.

There weren't a lot of kids our age on Grandmother's street either to play with, except the kids that would be over visiting their grandparents. Since summer was about over and school was about to start, they had all already returned home. Thinking about George and missing him so much, I started feeling sorry for myself and Chris. Why did it have to happen? Just yesterday, the three of us were digging in the dirt together, but from now on, it will be just Chris and me.

One thing I liked about George was that he wasn't the type of big brother who'd push us aside, not wanting to play with 'babies.' The truth is, he seemed to have as much fun playing with us as he did playing with his friends, who happened to also be our friends. We all hung out together.

Because of George, I had been looking forward to starting school, but now, I didn't know what was going to happen.

George had been at the same school since Kindergarten, so the teachers and staff knew our family. Through word of mouth and the media, news of George's death spread quickly throughout his school. Even those who didn't know George or our family were deeply moved by his death.

Not wanting to cry, I asked Chris to go with me around the side of the house to see if we could find more sticks.

Grandmother and Granddaddy had a nice one-story, three-bedroom, one-bath home with large shade trees in both the front and back yards. Like our house, a fence lined the entire backyard of their house.

On most sunny days, you could catch Grandmother in the backyard going back and forth over the fence, talking and laughing with adjacent and back neighbors.

Moving into the neighborhood when it was new, Grandmother and Granddaddy had lived there for well over thirty years and knew a lot of people in the community. Many of those folk, like our grandparents, were now up in age.

I enjoyed the community because, with the exception that there weren't a lot of kids, it reminded me a lot of our neighborhood and street. Everyone was so friendly.

Grandmother's closest friends, besides the ones from her church, lived right next door. Ms. Sanders, 'Mandy' as many called her, stayed to the right of our grandparents' home. She was a retired nurse and a widow who had adult kids and young grandkids.

To the left of Grandmother's house was Ms. Beatrice's house. Ms. Beatrice was affectionately known as 'Big Mama' or 'Mom B'. She was also a widow and, like Ms. Mandy, also had grown kids and young grandkids. Usually, Ms. Mandy's and Mom B's grandkids were the only kids we'd play with whenever we went to visit our grandparents.

While we were still looking for sticks, Daddy came outside, calling our names, looking for us. As soon as we heard him, we ran back to the front of the house. Daddy seemed panicked at first but then was okay when he spotted us coming from around the corner.

"Hey, what are y'all doing?" he asked.

"Just looking for sticks to play with," I answered, followed by Chris, who thought, because of Daddy's tone, that we were in trouble.

"Oh, okay. I have to go somewhere with Grandmother and Granddaddy for a little while, and Daddy needs for y'all to stay with Ms. Mandy until we get back."

"Can we stay with Aunt Della?" I asked.

"No, she's going with us too," Daddy said.

"Why can't we go?" Chris asked.

"Because we have to take care of some grown-up business, and it's best for you all to stay with Ms. Mandy until we get back," Daddy explained, drawing us both to his side.

He could see the look of disappointment on my face because we weren't allowed to go with them.

"It's okay, Cheryl, we won't be gone very long," Daddy said, gently placing his hand on my cheek, "…and Ms. Mandy will take good care of you all until we get back. When I come back, we'll go get some ice cream. How does that sound?"

"Okay. Yes, sir," I said, still somewhat reluctant to stay with Ms. Mandy but liking the idea of going out for ice cream.

I knew where they were going because, just as Chris and I were going outdoors, I overheard Aunt Della talking about having to make funeral arrangements for George. Daddy didn't want to tell us what they were going to do. No one had said one word about George in front of us. They hadn't mentioned him or Mama.

Staying with Ms. Mandy all of a sudden got a whole lot more pleasing when Chris and I looked up and out jumped Nicole and Junior from their mother's car. They were Ms. Mandy's grandkids. We were excited to see them, and I forgot all about how disappointed I was about not being able to follow Daddy. They were around our age, about 4 and 5. Nicole was the older of the two. We ran and met each other in Ms. Mandy's driveway.

"They'll be alright, Rudy," Ms. Mandy said, walking across the grass to meet Daddy.

All of us kids smiled as we tugged on and played with each other.

"Okay, Daddy will be back," Daddy said, walking over to us and giving us a hug before heading back across the grass to Grandmother's house.

"Hey Rudy," Ms. Mandy said, getting Daddy's attention and stopping him in his tracks.

"One day at a time, Rudy," she said, "We're praying for you. Just take it one day at a time."

"Yeah, that's it. That's where I am. Thank you, Mandy," Daddy responded before turning back around and continuing on to the house.

Ms. Mandy told us all to go inside her home and turn on some cartoons while she would go and make us a treat. She went into her kitchen and started popping us some Jiffy popcorn in her cast iron skillet. That's how Grandmother made it, too.

At one point, while we all sat on the sofa and watched TV, Chris looked at Nichole and said, "George isn't here anymore."

He looked as if he was waiting for Nichole to cry or something.

She looked sad, but the only thing she said was, "Yeah, Chris, I know. Our grandmother told us."

I looked at them and then turned away to watch cartoons again. We didn't talk anymore about George while over Ms. Mandy's house. Ms. Mandy gave us all the popcorn and Kool-Aid we wanted. Her Kool-Aid was almost as good as Mama's Kool-Aid.

Daddy and the rest of the family returned about the same time Junior and Nicole's mom came to pick them up, and we all said our goodbyes.

Chris and I milled around for a few minutes outside. Then, our grandparents' friends and church members began dropping by. The majority of them were in their 60s and 70s, close to our grandparents' age. They brought along with them plenty of food, including desserts, just like our neighbors had done yesterday. The Pastor from Grandmother's Church even came by.

Aunt Della called me and Chris to come inside while the pastor prayed for all of us together. We returned outside after the prayer but didn't stay very long because we were becoming bored of digging for worms. Chris and I decided to go back inside and just sit in the living room and listen to the grown folk talk.

Grandmother asked us if we were hungry, to which we responded, "Yes, ma'am."

She then gave us some fried chicken, mashed potatoes, green beans, and a small slice of cake—just some of the food the church people had brought with them.

After lunch, we continued to sit and listen to all of the conversations going on. Daddy had been sitting with everyone in the living room for a little while but then excused himself and went to the back room where we'd slept last night. I got up and walked back there to sit with him. When I peeked inside the room, he was just sitting on the edge of the bed watching television.

"Daddy, can I sit in here with you?" I asked as I walked into the room.

"Yeah, sure baby, come on," Daddy said as he scooted over to make room for me on the bed and then put his arm around me as I sat next to him.

At first, I just stared at the television, not really paying attention to what was on. I didn't want to watch anything. I just wanted to be with my daddy.

Not long afterward, Chris came into the room and sat on the bed with us. I turned to Daddy and asked, "Daddy, where's Mama?"

Chris leaned forward a little bit and looked at Daddy, waiting for an answer just like I was.

"Cheryl…Chris, your mother is very sick," he said with a blank look on his face.

"What's wrong with her?" I asked.

"Something's wrong with her…inside her head. Something's wrong with the way she thinks. You know, she's messed up inside her head," Daddy said, struggling to explain.

"Daddy, is that why she hurt George?" I asked, staring at him.

"Yes," he said as he turned to me and Chris, sitting next to me.

"Is she sad, Daddy? Does Mama miss us?" I asked as the questions that had been bottled up in my head started spewing out.

I was confused. Our family with Mama and George was no longer, and it just didn't make sense. We'd heard what our neighbors and others had said, but no one had at that point sat down with us to talk about Mama.

"Yeah, baby, I'm sure she's sad about what she did," Daddy answered, nodding his head.

"Cheryl and Chris, listen, your mama wasn't thinking right when she did what she did to George," Daddy said. "She loves you. She's just so sick and wasn't thinking right."

"Will she get better?" I asked.

"Daddy, where is George?" Chris asked before Daddy could answer my question.

"It's hard for me to explain to you what your mother did, uh… in a way that you can understand," Daddy said, bowing his head. "It's hard for me to understand it myself," he said, looking down and rubbing his hands together.

"That's okay, Daddy," I said, feeling sorry for him. He looked so sad. I didn't know if he'd even heard Chris' question about George because he didn't answer it.

Then Daddy, cutting the conversation short, said, "I tell you what, we'll talk about all this later. How about right now, we go get that ice cream?"

"Yes sir, okay." Chris and I said, nodding our heads while jumping off the bed.

Chris grabbed my hand as we walked behind Daddy towards the living room. I thought about his question about 'where George was.' Chris was the youngest of the three of us and just a baby, only four years old. I was having a really hard time with everything and couldn't even imagine what he might be thinking. I was told I was mature for my age, but that didn't help me figure out what was really happening to our family.

After saying 'Thank you' and 'Goodbye' to all of those who'd come to visit, Daddy told Grandmother he was taking us for a little ride to get some ice cream.

"Ok, you'll enjoy your ice cream, and we'll see you when you get back," Grandmother said, giving me and Chris a wet one on the cheek.

We walked outside and got into the car, and Daddy started driving, eventually getting on the highway. He exited and drove us to an ice cream parlor. He let us order whatever we wanted, within reason, of course.

I loved the chocolate-coated ice cream cone; it was my absolute favorite. Chris also liked it, so he asked for the same thing. Daddy got some kind of chocolate popsicle bar out of the freezer case. Daddy found us a booth to sit in, and he sat across from me and Chris. The three of us sat there quietly, eating our ice cream.

Breaking the silence, Daddy began talking about our dog, Shep. If Daddy was trying to get our minds off of George and Mama, talking about Shep would do the trick because we loved our dog. Our next-door neighbor was feeding him and giving him water while we were away.

Chris and I started laughing as Daddy talked about the first time he brought Shep home. He talked about how he would 'pee-pee' all over the house before we could get a cage for him and how 'bad' he would be at times, chewing up the floor rugs and, one time, even tearing up the sofa pillows, leaving a huge mess of cotton all over the living room.

Listening and giggling as Daddy brought up different stories about Shep, we joined in talking about the funny things Shep had done while Daddy was at work, stuff he didn't know about.

Even after we'd finished our ice cream, we still sat there for a little while longer as Daddy talked about the different dogs he had as a little boy growing up.

Finally, Daddy said, "Ok, that was good. We'd better go. It's getting late".

We weren't ready to leave but got up anyway. Throwing our trash away, we headed to our car, parked just outside the parlor's door.

Chris fell asleep less than five minutes into the drive back, and I was getting sleepy too. The drive back seemed to be longer than the trip to the ice cream shop. Daddy turned off the highway before our usual exit and drove through Downtown. As I sat in the back seat with Chris, I started gazing out the back window behind me. The sun was beginning to set. It was turning dark, and the lights Downtown lit up the city. It was so beautiful.

Noticing that we'd veered off the course back to our grandparents, I asked Daddy where we were going.

Answering, he said, "I thought you were asleep."

"No, sir. Chris is, though."

"I need to go somewhere before we go back to Grandmother's. It won't take long."

"Oh, where are we going?" I asked again, even more curious now.

By that time, we were pulling into a large parking lot, which sat in front of a tall building. Daddy turned the engine off, and we just sat there.

"Where are we, Daddy? What is this place?"

"Just a place," he said without elaborating.

"What's it called?"

Daddy quietly sat there with the back of his head resting against the headrest with his eyes closed.

Many years later, I found out that the place Daddy had driven us to was actually the morgue, where George's body had been taken.

Chris was still sound asleep in the back seat. I climbed over the bench seat so I could sit in the front with Daddy. Daddy opened his eyes due to my move to the front seat but then just sat there, staring straight ahead.

Out of the blue, I asked, "Is Mama in that tall building right there?" pointing to the building directly in front of us.

It was hard to tell how many floors it had, but it was one of the tallest buildings I'd seen.

"No…she's not in there," Daddy said.

 "Are we going inside, Daddy?"

"No, we can't go inside."

I was six and very inquisitive.

"Daddy?" I began to ask.

"Yes, baby," he answered.

"Do you think Mama's crying because of what she did to George?" I asked.

Daddy was still, and then he nodded his head, 'Yes.'

Then, looking at me sitting beside him, Daddy followed up with, "But everything will be alright. Daddy promises," while giving me a brief smile.

"Where's Mama right now?" I asked.

"She's somewhere where we can't go," Daddy responded.

Remembering how sick Daddy said Mama was, I asked him the question again that I'd asked earlier, "Daddy, will she get better?"

"I don't know, baby," Daddy said. Reaching for the keys still in the ignition, he said, "Ok, let's head back to Grandmother's. You go on and climb back in the back."

"Ok, Daddy," I said, yawning, turning and climbing back over the bench seat and sitting next to Chris.

I was too tired to ask any more questions, and my brain was starting to hurt, I believe, from thinking too much. We sat there in the dark for a couple more minutes, and then Daddy started up the car, and we headed back to Grandmother's house.

Mama's Life Without Us

The last time I saw Mama was when she was driven away from our neighborhood as she sat in the back seat of a police car. Chris had actually banged on the door of the police car in which Mama sat until one of the neighbors grabbed him while also peeking inside the car, trying to get a quick look at Mama.

In the eyes of many people, what she'd done was unforgivable. I heard them say that she deserved to die, to lose her life, just like she'd taken George's life.

Other than the people on the street who talked about Mama, I hadn't heard Daddy or my grandparents say anything bad about her other than that 'she was sick'.

Days turned into weeks, and weeks into months, following George's death, as Mama continued to be held at the county jail in the mental ward.

At Mama's court hearing, Grandmother Wilma was convincing in her argument that Mama was insane and did indeed need to be locked up, but not in a prison cell. She requested that Mama instead be committed to a mental hospital again, this time for as long of a duration as necessary, to be treated for her mental illness.

Mama's medical and psychiatric history helped paint a picture of the type of issues she'd dealt with over the years. Because she'd been committed to a mental institution before, a detailed record of her mental state was readily available for consideration in her court proceedings. Medical physicians and psychiatrists evaluated Mama. They concluded that the mental illness she had worsened by a deeper growing depression, eventually leading to her having a complete nervous breakdown and taking George's life.

For George's death, Mama was found '*Not Guilty By Reason of Insanity.*' The judge ordered that she be sent to the state mental hospital for confinement and treatment.

Initially, no one, except medical professionals, could see Mama, but eventually, as her condition improved, she was stable enough to receive visitors.

As for us, we did what Ms. Mandy told Daddy to do. We took life 'one day at a time' trying to adjust to our new life.

CHAPTER SIX

OUR FINAL GOODBYE

*Funeral arrangements for George had been made, and
we had to move forward with all of it. We had no choice.*

That next day, we spent the entire afternoon shopping. We had church clothes, but our grandparents wanted to buy us something new for George's services, and Daddy also needed to buy a suit for George to be laid to rest in.

Most Sundays, George and Chris wore slacks and button-down white or plaid shirts to Church and occasionally a tie to match. We'd all just gotten new clothes for Easter, but George had gotten taller and bigger over the summer months and had already outgrown the suit he had. The same was true for Chris. Grandmother often said we were growing 'straight up, just like weeds'.

Grandmother picked out a very pretty black dress with tiny white polka dots for me to wear. She then found some really sparkly black shoes to go with it. The shoes were so shiny that they looked wet. Walking over to the underclothes section, Grandmother let me pick out my own socks. Of course, she made suggestions, and I was glad that she did.

Mama did all of the shopping for us, and I wasn't used to making decisions like that for myself. We chose white ruffled 'baby doll' socks. Grandmother really knew how to put an outfit together.

Grandmother told me she was going to take me to her hairdresser to get my hair washed and pressed out and that Daddy would take Chris to the barber for a haircut. We met Daddy, Chris, and Granddaddy near the front register.

"Mother…," Daddy said, holding up two suits, one in each hand, for her to look at. The one in his left hand was much larger than the one in his right hand.

"I found this dark gray suit for George," he said, showing her the suit in his left hand. "The salesperson helped me pick out a shirt and tie to match it."

"Oh Rudy, that is such a nice suit. My grandson is going to look so handsome in it," Grandmother said with her eyes tearing up as she looked over the details of the suit.

Sensing Grandmother was starting to break down, Granddaddy stepped in and, gently taking her by the arm, said, "Ok, Mother, let's go ahead and get in line before a lot of folk get in front of us."

Just thinking about never purchasing anything else for George made Grandmother even more emotional, though, for our sake, she'd done her best to maintain her composure. She was such a source of strength for all of us.

"Let me show Grandmother my suit," Chris said while reaching to take his suit in Daddy's right hand.

"Look, Grandmother, look at my suit!" he said, holding up a black suit.

"Oh my Chris, boy, you're going to look so handsome in that suit. Did Granddaddy and your daddy get you some shoes?"

"Yes, ma'am, some black ones. They're in that box," Chris said, pointing to a box Daddy had already sat on the counter.

"What did you get for yourself, Rudy?" She asked, looking at Daddy.

"Oh, I found a black suit. It's hanging near the cashier. I also got a shirt and a tie to go with it," Daddy said, passing the boys' suits to the lady behind the counter as she was gathering our things to ring up.

It was our turn to be checked out.

"Is that your pretty dress?" Daddy asked as Grandmother passed it to the cashier.

I was just waiting for him to ask so I could show him what Grandmother was buying for me.

"Yes sir,…do you like it, Daddy?"

"Yes, Cheryl, it's very pretty. Did you tell Grandmother 'Thank You'?"

"Thank you for the shoes, and the dress, and the socks, Grandmother," I said, reaching to hug her.

"Oh, you're welcome, baby," she said, hugging me back.

"We have to take care of our babies," she said, smiling at both Chris and me, tenderly touching our chins.

It was early evening when we made it back home. Aunt Della had gone to her house to fix dinner, which she was going to bring over so we could all eat together. After Chris and I took our baths, we watched TV while waiting for the food to arrive.

By the time Aunt Della arrived at our house, which was about an hour after we'd gotten home, we were all starving and ready to eat. Seeing the headlights of Aunt Della's car as she pulled into the driveway, Daddy got up from where he was sitting and went outside to meet Aunt Della and help bring in the food.

"Hey everybody," Aunt Della said, greeting us as she walked through the door, heading straight for the kitchen to place a couple of containers on the countertop.

"Whew...let me sit down for a second," Aunt Della said, chuckling, bumping into and moving the dining room table a little as she sat down in one of the dining room chairs.

Grandmother was sitting in the chair directly across from her.

"Girl, you cooked a feast," Grandmother said, commenting on the abundant Pyrex and Tupperware containers Daddy continued to bring in and set on the kitchen counter.

"Oh, Mother," Aunt Della said, smiling, glad that she'd made Grandmother smile.

"Well, I wanted to make sure we had plenty and that you didn't have to cook for the next day or two."

"Well, I think you have that covered," Grandmother said, getting up from the table. "Thank you."

"No thanks needed, Mother. Just trying to help with what I can," Aunt Della responded, getting up and joining Grandmother in the kitchen.

She and Aunt Della then began to talk about George's funeral.

"Mother, I've called everyone out of town and told them about the services. Goldie and the others are planning to get a room when they get here," Aunt Della said. "I don't think they'll have a problem finding one. They'll need it just for a night unless they decide to stay longer."

"Ok, Della, good," Grandmother replied, looking at her.

"Oh, and George's teacher, Mrs. Drake, called me earlier while I was cooking, and I let her know about the arrangements, and she said she would let everyone at school know. She said so many people were asking about the services."

"Okay, I'm glad they have the information," Grandmother said.

"Yeah, she also told me that the school is sending a floral arrangement in George's honor," Aunt Della said, starting to remove the covers and foil from the bowls and containers of food.

"Rudy, Son…have you talked to any of your coworkers to let them know about the arrangements?"

"Yes, ma'am," Daddy replied, walking into the kitchen to talk to Grandmother. "I talked to Malone and Gibson, and they're going to put the information up in the break room. They said they would take care of letting everybody else know."

"My boss called me earlier to check on us, and so I let him know, too."

"You work with such nice people, Rudy, and the Lord has blessed you with good friends. He knows what and who we need in our lives," Grandmother said.

Daddy just nodded.

"Ok, well then, I think we have everything covered. Everyone has the clothes they're going to wear. The limousine will be here on Thursday at 6 pm to pick us up for the wake."

"Now, Della, you make sure you're here then so we can get to the funeral home no later than 6:30 pm," Grandmother said, giving Aunt Della a look.

"Oh, Mother, I'll be here…*on time*. I won't be late," Aunt Della said, a little embarrassed because of Grandmother's comment.

Aunt Della was known for being late for just about everywhere she went, and it irritated the heck out of Grandmother. Our aunt had no kids but was still usually the last one to show up at whatever function was going on.

Grandmother would say to her, "It just makes no sense for you to be late everywhere you go, Della. You need to move faster or get rid of some of the stuff on your schedule so you can get to where you need to get on time!"

We've all heard Grandmother say those same words over and over again.

Aunt Della would just usually respond in a very babyish, whiny voice, "Oh, Mother, don't fuss at me…I'm going to do better."

We've heard that over and over again too. Some things just never change.

THE WAKE WOULD BE IN A COUPLE OF DAYS, AND THE FUNERAL WOULD BE THE DAY AFTER THAT.

The morning of the wake, Daddy, Grandmother, and Aunt Della had all gone up to the funeral home to view George's body and to make sure everything was okay for the service, while Chris and I stayed at home with Granddaddy.

I guess everything was okay because no one said anything when they made it back. Aunt Della left to go home, meet Uncle Irving, and get dressed.

It was pretty quiet in our house as everyone got dressed. Family from out of town had come by the house earlier in the day and would meet us at the funeral home since the hotel they were staying at was on that same side of town. Grandmother and I got dressed in her room while Daddy had Chis in the back bedroom, helping him put his clothes on. Granddaddy got ready in his room.

The limousine pulled up to the front of the house at exactly 6 pm. Aunt Della, of course, didn't get there until 6:10 pm, *close enough* to being 'on time' for her. We were all dressed and waiting for her and Uncle Irving to arrive. I thought Grandmother was going to tear into her again, but this evening, she let it go. She whispered something under her breath to Daddy, to which he chuckled a little, but she refrained from making any comment to Aunt Della.

Some of the neighbors had also dropped by earlier to see if we needed anything and were just leaving as the limousine and motorcycle escort pulled up. We all gathered together just outside the front door and waited as Granddaddy locked up the house.

Making small talk with Daddy, the limo driver led us to the car, and we all filed into the limousine. It was my first time ever being so close to such a long car, much less actually sitting inside and riding in one. It was very spacious on the inside, and there was plenty of room for all of us to sit comfortably. Daddy sat between me and Chris with his arms around both of us.

The ride to the funeral home was a long one, as we traveled from the south side to the north side of town, almost the same distance as driving from Grandmother's house to our house on the north side. In fact, the funeral home was just a few miles from our family home.

Just minutes earlier, there had been talking, even a little joking, about Aunt Della's timeliness or lack 'thereof,' but now there was nothing but silence. No laughter. No talking.

The policeman escorting the limousine commanded such authority as he led us across town. It made me think about George, about how he would talk about becoming a policeman when he grew up. None of that would happen now.

Grandmother, who had been so in control of her emotions, now pulled out her handkerchief and began dabbing her eyes and softly blowing her nose. We were actually going to George's wake. It all seemed so surreal.

Aunt Della began to sniffle, too, and pulling out her tissue, she also began to wipe her eyes and quietly blow her nose.

Daddy, unlike Grandmother and Auntie, sat motionless. He didn't make eye contact with anyone. He just stared straight ahead.

Chris and I were very quiet too, looking down at the carpeted floor most of the ride. For me, it was hard coming to grips with seeing George again, only this time, lying in a coffin.

Arriving at the funeral home, we saw a lot of cars parked all over, even lining the streets near the funeral home.

"There are a lot of people here," Grandmother remarked, turning and looking at Daddy.

Daddy remained quiet, only nodding as he continued looking forward.

Grandmother's statement broke the silence that had begun the moment we stepped inside the limousine at home. We exited the limousine one at a time.

Meeting us at the front door of the funeral home was the funeral director. He was a very soft-spoken man, and after greeting us, he led us down the hallway to the chapel where everyone else was waiting.

Outside the room where George's services would be held, a few people greeted us, hugging and kissing us as we neared the doorway. There really were a lot of people there. Those inside, upon seeing us, stood as we entered the room and made our way to the front pew, escorted by the chaplain.

I'd never been to a wake, or even a funeral, of anyone and didn't know what to expect. My brother was the first person I'd known to actually die.

Many of the neighbors from our street and neighborhood were there, as were a lot of George's classmates and their parents. Many of Daddy's coworkers, Grandmother's and Granddaddy's neighbors and church members, and Aunt Della's friends and neighbors were also there. Even people who didn't know us personally but who had heard about what happened in our family came to be with us too.

We sat down just long enough for Grandmother and Aunt Della to put their purses down on the floor, and then we were escorted to George's casket, where his body lay neatly tucked inside.

Curious and afraid at the same time, I was even less prepared than I thought to see him again. He'd been dead going on five days now. I was there with him in the house after Mama killed him and remembered how he looked then with his eyes wide open. Now, they were closed, making him appear to be simply sleeping.

At least now, Daddy was with us, and there was no blood and no screaming. Still, there was a lot of weeping.

I slowly approached his casket, hesitant to take a longer look but unable not to. We all just kind of huddled in front of the casket as the others in the room looked on quietly. I stared at my brother.

Aunt Della commented on how handsome he looked.

There was a beautiful floral arrangement of blue and white roses draped over the bottom half of his steel blue casket. Surrounding his casket were many other plants and standing reefs, one of which was from his fourth-grade class.

"He looks so peaceful...just like he's sleeping. Well, he is sleeping," Aunt Della commented. Then Aunt Della leaned over into the casket and kissed George on the forehead.

I was stunned, so taken aback that I almost tripped over Daddy's shoe.

Was it OK to do that? Were you allowed to kiss a dead person? He was my brother, my big brother, but I was too afraid to kiss him. Aunt Della offered me the opportunity, reaching for me to pick me up, but I refused, shaking my head 'NO' in objection.

Moving closer to Daddy and clinging to his jacket, I peeked at George again.

Because he really did look as if he was just sleeping, some of my fear eased up. Gazing at him, I noticed that his eyes looked like they were glued shut. His hair was neatly cut, sideburns perfectly trimmed, and his thick eyebrows were well groomed.

Chris, George, and I all had these thick eyebrows that looked like black caterpillars above our eyes.

His lips, pressed together, were a little shiny but not too much. My brother looked handsome in his gray suit, more handsome than I'd ever seen him look, even on Sunday mornings when we'd gone to church.

As I stood there, I thought about how I'd never hear his voice again and how I'd never hear him call my name, especially when he'd try to help me find him when we played 'Hide and Seek.' I'd never see him smile again or hear him laugh at the cartoons we all watched together on rainy Saturday mornings. I was looking forward to seeing him in the hallway at school during the day or at lunch, but now I'd have to start school without him. We'd never dig for doodle bugs in the dirt together; we'd never play together again at all.

My brother meant more to me than I'd imagined, and it was at that moment that I realized just how much I was really going to miss him.

Then, feeling even sorrier for him than I did for myself, I wondered, 'Did he know that it was Mama who hurt him?' 'Did he even realize what was happening?''How long was he in pain, and what was going through his mind as he lay on the floor in all that blood?'

Now that he was dead, what would happen to him? Would he be lonely where he was going, or would he see other people from our family who had also died, like our great-grandparents, whom we'd never met?'

Everyone kept saying how he was now in Heaven with God, even though I could still see his body. They said his spirit was with Jesus. I didn't know what that meant. I just knew he wasn't with us anymore.

I thought about whether there were other kids up there for him to play with so he wouldn't be lonely or afraid.

He was a good big brother to me and Chris, so maybe God had some kids up there who wanted a big brother, and George could be their big brother, too. Having others to play with, I believe, would make George smile. He loved to smile. I guess God would take care of him so he wouldn't be scared.

I tried to process it all, but each question in my head only led to more questions.

"Come on," Daddy said, distracting me from my thoughts and reaching for me and Chris.

His eyes were the same blood-shot red color that they were the day he came home and found out that George was dead. I was so consumed with my thoughts that I hadn't noticed how everyone was leaning over and sobbing as they looked at George. Daddy just stared at George, not crying, just staring with the saddest face I'd ever seen him have.

Following Daddy's lead and turning to the usher, we were all escorted back to our seats. Then, the minister in charge did something he said he didn't ordinarily do. Standing in front of the congregation, he asked all the people to get up out of their seats and give somebody nearby a hug and then asked them to make their way up to where our family was sitting and hug us as well.

Without hesitation, everyone got up and began moving around, embracing those closest to them, and then came to where we were seated and began, as the minister put it, 'loving on us.'

My other grandmother, aunts, uncles and other family were also sitting on the same side of the chapel as us, in the 'family' section. It was a difficult time for everyone in the room, especially for our family, and that minister obviously knew what everyone in the room needed.

In a matter of minutes, a very solemn gathering turned into what looked and felt like a huge family reunion. Family, neighbors, friends, strangers, coworkers, church members, George's teachers, and George's classmates and their parents came up one after the other and comforted us with hugs and kisses, expressing their sympathy and letting us know that we were in their prayers.

We all returned to our seats as the minister began speaking, asking everyone to take their seats.

The service began. Time couldn't pass quickly enough for me because it all hurt so much, but at the same time, time couldn't go slow enough because this was almost it. We would soon be saying our final 'Goodbye' to George and laying him to rest in a cemetery many miles away from our home. For me and my family, it was the most difficult thing we had to do.

There was a lot of activity going on in the room: words were being spoken, and sentiments were being expressed. It was tough for each one who stood and spoke, evidenced by the many pauses and breaks taken to wipe tears from their eyes.

I drowned out much of it as I continued to gaze at George. He simply didn't deserve to die and shouldn't have been lying in that casket. I could still see part of his face as his head rested on the white silk pillow inside his casket.

The minister in charge took the podium last and gave a short eulogy filled with words of encouragement for everyone there, especially our family.

As the service was coming to a close, Grandmother's Pastor, Pastor Jammer, went to the front of the room to deliver the closing prayer.

Lifting up his arms and bowing his head, he prayed for our family, friends, and all of those who were there. Pastor Jammer even prayed for Mama. His prayer did seem to lift spirits as the crying got quieter. Either the prayer worked, or the people were just worn out from so much crying.

After the benediction of the services, everyone moved to the outside of the funeral home, with me, Chris and Daddy being the last to leave out. Walking closely behind Daddy, with his hand tightly holding mine, I turned back to look at George.

At about that time, a funeral home attendant turned on a red light over George's casket and then turned off the main light in the room. The casket looked like it was glowing, giving me the feeling that George was going to get up.

Though I believed that even if George had woken up, he wouldn't have hurt me, I'd already seen so much, too much, which made me quickly get in front of Daddy.

After saying our 'Goodnights' to everyone, we loaded back into the limousine, and the driver took us back to our grandparents' home on the other side of town.

Chris and I fell asleep next to Daddy.

Just as during the ride to the funeral home, very little was said during the ride back. By the time we finally made it home and took our baths, it was a little past 11 pm. The last service for George was less than twelve hours away.

Still sharing the bed with us, Daddy seemed to toss and turn a lot, waking me up a couple of times as the bed shook. It seemed like, by the time Daddy finally fell asleep and stopped moving the bed, it was time to get up.

THE FUNERAL.

At 9:30 a.m., we were awakened by a small alarm clock placed on the nightstand in our room. Daddy stepped just inside the room and said, "Good Morning. Y'all get up. It's time to get up, Cheryl and Chris."

We sat up in bed, trying to focus our eyes while stretching for a moment. Grandmother also came into the room, passing Daddy and walking over to the bed.

" Come on, y'all, we don't have a whole lot of time, babies. Let me help you get ready," she said, pulling the blankets completely back.

"We're supposed to leave in about an hour, and we all have to be ready to go. Grandmother let you all sleep too long, but I knew y'all were really tired from last night and all," Grandmother continued on while taking us both by the hand, getting us out of bed.

Grandmother, Granddaddy, and Daddy were already dressed.

"Come on now," she said, leading us to the bathroom, "Let's go brush your teeth and wash your faces. Then we'll come back and get dressed."

Grandmother moved quickly, handing us toothbrushes and wiping our faces as we finished brushing our teeth.

"Grandmother, what time is it?" Chris asked.

It's a little after 9:30," she answered.

"Are we going to ride in that same long car that we rode in last night?" He also asked.

"It's called a limousine, and yes, but we have to hurry. We need to be ready."

"Grandmother?"

"Yes, Chris,"

"Uhm, I'm scared to see George again."

"Oh, it's ok, baby. Just close your eyes and walk with me. I'll hold on to you. It will be alright. Nothing will hurt you."

Chris didn't say anything back but just looked at Grandmother. I could tell how afraid he was, so I tried to help him not be so afraid. He was my baby brother, and I completely understood how he felt because I was still afraid myself.

"But Chris, you know that there's nothing to be afraid of. George won't hurt you. He's already in Heaven with God," I said.

"That's right, Cheryl. He has gone to be with Jesus," Grandmother added.

"Grandmother?" Chris began, looking at Grandmother.

"Yes, baby?" Grandmother gently responded.

"Is George happy in Heaven with Jesus?" Chris asked.

"Yeah, baby...I'm sure he's very happy. He's not sad at all. God has him, and you know what else?" Grandmother continued.

"What?" Chris asked, looking up at Grandmother with his big, beautiful, round eyes.

"He's watching over us right now, so we're going to be alright. God is looking at us this very moment, and He'll help all of us to one day not be as sad as we are now," Grandmother said, giving Chris a light pinch on the cheek.

"Grandmother, do you think George sees us too?" I asked.

"Maybe so, baby...maybe so. I bet you that if he does see us, he's smiling," Grandmother said, smiling while tearing up and stroking Chris' chin.

"Yeah, Grandmother, I bet you he is smiling. That boy loved to show his teeth," I said, as we all began to chuckle lightly.

Grandmother always knew the right thing to say to make us feel better. She fed us a really light breakfast: a bacon sandwich made with bacon leftover from yesterday's breakfast.

The limousine arrived on time, and this time, for once, so did Aunt Della, along with Uncle Irving. We all got into the limousine and rode back across town for George's funeral.

When we pulled up in front of the funeral home, there were a lot of cars everywhere, even more than at the wake. We got out, and the director of the funeral home and the Pastor came out to greet us.

Grandmother Wilma, Aunt Doris and other aunts, uncles, and cousins were waiting in a car for us to arrive. We all gathered together and walked in together.

As soon as we entered the Chapel, which was standing room only, those who were seated stood as we passed, making our final trip up to the casket.

Chris and I held on to Daddy as we cried loudly, and he hugged us tightly. Tears flooded my eyes and streamed down my face because we were told that once they closed the casket, that would be it.

For the first time ever, Daddy cried in front of us, not trying to hide his tears or the sound of his weeping. He wiped his face and then held his face in his hand. I could see the tears streaming down his face and over his hand, as he hung his head. While standing in front of George's casket, his tears just flowed, one after the other, but his cries became silent. Everyone allowed Daddy to weep for a moment alone.

We all then embraced each other and wept together.

Following the usher, Grandmother turned and took us with her to the pew where we were to sit. As Daddy turned to walk to his seat, his face was still wet, and that made me cry even more. George's casket was slowly closed, and the wails got louder.

Not being able to hold back the tears any longer, even Granddaddy cried out loudly, calling out George's name, "Oh God, my grandson... George!"

During the service, many expressions and thoughts were shared, a poem was read, a couple of hymns were sung, and then the last eulogy was delivered.

The students that would have been George's fourth-grade classmates served as 'Honorary Pallbearers.' It was one of the saddest days of our lives, only second to the day George died. Although there were moments of laughter from a story or two being told about George, it was a very difficult service to get through. A young life had been taken way too soon.

The funeral was over, and George was laid to rest in a beautiful cemetery. It was late summer, the grass was a vibrant green, and the grounds were well-kept. Many of the graves were adorned with lovely, bright-colored flowers.

The Pastor gave the final benediction at the cemetery, just after those in the immediate family were offered roses from the reef lying atop George's casket. The floral arrangement was huge, enabling most of the people there to take a flower. Daddy gave Chris and me one each, as he also took one. Daddy looked down at the rose and clutched the stem of the rose in his hand so tightly I could see his knuckles rounding out.

After the service ended, Chris and I stayed close at Daddy's side, only moving when he moved, as everyone walked around, kissing cheeks and hugging tightly.

We'd later on see many of them again at the repass being held at Grandmother Wilma's house.

As we walked back to the limousine, it struck me that this was it. This was our final 'Goodbye' to George. We walked slowly back to the limousine, climbed in, and headed back to our grandparents' home to change clothes. After that, we were to meet everyone at Grandmother Wilma's house.

What a long day it had been, and I was looking forward to being around family, around my cousins and friends who'd be there.

Not much was said during the ride back home. Daddy was silent, with his arms around us, staring straight ahead once again.

Daddy had an inscription put on George's headstone, along with his name, date of birth and date of death, which read:

'OUR SON'

GEORGE ANTHONY BATTLE

JULY 7, 1964

AUG 26, 1973.

George was Daddy's and Mama's son.

Throughout the funeral, I didn't think much about Mama, but after leaving the cemetery, I couldn't stop thinking about her, remembering how frightened she looked the last time I saw her as she ran away from our house. George was dead because of her. I wanted to believe that Mama loved us too much to hurt us, but George's death said the opposite to me.

A couple of days ago, I'd overheard Daddy telling Grandmother that the people at the jail were watching Mama, making sure she wouldn't try to hurt herself. I guess her pain had to be as deep as ours but for different reasons.

CHAPTER SEVEN

OUR NEW NORMAL

George Had Been Laid To Rest. Mama Was Transferred Out of Town.

Our family was in shambles. Just like our lives had changed, Mama's life completely changed, too. She, at 33 years of age, went from being a wife and a mother of three young children living at home with her family to being committed to a maximum-security psychiatric institution, where she would be completely dependent upon others for even the most basic needs of life.

The only constant thing we still had that hadn't been destroyed or fazed by what Mama had done was the love Daddy had for us and his determination to still provide a stable home for us.

Now a single father, Daddy's top priority was finding someone to take care of us full-time once he returned to work at the steel mill. While nothing would have made us happier than to live with Daddy, we understood that he had to work to pay the bills and take care of us financially, which meant someone would have to step in and help him raise us.

For a little while, it wasn't exactly clear as to who that 'someone' would be. I only knew I really missed Mama and, for a while, dealt with what I guess was depression, causing me to bury my feelings eventually. It seemed to be the only way I could survive. We were really too young to understand just how deeply our mother's actions would later on, even many years later, impact our lives.

Initially, Chris and I lived with our Aunt Katy, Grandmother Wilma's sister. Aunt Katy was married but didn't have any children of her own. For some reason, after a brief stay with her and her husband, we were then shuffled around, eventually moving in with Aunt Della, whose actual name was Idella, and Uncle Irving. She and Uncle Irving, who was a reverend, had been married for several years. It seemed that Daddy was trying to put us with someone who'd be able to devote a lot of personal time to us.

The great thing about staying with Aunt Della and Uncle Irving was that our grandparents were just a few blocks away. We were so crazy about our grandparents, especially Grandmother. Though they were up in age, we still enjoyed being with them. On most weekends, we'd stop by on Saturday and pick Grandmother up so she could go shopping with us. For certain, every Sunday, we'd go over there after church to eat.

For the first few weekends, that's how it was until Daddy was able to change his shift at the steel mill so he could get us on weekends and spend that time with us. As soon as his shift change went into effect, he'd pick us up late Friday evening and would keep us at our home on the north side of town until early Sunday evening.

Daddy started working on a major project in our backyard. He was building something. Because it was a surprise for us, Daddy wouldn't tell us what it was until it was recognizable. After a few weeks, Daddy took

Chris and me to the backyard one weekend we were over and revealed that he was building us a playhouse! Daddy had bought wood, all kinds of screws, nails, and even light fixtures to build our playhouse.

After that weekend, each time Chris and I went to spend time with Daddy, we'd excitedly head straight for the backyard to see how much more Daddy had done. That playhouse kept Daddy busy during his off time from the steel mill for a little while. He wouldn't spend all of his time with us working on it, but he would work on it for an hour or two each day we were there. That was perfectly fine with us because we'd soon have our very own playhouse!

Daddy finally finished it, and it stood as a masterpiece! Wow!!! We'd never seen anything like it! It actually had windows and a working light, operated by the same kind of switch we had inside our home. Even our neighbors' breath was taken away as they dropped by to check it out. I already knew Daddy was smart, having come across notebooks full of all kinds of mathematical equations and calculations that he'd learned while serving in the army. However, looking at that playhouse gave me an even greater respect and admiration for him. He built that house for us, and Chris and I were simply beside ourselves. Our friends couldn't wait for us to come over on the weekends so that they could play in it too.

Daddy did all he could to make Chris and me happy. He'd never be considered a 'part-time' daddy in my eyes. Besides doing very special things for us, he'd come over to Grandmother's as often as he could to spend as much time with us as he could. Many times, we'd even see him during the week after school after he'd gotten off work. It took about 30 minutes to get from our home on the north side to our home with our auntie and uncle on the south side of town, and even longer if Daddy was coming from work. However, Daddy never let that keep him away from us. He was still there with us, and he still took care of us.

Understanding that would later make a bigger difference in my life than I could ever imagine. Daddy tried to make our time together as 'normal' as possible and what we were used to with our grandparents, with the one exception being that he didn't take us to church on the weekends when he had us.

After living with Aunt Della and Uncle Irving for about a year, we were suddenly moved to Grandmother's and Granddaddy's home.

A year after George died, Uncle De'Walter, whom our grandparents continued to take care of, also died. Daddy was very close to Grandmother and all along preferred that we lived with her and Granddaddy, knowing that they would take good care of us. Now that Uncle De'Walter had passed, our grandparents would take us and raise us with Aunt Della's help.

When we moved in with our grandparents, Daddy continued to pick us up on Friday evenings, but one major difference now that we were living with our grandparents was that Daddy would take us back late Saturday evening so we could go to church on Sunday morning. It was important to Grandmother that we go to church, and Daddy honored that.

Oddly enough, Grandmother and Granddaddy went to different churches. Granddaddy went to a Baptist church, and Grandmother attended a Methodist church. While Granddaddy drove his car to church, Grandmother, with us in tow, would take the city bus to her church, which was much further across town. On most rainy days, however, Granddaddy would either drop us off or take us to his church and from there, we would ride the bus the remaining way to Grandmother's church.

I have no idea why they went to different churches, but Chris and I enjoyed riding the city bus with Grandmother across town. It was fun waiting for the bus and then getting on the bus and seeing all the different people who got on and off the bus. The bus driver, who got to know us from our regular trips, was very nice and began dropping us off right in front of our house, which was along the bus route. That saved Grandmother, who was in her upper 60s, from having to walk down the street with two small kids. It was nice receiving 'front door' treatment like that.

Daddy would always come back after we got home from church to spend time with us so that we could eat Sunday dinner together. We hated leaving Daddy so soon on the weekend, and other than riding the bus to church, we weren't *that* excited about cutting our visits short. Also, knowing that Daddy would be joining us after church for a feast also made our weekends 'not so bad'…as Grandmother would really 'throw down' cooking on Sundays!

Her Sunday meals were so delicious. We'd have a spread of foods, ranging from meatloaf, fried ribs, pork roast, and fried chicken to oven-roasted hen or pork chops. Of course, whatever meat we had would also be accompanied by plenty of sides, like mashed potatoes, rice, green beans, yams, mustard greens, creamed style or whole kernel corn. Occasionally, we'd also have a side of red beets, which I wasn't particularly crazy about but ate anyway because Grandmother ate them, and she said they were good for us. To top it all off, Grandmother would make dessert for us. She'd surprise us with rice or bread pudding with raisins, peach cobbler, sweet potato pie, blackberry pie, or my absolute favorite, banana pudding!

At the dinner table, everyone would be chewing and enjoying the food so much that there would be very little talking until everyone had finished. Afterward, we'd all just usually sit on the sofa, full from eating.

During the week, we'd have much smaller but still tasty meals for dinner. That is unless Daddy put in a special request, which Grandmother would always fulfill without hesitation. Most times, Daddy would either buy the food he wanted Grandmother to cook or give her the money to buy the groceries.

Although I never learned to cook like my Grandmother, I did learn early on how to clean a house. Grandmother was an especially neat and tidy person, teaching me that 'everything has its place.' Keeping a clean house was more involved than I thought, though Grandmother made it look so easy and effortless. Every day, she would busy herself with cleaning, dusting, or straightening up something. That's why our house always looked so uncluttered and smelled so good.

Grandmother would give me money, an allowance, for helping her clean the house. Grandmother, however, would tell me 'not' to tell Aunt Della whenever she gave me money.

I asked her, "Why not Grandmother?"

She simply said, "Because your Aunt Della will get jealous," and then she'd shake her head, as if being a little disgusted, and would then follow it all up with a chuckle.

I laughed, too, even though I didn't get that at all.

At first, I thought it was just a joke, but later on, I learned that it was no laughing matter, experiencing the undisputable truth firsthand. Life was what it was.

Our time with Daddy, on the weekends especially, was so special and something we looked forward to. Daddy wasn't the cook that Grandmother was, but he absolutely had his own signature dishes that Chris and I loved. At the top of the list were his perfectly fried bologna and cheese sandwiches! Daddy knew how to fry the bologna just right, perfectly darkening the edges of the meat just enough and laying the cheese in the right position between the two slices of bologna. He would also give us dessert following most meals, with our favorite dessert being cherry cobbler with whipped topping. Of course, Daddy would cook other things as well, but the fried bologna and cheese sandwich was our favorite.

Chris and I were becoming adjusted to our new lives. We were happy with our grandparents. We were happy with Daddy.

One particularly strange thing Chris and I had begun doing when we wanted to ask Daddy for something, and it didn't matter what it was, was we'd count down from three and then ask for what we wanted at the same time.

We'd start by practicing with each other, rehearsing what we were going to say together, and then would begin, "Ok, ready, 1, 2, 3, *Daddy...*"

It's not that we were afraid of Daddy; we were just afraid of being told 'No.' A 'No' response seemed a lot less embarrassing when you weren't the only one being told 'No,' so we concocted a way to keep either one of us from celebrating or suffering alone, depending upon the response we got. We thought we were being smart, but Daddy probably gave in most of the time because perhaps he thought what we did was cute. He never asked us why we asked him for things that way. I looked up to him so much because he didn't complain, at least not in front of us, about how unfair life was.

As a single parent now, Daddy stayed positive about life, never taking his frustrations out on us. I guess Daddy was just so grateful to still have me and Chris. The most fun we'd have with Daddy would come during the summer months. That's when we were able to spend more time with him since school was out, and he'd usually take two weeks off during the summer months to be with us. Just about every summer during those two weeks, Daddy would pack our bags, and we'd head out of town. Destination? *Fun*!!!

We made several trips to San Antonio and the surrounding areas like Seguin (where we had relatives), New Braunfels, and San Marcos. Chris and I liked staying up late nights at nice motels and eating out for every meal.

By far, our most memorable vacation trip was our visit to The Wonder Cave in New Braunfels and Aquarina Springs, located just a short distance from San Marcos, Texas. It was the first time I'd ever ridden in a glass-bottomed boat and seen a pig up close; a pig that actually swam!

We would be excited from the very moment Daddy told us we were going on vacation. While going out of town with Daddy was something we absolutely looked forward to, even more than that, we just enjoyed spending any amount of time with him.

Every Friday, Chris and I would be in a state of excitement, waiting for our daddy to pick us up. Though our time together was fairly routine, with us doing the same thing, Friday nights with Daddy were still always special. We'd arrive home, put our bags away, and eat dinner- either one bought or made by Daddy. Sometimes, when Daddy didn't cook, we'd be treated to fried chicken or a burger at one of the local fast-food restaurants.

Usually, after eating, we would put on our pajamas and, weather permitting, go outside, climb on top of the hood of Daddy's car, sit there with him, and listen to music for two to three hours, well passed dark.

It was so peaceful at night. Except for the occasional mosquito attack for which Daddy was armed and ready with 'bug repellant,' we'd sit back motionless against the windshield and gaze at the stars on a clear night. How beautiful and brilliant they looked, not having a care in the world. All they had to do was hang up there in the sky and twinkle. How funny it was that something as complex as a planet looked so simple from far away.

Those were some of the best nights and times ever. We were already learning to appreciate moments like that, knowing how quickly life can change.

Our time with Daddy was simple and uncomplicated, and that kept us very close. The music was soothing. That's when I began to have an appreciation for musicians like Otis Redding, Dinah Washington, Brooke Benton, Ray Charles, the Platters, Gladys Night and the Pips, the Temptations, the Spinners, and a host of other singers/groups.

Daddy did drink, but never to the point of becoming intoxicated. As the radio played, he'd normally have a drink with ice in a glass while Chris and I sat quietly on the hood and enjoyed the music with him.

Eventually, learning the lyrics to just about every song he played, Chris and I would sing along with our favorite tunes. That made Daddy rock and smile.

Sometimes, if we were somewhere else and heard those songs playing, we'd immediately start singing, which often made other grown-ups laugh or grin, too.

LIFE WITH OUR GRANDPARENTS

Chris and I already felt at home with our grandparents, having previously spent so much time with them during the summer months. We shared the back bedroom that we'd shared with Daddy following our family tragedy. The full-size bed that once occupied the room was replaced with twin beds so we could each have our own bed and still be able to stay together in the same room.

Our grandparents' entire home, except the bathroom and the kitchen, had hardwood floors.

Granddaddy snored loudly, so he and Grandmother no longer slept in the same bed, now having separate rooms. Granddaddy's bedroom was directly across the hallway from ours, and Grandmother's was just down the hall, across from the bathroom. Grandmother's room had a huge queen-sized bed, and her bedroom was the only one with an air conditioner. There was also an air conditioner in the living room. Our room and Granddaddy's had box fans to help keep us cool in the summertime.

In the living room sat a huge Deer Borne heater, adequate enough to heat the entire house during the winter months. Our new home with Grandmother and Granddaddy was very comfortable and cozy, like the way our old home had been. The only television in the house was a floor model Zenith, which sat in the living room, surrounded by a long sofa, a recliner, and a love seat.

Our dining area, though small, was furnished with a brown, round wooden table and six matching chairs, which was more than enough room for us all. Other than at the dinner table, we weren't allowed to eat anywhere else in the house. Generally, Granddaddy led the prayer before every meal, and whenever Chris and I were the only ones eating, Grandmother would make sure we said our Grace, which I learned to say in school, with Chris learning from me.

Our lives with our Daddy and grandparents became our new normal, and we settled into it. If, for some reason, Daddy couldn't pick us up on Friday evening, our Saturday would be spent doing the same thing we did when our family was still intact—playing!

Chris and I would grab toys and head for the backyard. Though it wasn't as big as our backyard at Daddy's, there was more than enough room for us to run around and play, including playing kickball; though many times we had to go next door neighbor to Mom B's, ring the doorbell, and ask her if she would kindly retrieve our ball from her backyard after we'd kicked it too hard. It became such a common occurrence that we stopped bugging 'Mom B' and just waited for her to come out and see our ball in her backyard and toss it back into our yard. I'm so glad she was such a sweet old lady because she never seemed to mind or become irritated about having to throw our ball back to us. In fact, she'd always just toss it back to us if we were still outside, saying, "Here you'll go," while giving us a huge smile.

Our grandparents had some of the nicest neighbors. They looked out for us as if we were their grandchildren.

The elementary school that we would now attend was right down the street from our grandparents' home. Chris was now in the first grade, and I was in the second. Because school was just down the block, Granddaddy would walk us to school every morning unless it was raining hard, in which case he'd drive us. Once school ended, Granddaddy would come back and pick us up at our designated area.

We continued the same routine until the following year when we were a little older and allowed to walk to and from school by ourselves. Being able to walk home from school by ourselves made us feel like 'big' kids.

Without fail, however, every morning, Granddaddy or Grandmother would still watch us from the end of the driveway as we made our way to school. One or both of them would do the same thing in the late afternoon, standing there at the edge of the driveway, looking for us and watching us until we made our way back home.

As soon as we reached them, we'd be asked how our day went. If we said anything other than 'good' or the like, they'd want to know right away what happened and would be ready to go right back up to the school and fix whatever problem we had. I loved them for that because I knew that I could always count on them to protect us and take up for us if need be.

Our grandparents in *no way* condoned any wrongdoing on our part, and they made sure nothing and no one interfered with our getting a good education. Our grandparents had 'zero tolerance' for bullying of any kind from kids or from teachers. I looked forward to going to class every school day.

Walking home from school, I can remember how, during some Spring days, the wind would blow so strongly that we'd have to literally walk against the wind with our heads bowed to stay on our feet. The wind does not blow like that anymore, at least not unless there's bad weather in the area.

Also, very intriguing during our life with our grandparents was the presence of a multitude of fireflies that would literally light up the yard at nighttime. Wow, what an awesome sight that was!! We would run to them and just look in amazement as they fluttered around. Though our nights were pitch dark because there were no streetlights in our grandparents' neighborhood, these little round lights would be floating around everywhere, lighting up the area. It was so magical!

Our daytime outings with our grandparents were different from our outings with Daddy. Now in their late 60s, approaching their seventies, there were things they simply couldn't do with us because they tired easily. They did, however, spend time with us watching television, going grocery shopping, and even making occasional trips to the outdoor mall, which was not too far from our home.

Grandmother never learned to drive, so Granddaddy did all of the driving. Granddaddy owned a mint condition silver and black 1962 Chrysler New Yorker, with '*push button*' everything. You had to push a button to put it in reverse, to put it into drive, to change the radio, etc. To us, it was such a neat car.

I could tell Granddaddy had a lot of confidence in his car and was proud to show it off because, at the drop of a hat, he would prompt much younger drivers to race him. I thought that was so crazy and wild for him to do, especially with us in the car with him. He'd become especially annoyed whenever one of them would cut in front of him, which would cause him to maneuver to get alongside them and rev his engine as an invite to a duel. It would be on, and many times, we'd be scared to death!

Granddaddy was confrontational, but for the most part, people would just ignore him, seeing that he was an old man. Grandmother would fuss while holding on to her door handle tightly, but Granddaddy would continue driving fast as if he hadn't heard a word she said. Grandmother's voice would begin to crack as she raised her voice even more, and then, as spiritual as she really was most times, she would let loose a couple of 'not so spiritual' words, though most times she tried not to curse, especially in front of us. Sometimes, however, Granddaddy would *push her buttons* beyond her limit, and she'd let him have it.

'Amusing' is the best way to describe our grandparents' relationship. Having been married close to fifty years, there was no doubt they loved each other. They just sometimes didn't *like* each other. More often than not, Granddaddy would be in the 'doghouse' for one reason or another.

Granddaddy was up in age and would say or do things without thinking—things that sometimes caused embarrassment for us. One such thing that Granddaddy did that mortified me and Chris was how he'd tuck his shirt inside his pants when we were out in public. Of course, tucking your shirt in your pants is a very normal thing to do, except Granddaddy would actually unbuckle his belt, unzip his pants, and allow them to fall down low enough to expose his underwear as he stuffed his shirt in his pants, and it didn't matter to him where we were! Whether we were on a grocery store aisle that had a few shoppers or at the very busy outdoor mall, his ritual never changed! Oh, if we could have just crawled under something. Anything! Granddaddy had little shame about anything. That took some getting used to, though I'm not sure we ever did.

We also had to adjust to the kind of music our grandparents listened to. Because I'd never done it, I didn't think it was normal for Black people to listen to or like country music. Our grandparents taught me differently. Unlike our daddy, our grandparents were lovers of country music, so while we would listen to rhythm & blues with Daddy, with our grandparents, we'd listen to country music singers like Charlie Pride, Johnny Cash, Dolly Parton, Kenny Rogers, and Crystal Gayle (my personal favorite country star). After a while, I came to love country music, with Crystal Gayle's *Don't It Make My Brown Eyes Blue* becoming one of my favorite songs!

Now, when it came to television, the adjustment was not so easy. Grandmother and Granddaddy liked to watch 'Nashville Tennessee,' 'Hee Haw,' and 'The Lawrence Welk Show,' which meant we also had to watch those shows. Though it was tough in the beginning listening to orchestra music, as we were 'bored' to tears, after a while, we got used to it, and later on, like country music, we even developed an appreciation for it.

Other than the few exceptions, life with our grandparents wasn't very different from what we were used to. They took care of us, feeding us, making sure we were clean, and letting us 'be kids' and play. We missed being at our old home every day, and we missed our huge backyard, playhouse, swing set, and friends. Still, our grandparents provided a safe place for us to grow up.

We were also already making new friends, some of whom lived just around the corner. Our grandparents made sure they knew where we were at all times, also making sure they met the parents or guardians of every kid we played with. Most times, however, instead of allowing us to go to our friends' homes to play, our grandparents would invite our friends over to our house to play, especially on weekends. Finally, life was happy for us again.

The most special thing about living with Grandmother and Granddaddy was that daily, we were flooded with so much love.

Grandmother covered our family with so much love and with so many prayers. She was known for praying, and what a 'praying' Grandmother she was! She'd get up in the middle of the night to go to the bathroom, and I could hear her praying for us: me, Chris, and Daddy especially, specifically calling out our names.

I'd become a very 'light sleeper,' waking up at the slightest sound. During those times when I could hear Grandmother in the bathroom praying, she sounded as if she was 'whispering' to God. I could hear her say words like 'protection,' 'strength,' 'guidance,' and many others.

LIFE LESSONS

"Cleanliness is next to godliness," Grandmother would say, stressing how crucial it was in particular for me as a young lady to practice good hygiene and develop good manners, especially since I was beginning to blossom into a young woman. I would eventually start having periods, *ugh*, and I needed to know how to keep myself clean and presentable.

Also important to Grandmother was taking us to church and teaching us how to behave. Grandmother's Church was a very traditional Methodist church. There were considerably far *more* older people there than young people. That was okay with us because those old people loved to hug and kiss on kids.

One sweet old lady, in particular, would search us out and land a big one right on our cheeks! We always felt her teeth on our skin for some reason, so we affectionately and very secretly (just between me and Chris) nicknamed her 'Sharky.' Every time she'd kiss or *nick* us on the cheek, we'd look at each other and try our hardest not to burst out laughing in front of her, getting such a big kick out of it. We'd even start betting on which one of us she'd get first. Honestly, that was probably the one thing we really looked forward to at church on Sundays. Each time, after being seated, we'd look around, trying to spot her to see if she was at church that Sunday, and whenever we spotted her, we'd giggle to ourselves.

At church, we learned how to behave when it was quiet. A couple of times, Chris and I kept ourselves entertained by passing licks; that is until Grandmother passed the final lick, after which we quietly wept 'ourselves to sleep.' We weren't bad kids, but for some reason, we chose the time we needed to be the quietest as our time for irritating each other. Grandmother taught us early on that 'fighting' in church was a big 'NO, NO' and that it wouldn't be tolerated. We would learn to straighten up quickly whenever Grandmother would give us that 'stern' look. It didn't take too many Sundays for us to learn to be quiet in church.

Though Mama did take us to church, the church we went to with her was a very loud church, a 'sanctified' church. Most times, there was a lot of noise and plenty of folks who amused us as we watched them 'get happy,' as Mama called it. Grandmother's church, however, was the total opposite. No one 'got happy,' and there wasn't any dancing around the church. Even the music was different—much quieter. Grandmother's church took some getting used to, which eventually happened.

Though extremely loving, Grandmother was firm at times, not wanting us to grow up believing that 'the world owed us something.' She would not tolerate disrespect of any kind, and we were expected to say *"Thank you," "Please," "Yes, ma'am,"* and the like. Being courteous, especially to grown people, became like second nature to us. That's not to say that Daddy and Mama never taught us manners because they did. It was just that now, being around so many older people gave us more than enough opportunities to practice our manners.

Our grandparents, along with showing us a lot of love, told us that we could be whatever we wanted to be in life. They didn't make us feel different from anyone else in the family and didn't give us special privileges or try to make up for what Mama did.

Our new life with our grandparents, however, didn't stop me from thinking about Mama. We hadn't seen or talked to Mama since the day of 'the tragedy.' Eventually, as time passed, Mama was no longer mentioned. It was almost as if she was nonexistent.

CHAPTER EIGHT

PLEAS FOR FORGIVENESS

UNANSWERED LETTERS

A few months after being sent to the hospital, Mama began frequently writing letters to Daddy, letters that, for well over a year, Daddy didn't respond to. However, her letters kept coming. Repeatedly, Mama would beg Daddy for forgiveness and even ask him numerous times to get her out of the hospital so she could return home and be a wife to him and a mother to us again. That was not going to happen. Mama hadn't even been confined for a year before she began offering up reasons as to why she should be released.

In one of her letters, Mama told Daddy that she'd heard from someone that George was still alive. Daddy didn't know if someone had actually told her that or if she'd made it up. Believing that George was still alive gave Mama greater hope for reconciliation with us. Maybe things were not as bad as she thought, and maybe Daddy would give her a second chance. After all, she'd been committed before, and Daddy took her back.

The reality was, however, that George wasn't still alive. Even if George had, by some miracle, survived the attack, there was no way Mama could return home to us in the same capacity as before. All our lives had changed, and we could never go back to the way we were.

Daddy actually held on to all the letters Mama had written him, and to my surprise, I discovered them one day years later while going through a box of odds and ends that had been neatly tucked away in a closet. Most of the letters sounded the same, with Mama saying how she had to have been sick to do what she did but that now she was better and ready to come back home. Moreover, her letters ended pretty much the same way as well, requesting to see us and telling Daddy that she loved him.

At the time, not only did Daddy not write Mama back, but he also ignored her pleas to see Chris and me. Accepting that Daddy wanted nothing to do with her because he hadn't replied to any of her letters, Mama eventually stopped asking him to bring us and instead asked if he would allow Chris and me to travel with our Aunt Doris to come for a visit. That request was also denied.

One of her pleas in her letters to Daddy was, "Make sure the kids don't forget me." I did wonder if we would ever see Mama again. Honestly, upon first reading the letters, I became very angry because it seemed as if Mama was downplaying what she'd done as if my brother's life and the fact that she'd taken it was a small matter that could be resolved. Taking everything into consideration, I had to remind myself that those letters were written by a mentally ill woman. None of us would ever be the same or forget what she'd done because George's absence in our lives was a constant reminder. Mama wanted us to start over, but we had already moved forward, knowing that we would never live together again as a family.

Not doubting for one moment that Mama missed us, I did feel sorry for her. She'd do anything to have her 'old' life back, but it was too late. In her letters, she stated how she *now* understood 'what it meant to be a wife' and was now willing to listen and do what she was supposed to do.

Because 'the tragedy' was treated like some 'taboo' subject that we weren't supposed to talk about openly, I didn't know how we were supposed to feel about Mama. Having compassion and pity for Mama was one thing, but trusting her was a *completely* different matter. The fact that she had mental health challenges caused me not to hate her, though I did later develop some resentment towards her, thinking that if she hadn't done what she did, we'd all still be together. That resentment did, however, disappear once I honestly faced it. Even the love that I had for her confused me because I didn't know how to process that, along with all the other emotions I also felt towards her. From reading the letters, I could tell how badly Mama wanted forgiveness because she repeatedly said how sorry she was for taking George's life.

While Daddy, like our grandparents, never talked badly about Mama in front of us, he never spoke highly of her either. In fact, he chose not to talk about her much at all. I didn't ask Daddy if he forgave Mama for what she'd done. I wasn't sure if I'd forgiven her myself or if I just felt too sorry for her to hate her.

Out of the blue, after more than a year of not seeing Mama, Daddy decided to take us to visit her. At the onset, I was excited when he told us. Being the only girl, and in spite of all that had transpired, I still yearned to have some kind of relationship with my mother. I wasn't sure how Chris felt about it or Mama.

We left home early in the morning and headed for the state hospital.

Daddy said the drive to Austin, Texas, would take about three hours. In 'kid's time,' it seemed like an eternity.

Finally arriving, we entered the hospital parking lot after passing a security booth. Chris and I had dozed off a few times during the ride but were now fully awake and looking forward to seeing our mama. The hospital had lots of what they called 'check points.' There were security guards, doctors, and nurses everywhere. At the front desk, a man made a phone call so that Mama could be escorted down.

On the way up to the hospital, Daddy told us how Mama really wanted to see us, and that was why we were going. Daddy didn't seem thrilled about the fact that he'd soon be seeing Mama. One of the hospital workers took us to a large waiting room. The room was very pretty, decorated with colorful pictures on the wall. There were huge, comfortable sofas and chairs throughout the area where we were standing. It reminded me of our living room at home with our grandparents, though our living room was much smaller.

"Come on, let's sit here," Daddy said, sitting on an oversized tan sofa.

We did as he said and sat down on the sofa, staring at the doorway, which actually didn't have a door. You just walked right through it into the room.

Rocking back and forth on the sofa, I could hardly be still because I was so eager to see Mama. I wondered, 'What would she look like?'

'What kind of clothes would she have on?'

In anticipation of our visit with Mama, I'd made a doll for her. Making the doll from an old, white bed sheet, I cut and sewed together two identical pieces from the sheet to serve as the whole body, including a head, the body, two arms, and two legs with feet but no toes. I then stuffed it with more bed sheet fabric. Two black round buttons served as eyes for the doll, and the nose and mouth were drawn on the face with a black marker. Grandmother did a lot of sewing and had plenty of scrap material and other stuff for me to choose from to make my special gift for Mama. Using needle and thread, I carefully attached yellow pieces of yarn to the top of the doll's head for hair. Grandmother thought I'd done an exceptional job and told me how pretty the doll was, which made me smile. Hoping Mama would like it, I reached into the bag I'd been carrying, pulled the doll out and sat the doll in my lap.

The three of us, Daddy, Chris, and I had our eyes on the entryway when Mama came in, escorted by two men in white uniforms. I believe they were her nurses, which was odd to me because I hadn't seen too many male nurses, but then again, I hadn't been in too many hospitals either. Jumping from the sofa, I ran towards Mama. Her eyes lit up when she saw us, and she took off running towards us, too, with her arms stretched out wide. Chris was on my heels, running right behind me, almost tripping as he ran directly into Mama's waist. Mama grabbed and hugged us, crying as she squeezed us tightly.

"Oh, my babies!" she exclaimed, kissing me and Chris.

Her kisses were long and plenty wet and were planted all over our faces. Just as happy to see her, we hugged and kissed her back. I hadn't realized just how much I missed Mama until that moment.

Daddy, watching it all from his seat, eventually got up from where he was sitting and walked over to us and Mama. He stood there, waiting for her to finish kissing on us, and then hugged her back as she reached for him also.

"Thank you so much, Rudy, for bringing my babies to see me! They are so beautiful!"

"Oh my, just look at you all!" She said, staring at us with a huge smile on her face.

Daddy replied, "You are welcome, Alice," walking back to take a seat on the sofa.

Mama led me and Chris by the hand to the place we'd all been sitting before she came in. Putting her hands on our faces and kissing us about three or four more times each, Mama looked us all over; she looked at our eyes, our hair, our fingers, our clothes. It was kind of odd, and Chris and I just giggled.

Though she had lost some weight, Mama still looked very pretty. Wearing a brightly colored yellow dress and red lipstick, she had her hair pulled back in a bun. Mama still looked pretty much the way I remembered.

"Oh, Mama misses y'all so much," she said. "I'm so glad y'all came to see me! Stand up again, and let me look at you!"

As we stood, she started to weep again, looking at us up and down, saying, "My goodness! Look at how much you'll have grown!"

A little shy, Chris and I shook our heads while continuing to smile.

Daddy reached for a conveniently placed box of tissue and passed it to Mama.

"Oh, thank you, Rudy," Mama said, dabbing her eyes.

"Cheryl, you are more pretty than I remember, and Chris, my! How handsome you are, looking like your daddy!"

Giggling some more, I anxiously reached for the doll I'd made for Mama. It was tucked behind Daddy's back, placed there so that it would be a surprise to her.

It's funny that I'd longed for so long to see Mama, demanding to see her the day she was taken away, but now overcome with all sorts of emotions, I found it hard to even utter a word. Giving Mama the doll seemed to help my words come out. I proudly gave her the doll as she sat Chris on her lap. Taking a seat between her and Daddy on the sofa, I watched her facial expressions light up even more as she took the doll from my hands.

Mama looked at the doll and then at me and said, "Oh Cheryl, what a beautiful doll! Is this for me!?

"Yes, ma'am," I replied, smiling and looking down while fiddling with my hands.

Finally able to speak, I said proudly, "I made it myself."

"Really? You made this all by yourself? I don't believe you. You bought this at the store, didn't you?" Mama said, giving me a look as to jokingly say she didn't believe me.

"No, ma'am, I made it. Grandmother helped me a little, but I did most of it by myself," I said proudly, still grinning.

"Well, it's the prettiest doll I've ever seen! Thank you sooo much, baby! I'm going to find a special place in my room to put it and show it to everyone who comes in what my little girl made for me!" Mama said, hugging the doll and then giving me another huge kiss on my cheek.

"You're welcome," I said, beginning to feel more at ease talking to Mama.

I could tell she loved the doll. It made her happy, and that made me happy.

Chris had drawn Mama a picture during our drive up to the hospital, and as Mama hugged the doll, he beckoned for Daddy to pass him the picture, which was on the table next to the sofa. Daddy handed the picture to me, and I gave it to Chris, and he proudly gave it to Mama.

"Oh, this is just too much! Wow! Did you draw this, Chris!?" Mama asked, holding the picture up to her face.

"Yes, Ma'am," he said, grinning from ear to ear.

"Why, I tell you, it is perfect and the best picture I've ever gotten!"

"My goodness, you are really the artist, Chris! Thank you so much, my little man! I'm going to hang it up on my wall in my room where everyone can see it. I'll tell them my son drew this for me," Mama said proudly, also hugging the picture but gently so as not to tear it.

"Thank you, Chris!" Mama said, also planting a big kiss on his cheek, wrapping her arms around him, and giving him a tight squeeze.

Chris bent over, sniggling, showing all his teeth. The attention I'd longed for from Mama was coming in buckets! Not to discount the way Daddy and our grandparents showed us love because that was beyond comparison. It's just that we'd missed Mama so much, missed seeing her, hearing her voice. After all, for well over a year, we hadn't had any contact with her at all. It was almost as if she'd dropped off the face of the earth, and now, today, she was back, even if only for a little while.

On the way up to the hospital, Daddy talked to me and Chris, explaining to us that we were just going to visit Mama for a couple of hours, making it clear that she wouldn't be coming back home with us. That was actually a relief for me because though I missed Mama, I wasn't ready for her to come home. I just wanted to see her, but remembering what she'd done terrified me when thinking about ever staying with her again.

The rest of our visit went very well. Mama asked us about school, our teachers, and our friends. She asked us if we were being good and not giving Daddy and our grandparents a hard time. Just about every question was quickly followed up with a grin and another question after we'd answered her.

After talking to us for about thirty minutes, while Daddy just sat there and watched us interact with Mama, she then turned to talk to him. Looking at Daddy, she asked, "And how are things with you, Rudy?"

"Everything is fine," Daddy replied, not saying anything beyond that.

"Oh...ok, that's good," Mama said, smiling through the uncomfortable moment.

"Well, how are the kids doing in school?" she asked, smiling and looking at me and Chris.

"I heard from Doris that they were doing good. Is that true?"

"Yep, both of them are doing really well," Daddy responded, confirming what we'd already told her. He added, "They get their studies like they're supposed to. Mother and Daddy always see to that. We're all very proud of them."

"Oh, yes, me too," Mama said, continuing to smile at me and Chris.

"I bet they do get good grades," Mama said, clutching her hands, looking down at them, and then up at us again as if her mind had wandered for a moment.

Looking back at Daddy, she asked with teary eyes and cracking in her voice, "Is Mrs. Battle taking them to church?"

"Yes, Alice, Mother takes real good care of the kids," Daddy said. "I don't know what I'd do without my folks. They've really been there for us."

"I'm sure she does, well, both of them, your mother and father. They've always been good people. I'm grateful they are there for you and the kids. Whether they know it or not, I've always had a lot of respect for them. Please tell them that for me, that I really respect and appreciate them both."

"I will," Daddy responded, staring, neither smiling nor frowning, just looking, almost emotionless, at Mama as she continued to speak.

"Tell them, and Idella too, that I said hello and tell them all that I said, thank you. They are taking such good care of my babies."

"Yeah, ok…I'll tell them," Daddy said, abruptly getting up from where he was sitting and walking over to make himself a cup of coffee.

We all watched as he grabbed the coffee pot. Mama, a little startled by the way Daddy suddenly stood up, stuttered a little as she offered, "I… I can make that for you if you'd like, Rudy."

"No, that's okay. I've got it," Daddy said, not making eye contact with Mama.

We could tell Mama was a little disappointed at Daddy declining her offer. With his back slightly turned to all of us, Daddy still kept his eyes on us as he opened his cream and sugar and then poured it into his cup of coffee. Walking back over to the sofa, Daddy joined us again, sitting down and staring into his cup of coffee as he blew on it and sipped it.

Attempting to start up another conversation with Daddy, Mama said, "So, I know Cheryl and Chris are with Mr. and Mrs. Battle during the week. Doris said that they go home with you on the weekend. Is that right?" Mama asked.

"Yeah, that's right. I pick them up Friday afternoon after they get out of school, they stay the night with me, and I take them back Saturday night so they can go to church on Sunday with Mother," Daddy replied.

"Oh, I see," Mama said in response.

After saying that, Daddy looked at Mama and went silent again. Daddy appeared to be uncomfortable, struggling with the visit and not really wanting to be there. However, he agreed to let Mama see us and was making good on his word.

While Daddy wasn't really rude, he did watch Mama like a hawk. I felt safe because Daddy was there and also because the two men in white clothes remained in the doorway our entire visit, never leaving us alone with Mama.

Turning her attention to us again, Mama kept the questions coming, one after another, including asking what boy I liked and what girl Chris liked.

We giggled bashfully and laughed as we told on each other. With our most recent vacation trip to San Antonio still fresh on our minds, we initiated a conversation about the great time we had with Daddy, not sparing any detail. It had been so long since we'd seen Mama, much less talked to her, and our visit with her was passing so quickly. Not one word was mentioned about George, not on purpose or by accident. I did wonder, though, if she thought about and missed him.

It was getting close to the end of our visit, and before we began preparing to leave, Mama stood up and asked Daddy if he would go with her to the other side of the room so that they could talk in private.

"Rudy, can I have a word with you in private?" She asked humbly.

Daddy, almost dreading her request, sighed a little and responded, "Yeah, I guess so, Alice."

They both stood to walk across the room, not far from where the nurses were standing.

Whatever Mama had to tell Daddy, she didn't want me and Chris to hear.

Daddy looked at us and said, "I'll be right back, Cheryl and Chris."

"Yes, sir," we responded.

There was a television mounted on the wall in the upper right corner of the room. Our favorite show, 'The Little Rascals,' was on, which we turned to watch.

We don't know what they talked about, but whatever it was, it didn't take very long. Mama and Daddy tried to whisper, but some of their words were loud enough for us to hear, and it even looked like they were arguing. After just a few more minutes, Daddy, frowning for a second, turned away from Mama and walked back over to where we were sitting. Placing his hands in his pants pockets, he stood there watching Mama as she continued to have her back turned to us. We could see Mama wiping her eyes and cheeks with a tissue she'd had in her pocket. She then turned to walk back over and join us. She walked towards us with her arms outstretched, the same way they were at the beginning of our visit.

"Come here, my babies," she said,

We stood up and hugged her. She wept some more as she kissed us on our foreheads and hugged us, almost clinging to us.

"Mama's going to really miss you all, but it was so *WONDERFUL* to see my babies!" she said, with a squeeze so tight and so long, I thought maybe this was going to be our last visit.

"We're going to miss you too," we said back as the three of us huddled together.

Sad to be leaving her, too, I could feel the tears forming in my own eyes. One thing I knew was that Mama did love us. I could tell by her hugs and kisses—they hadn't changed. Showing little emotion, Daddy embraced Mama just briefly as she turned to him to hug him too.

"Okay, kids, you all come on. It's time to leave," Daddy said.

We waved goodbye to Mama as we walked out of the room, with Daddy leading us both by the hand. At first, we could only hear sniffles from Mama as we exited the room, but her cries got louder as we continued down the hallway. Turning back to look at her, I saw the two attendants who'd been with us the entire time, talking to her just outside the room, trying to console her. It hurt my heart to see Mama so sad, and as we left that day, I didn't know if we'd ever see Mama again.

CHAPTER NINE

MAMA'S RETURN HOME

Turns out the first time we visited Mama in the mental hospital would be our only visit.

GOING HOME

After being confined for a little over two years and receiving intense therapy and counseling following extensive evaluation, Mama received the news she'd wanted to hear for many months: she would finally be going home!

Less than a year after we'd gone to visit her, Mama received approval by her doctors to be released into Grandmother's Wilma's care. Mama was coming home, and I, though I loved her and missed her, had very mixed emotions about it.

Was it safe for us?

Would old thoughts and memories trigger something bad in her head?

The day she killed George, she'd planned to kill all of us. I'd even come face to face with her, still carrying the knife in her hand. Did she want to finish her plan?

Not being convinced either way, I was as nervous and anxious as I was excited about Mama's return home. She was *still* Mama.

Chris and I hadn't openly talked to any adult about how we were feeling. In fact, no one in our family opened up the conversation, so we just kept our emotions to ourselves, bottled up inside. Maybe I could have talked to Daddy, but it seemed like he really didn't like answering questions that had anything to do with Mama.

PREPARING FOR MAMA'S REENTRY INTO OUR LIVES

Neither Daddy nor our grandparents said much about Mama's release, so I was curious about quite a few things like:

Where would she stay?

Would we be able to see her more now that she is being released from the hospital?

Was it possible that she'd still want to hurt us?

Because 'the tragedy' was such a closed conversation, I wasn't surprised when Daddy told us that Mama was being released and didn't say much more than that.

The day after we were told Mama was coming home is one I won't likely ever forget: Having begun Second grade, I had an awesome teacher whose name was Ms. Halcarz. One of only a handful of white teachers at my predominately Black elementary school, she was by far my favorite teacher!

Being nervous about Mama's return home, I drew a picture while in class, expressing how I felt about it. Ms. Halcarz removed the picture from the top of my desk and just stared at it. The drawing was a picture of a knife going through a hand. I don't really even know why I drew that particular picture. Mama didn't stab George in the hand.

With Mama's release on the horizon, I needed to talk about it. I guess I wanted to talk about it with Ms. Halcarz. Ms. Halcarz didn't question me at all about the picture and instead took it and didn't give it back to me.

Soon, I regretted drawing that picture.

We lived with our grandparents but would sometimes go to Aunt Della's after school when our grandparents had doctor appointments, etc. The day I drew the picture, I wished we'd been able to just go home to our grandparents. But as fate would have it, Aunt Della picked us up from school that day. I knew something was wrong because she wasn't smiling like she normally did when she'd get us after school. She told us to get into the car and didn't say a word all the way home, not even asking how our day went. It was apparent she was very upset about something.

What had we done?

Then, I realized I was the one she was angry with because as soon as we arrived home, she ordered Chris to the back bedroom but made me stay with her in the dining room. The back bedroom had been set aside for Chris and me for whenever we'd come over.

As soon as Chris left the room, she immediately began questioning me about the drawing. She angrily grabbed the picture off the table and began pointing to it, hitting the paper with her hand. Raising her voice at me, she asked, "What is this, Cheryl?! Why did you draw this?!"

How in the world had she gotten the picture??? I had just drawn it that afternoon during class. Oh no! I didn't want to believe that Ms. Halcarz had told on me and turned me in, but that's exactly what had happened! My heart sank.

Sometime during that afternoon, unbeknownst to me, Ms. Halcarz made a phone call to Aunt Della and told her about the picture. Aunt

Della went to the school to pick up the picture without my even knowing she'd been up there. Though we stayed with our grandparents, her name was still listed on our school records as a primary contact person.

Given her bulging eyes and loud voice, I was sure I was going to get a beating for the drawing.

"Cheryl, I asked you what this means?!" she asked angrily, inadvertently spitting as she spoke.

Staring at the picture in her hand, I was speechless, not being able to say a word. I wanted Ms. Halcarz to ask me about the picture so that I could talk to her. Because I admired her so much, I just knew I would be able to talk to her, and she would understand.

"What does this mean, little girl?!" she said, demanding an answer, this time moving closer to me, getting right in my face as if she was going to hit me.

She then grabbed me by my left arm and started shaking me.

"Say something!" she demanded.

"I don't know!" I replied out loud, covering my face with my hands and starting to cry out loud.

"What do you mean you don't know?! You drew it!" she yelled back, shaking the drawing in my face.

"Yes, ma'am...but I...," I said, trying to explain but not being able to get the words out.

"You stop crying right now and tell me why you drew this!" She insisted, not at all moved by my crying.

"I just drew it. I didn't mean anything by it. I just drew it in class," I said, speaking through my sobbing.

I just wanted her to leave me alone. What a huge mistake I'd made believing I could trust my teacher!

Aunt Della paused for just a second. Expecting to hear her curse me or hit me, I stared at the floor, trying to brace myself. But Aunt Della was relentless, not at all letting up on the interrogation.

"You didn't just draw it!"

"You drew it for a reason, and I want to know right now what this darn knife going through this hand means…what are you trying to say, Cheryl? Huh? What does this mean?!"

She just kept yelling, insisting on an answer. I knew that there was no answer that I could give that would satisfy her. Continuing to try to brush off the picture as just a meaningless drawing, I continued to sob.

"It means nothing. I'm sorry for drawing it," I said, apologizing over and over again.

Had I known I would have caused myself that kind of trouble, I would have kept my feelings to myself.

"Do you think this is a good thing to draw?" she said, finally starting to lower her voice.

"No, ma'am…I'm sorry," I said, wiping my face with my hands, "I'm sorry, I won't do it again."

"I should beat your behind for this!" she said, staring at me.

I stood there motionless, sniffling, almost wanting her to just go ahead and whip me so it would be over with.

"You go in there and get on your homework!" she said, almost pushing me as she let go of my arm.

My arm was sore from all the jerking, and I was sure there was a bruise. I didn't want to look, though. I just wanted her to let me go and leave me alone.

"I'm going to talk to your daddy about this when he gets off work," she said, rolling her eyes at me as I moved quickly, out of her arm's length.

Going directly to the back room, I fell face down onto the bed where Chris was sitting, scared from hearing all the yelling, wondering what I'd done. Burying my face into a pillow, I tried to muffle the sounds of my crying. Chris, trying to console me, began patting and rubbing my back.

"What happened?" he softly asked.

I just shook my head 'No' because I didn't want to talk about it anymore.

I wondered, 'Why had Aunt Della reacted that way?' The more and more I thought about it, the angrier I became.

She completely disregarded my feelings and didn't think that maybe the drawing had something to do with the fact that Mama would soon be released from the hospital, and I was scared about it.

I'm sure she couldn't wait to tell my Daddy, but I was certain he wouldn't yell at me like she did. Maybe he'd talk to me and try to find out what was going on in my head. Daddy, however, never said a word about the picture; he *never* even mentioned it. The subject stopped with Aunt Della, and we just moved forward.

For years, I walked around with horrible anxiety about Mama but felt as though I could not share it with anyone, for fear they just might 'go off' on me and attack me like my aunt did. I eventually forgave Ms. Halcarz because I thought she was trying to help, but because of that incident, I remained silent for years.

Joy

The day Mama was released from the hospital, we went to Grandmother Wilma's house to see her. Mama would be staying with her now that Grandmother would be responsible for her.

My heart began to beat so fast and hard as Daddy pulled into Grandmother Wilma's driveway that I thought it was going to come out of my chest. Grandmother Wilma only stayed about a five-minute drive from our family home on the north side. It's very likely that Mama and Daddy moved close to Grandmother Wilma so that she'd be nearby to help.

Getting out of the car, we started walking up the winding sidewalk that led to the front door steps. Grandmother Wilma's house sat high off the ground on cement blocks. The huge, white, wood-framed home had a detached garage to the rear of it. Her backyard was almost as large as ours, giving us plenty of room to run around and play. However, unlike Daddy's house, Grandmother's house did not have a fence. Inside the house were several rooms, including a very large kitchen. There were beautiful paintings on the wall, some of Jesus and some displaying bible verses. Grandmother Wilma was religious like Mama. Family pictures also hung along the walls throughout the house, some of which were very old pictures of people who'd already died. Very nice furniture was laid out in each room, especially in the family room. Grandmother had a 'what-not' cabinet with little glass figurines in it. None of us kids were allowed to play with anything inside that cabinet. It was hands-off! We were very familiar with the 'rules of the house' because, staying so close to her, we'd gone over many times for regular visits.

Today, however, wouldn't be one of our usual visits but rather a family celebration with aunts, uncles, and cousins from Mama's side of the family.

Reaching the front door, Daddy knocked, and Aunt Doris immediately answered the door. I guess they had been waiting for us. Excitedly stepping outside, Aunt Doris started hugging us, acknowledging our presence, "Hey, you guys! Oh my, it's so good to see you all!"

"How are you, Rudy?" Aunt Doris said, smiling real big, embracing Daddy, and patting him on the back.

"Hey, Doris," Daddy said, hugging her back. "I'm good," Daddy answered, "How are you?"

"Oh, I'm great now that I see you all. It's been a while," she said, continuing to smile.

That was true. We hadn't seen much of Mama's family since we'd begun staying with our grandparents.

"Cheryl and Chris, my goodness, how you two have grown!" she said, looking us up and down, making us grin.

"Well, you all come on in. Everybody, especially Alice, is waiting to see you. Y'all are all she's been talking about since we picked her up. Well, you all are all she ever really talks about," she remarked, chuckling.

Aunt Doris led us inside to the family room after closing the door behind us. Everybody was gathered in the kitchen, which the family room opened up to.

"Look who's here!" she announced loudly as we walked through the house.

Mama had gone to the bathroom, but the rest of the family was in the kitchen. Everyone else, including Grandmother Wilma, stood up and walked over to us before we could even make it to the kitchen. We were greeted with more smiles, hugs and kisses. It was like a big family reunion! In fact, that's exactly what it was because Mama was being reunited with her family.

Our cousins were out back playing, but my Uncle Earnest called them all in when he saw we'd arrived. Uncle Earnest was our Aunt Doris' husband, and they had one daughter, our cousin Bridgette. Also in the room were our Uncle Charles, our mother's brother, his wife Greta, and their son Eveleo. They'd have another child later on, a little girl named Amber. My Uncle Nathaniel was also sitting close by with his wife Lois and their only child LaTanya.

Chris and I were so happy to be there with our cousins. Since George's funeral, we hadn't seen much of them.

Grandmother stood off to the side smiling, watching as we greeted everyone else in the room, except for Mama, who still hadn't returned from the bathroom. It was Grandmother's turn, and she approached us, reaching out for us with her arms, waving for us to come to her. Grinning, we ran into her arms.

"Grandmother's gonna take all the love!" she said, grabbing us and squeezing us so hard that our arms just flung down at our sides.

It was a Grandmother Wilma hug.

"It's been way too long! Grandmother really missed y'all," she said, kissing us on the forehead.

"Cheryl, you're just as pretty as you can be," Grandmother Wilma said, touching my face.

"And look at you, little man," she said, looking at Chris and pinching his cheek. "You're just as handsome as you can be. Grandmother is so happy to see you all."

Turning to Daddy, Grandmother asked, "Rudy, how you doing, Son?"

"Oh, I'm doing okay, Ms. Johnson. You been doing okay?" Daddy responded after giving her a hug.

"Oh yeah, you know, I'm making it. This ole sugar tries to get me, but I'm putting up a good fight," Grandmother Wilma said, chuckling.

Daddy responded, "Yes ma'am, I understand that. Well, you look good."

"Thank you, Son. You too, Rudy. You looking real good yourself," Grandmother Wilma said, smiling and looking at Daddy.

Grandmother Wilma took me and Chris by the hand and led us over to the sofa back in the family room, where we all took a seat.

"How's school?" she asked.

"Good," Chris and I said, grinning, responding almost simultaneously.

Once Chris and I finished talking to Grandmother, we stood up and walked over and started talking to our cousins, friendly pushing each other and giggling. Daddy was also talking to other family members in the room. We were looking for Mama, but she was *still* in the bathroom.

Daddy made his way back to Grandmother Wilma, and they began talking again.

"Thank you so much, Rudy, for bringing Cheryl and Chris and for coming too. It really is good to see you all. You just don't know what it does for me to see my other grandbabies," Grandmother Wilma said, glancing over at us.

"Yes, ma'am, it has been a while," Daddy responded.

"How's your job going?" she asked.

"Oh, busy, but I can't complain. Things are pretty good."

"That's good, Rudy. You always were such a hard worker," Grandmother said, smiling, complimenting Daddy.

"Thanks. I have to take care of my babies," Daddy replied, also looking at us.

"Well, I can tell you are doing a great job…you and your parents. How are they?"

"They are fine. I'll tell them you asked about them," Daddy responded.

"Yes, please do that, Rudy. I was hoping they'd come with y'all, them and Della."

"Yes, ma'am, well they couldn't make it, but I'll give them your regards."

"I hope they know they are welcome."

"Yes ma'am, they know."

"Ok, well....," just as Grandmother was getting ready to say something else, we heard a loud scream, and Mama came rushing towards us with her arms extended.

"Oh my babies, my babies!" she exclaimed, so overjoyed to see us.

Everyone in the room stopped what they were doing and looked on as Mama grabbed us, lifting us up as far off the floor as she could, kissing us on our cheeks and our foreheads. Mama then began to cry and just held on to us both at the same time. Not saying anything, Chris and I showed all our teeth as we hugged her back. Mama cried some more.

"Ok, Alice, let those kids breathe," Grandmother Wilma said, as others in the room were also overcome with emotion and laughter.

Our cousins, who were around our ages, were ready to go outside and play, but Mama wasn't about to let us go and play just yet.

Mama, noticing that Daddy was standing close by against a wall, finally let us go.

"Oh, hello, Rudy," she said, walking over to hug him too.

He hugged her back, and she immediately returned to where we were standing and said, "You'll come and sit with me over here. You too, Rudy," Mama said, leading us to the same sofa we'd been sitting on with Grandmother Wilma.

Grandmother had gotten up and gone into the kitchen with the others, giving us some alone time with Mama.

"Oh, this is the best day of my life! It's good to finally be home and be next to my babies. Did y'all miss me?" Mama said, beaming.

"Oh Alice," Grandmother said from the kitchen," of course they missed you." Grandmother wasn't close by, but boy, was she listening to our conversation.

We nodded our heads 'yes,' prompting Mama to come in for another hug.

"I missed y'all more than you'll ever know! Oh, it's so good to be home," Mama repeated again.

"I love your dress, Cheryl. Did Grandmother Hilda pick it out for you?" Mama asked while stroking my lap.

"No ma'am, she bought it, but I picked it out", I said proudly as the others listened and smiled, praising me for being a 'big' girl.

I was glad Mama had noticed my new dress since I wore it, especially for her.

"Oh, you're a big girl now, huh?" Mama asked, leaning over and kissing me again on the cheek.

"Yes, ma'am," I responded, a bit bashful because all eyes were on me and Chris as we spoke.

"What about you, Chris? You look so handsome in your jeans and shirt. Did you pick out your own clothes too?" Mama asked.

"Yes, ma'am," he replied with a huge grin on his face.

"My goodness, Mama's babies are really growing up so fast," she remarked proudly.

"Well, we have all kinds of food in the kitchen, including cookies, cakes, and pies. Are you hungry? We can go in the kitchen, and I can fix you some plates," Mama said, anxious to wait on us just like she did before she was sent away.

It would be the first time we'd eaten together since our family was torn apart.

"Yes, ma'am," we said, hoping to bypass the food and go straight to the cakes and pies and anything else sweet.

It didn't go down like that, though. We stood up with Mama, ready to walk with her into the kitchen, when she turned to Daddy and asked, "How about you, Rudy? Would you like for me to make you a plate too?" Mama asked Daddy while holding our hands.

"Yes, Alice, that'll be good. I'll take a little something, not too much, though. We had a big lunch at my mother's earlier."

"Oh, okay, well, we have fried chicken, turkey and dressing, rice, and green beans. I know there's also some potato salad, rolls, and dessert: sweet potato pie, chocolate cake, pecan pie, all kinds of good food," Mama said, excited to be fixing plates for all of us, including Daddy.

Just hearing Mama talk about all that different food made my mouth water. It was like Thanksgiving! In our family, good food had a way of bringing out the best in people, regardless of the purpose of the gathering.

"I'll take just a little bit of turkey, dressing, and some green beans. No sweets right now. I'll get that later. Thank you." Daddy said.

"Y'all, come on then. I'll help your mama get your plates together," said Grandmother Wilma, motioning for us to join her in the kitchen.

I don't know if that was her way of supervising Mama around us, but I honestly felt safer having someone else in the kitchen with us and

Mama anyway.

"I think I'll have some dessert now myself," said Aunt Doris, also following us over to the kitchen counter.

One of my uncles walked over and sat on the sofa next to Daddy and sparked up a conversation with him while we disappeared into the kitchen.

Most of our other relatives had eaten earlier, but a few of them still wandered into the kitchen in search of dessert or just to talk to us while we ate. We had a really good time 'catching up' with Mama's side of the family. Now that Mama was home, maybe we'd be able to spend more time with them, especially our cousins.

Grandmother Wilma had some little gifts and trinkets for us to take home with us.

"Now y'all make sure y'all think about Grandmother and call me sometimes, ok?" she said as she handed the items to all of us kids.

"Yes, ma'am," we said, excited to get and open the gifts.

We stayed at Grandmother's for over three hours.

Chris and I spent most of our time outside playing ball and singing and dancing to music that was playing on Grandmother's portable radio. Running, laughing, and joking around, Chris and I had so much fun with our cousins. Daddy stayed indoors with the grownups, peaking out every once in a while to check on us.

It was starting to get late, and Daddy had to take us back to our grandparents' house so he could get back home and rest up for work the next day. Mama didn't want us to leave, but she knew we had to go.

Leaving before most of the others did, we went around and hugged and kissed everybody again, saying 'Goodbye.'

Mama walked us out to the car.

"Rudy, please bring them back soon. Will you do that?" Mama asked.

Before he could answer that question, Mama asked, "Is it okay for me to call them at your mother's?"

"Okay, Alice, and yeah, I'm sure Mother and Daddy won't mind, just not too much," Daddy responded, taking his keys out of his pants pocket to unlock the car door.

Mama smiled and nodded. Mama turned to each of us and gave us a big hug, blowing on each of our cheeks, to which we laughed and bent over.

"Mama will see y'all again real soon, babies," she said, holding our faces in her hands.

"Ya'll ask Daddy to bring you back soon. Here's our phone number, just in case you don't have it and want to call," Mama said, handing me a piece of paper with Grandmother Wilma's number written on it.

"You'll call me as much as you want to, okay? Every day is fine with me. I just love to hear my babies' voices. Mama loves you," she said with tears in her eyes.

"Take care and call me tomorrow, okay?" she said, helping us into the car.

"Ok, bye, Mama," we said, waving at her as we settled into our seats in the back of the car.

"Bye, babies. Y'all have a good night, and don't let the beddie bugs bite," she said smiling.

We, too, giggled at such a silly saying.

Looking at Daddy as he got into the car and closed his door, Mama, pleading with Daddy again, said, "Rudy, promise me you'll bring them back to see me again."

"Alice, they'll be back. I'll bring them back," Daddy said, looking up at Mama.

"I just missed them so much…and you too, Rudy," Mama said, touching Daddy on his shoulder.

"Okay, Alice, I'll bring them back to see you," Daddy said, reaching to start the car.

Daddy didn't say that he missed her too, and Mama didn't question him about it. Mama reached down to give Daddy a hug through the window.

"Okay, Alice, take care," Daddy said as he awkwardly hugged her back with his free arm.

"See y'all soon," Mama said, moving away from the car door so Daddy could back out of the driveway.

As we pulled out, we waved back to Mama as she stood in the driveway, also waving, following our car out to the street. Standing at the end of the driveway, Mama watched as we drove down the street and out of sight.

Daddy turned on the radio as we continued traveling down the main road to the freeway.

"Daddy, are you going to take us to see Mama again?" I asked curiously.

Pausing for a few seconds, Daddy replied, "Yes, baby. Y'all will get to see her more now that she's home. Is that what you'll want?"

"Yes sir," I said.

I now understood that because of what Mama did, we'd never be able to live together as a family again, but I wanted confirmation from Daddy that we would still be able to visit her.

I then asked, "Daddy,…is she better now?"

"Well, I hope so, but you're going to continue to stay with Grandmother and Granddaddy. Your Mama is not able to take care of you."

"You mean she doesn't have any money?" Chris chimed in.

Daddy chuckled, "No, it's not about money. She just can't take care of y'all like Grandmother and Granddaddy. She's your mother, and I want you to always love her," Daddy said, "but you all will never be able to live with her like before. You'll understand that?"

"Yes sir," Chris said, obviously okay, and even somewhat relieved, with the fact that we won't be living with Mama.

"Do you still love Mama?" Chris very innocently asked.

"Uh, yeah, well, I still love her. She's your Mama, but Mama and Daddy will never be together like before." Daddy said, again addressing the living arrangements for us.

"Yes sir, that's fine with us," I responded. "We just miss Mama, but we don't want to stay with her," I said, finally sharing my honest feelings.

"Will we see her every day?" Chris asked.

"Oh no, Chris, not every day. Daddy has to work, and y'all have school. No, not every day, but you'll be able to see her more than before." Daddy said.

"More than when she was in the hospital?" Chris asked,

"Yes," Daddy responded.

We resigned from questioning Daddy anymore that night. His answers were good enough for us for the time being. That was about the longest conversation we'd had about Mama in a while and one of the few ones in which we were actually asked about our feelings.

Keeping his promise to Mama, Daddy took us over to Grandmother Wilma's house often to see her. Just about every weekend, we got to see

Mama, even if it was for only a few minutes. Daddy, however, would never leave us alone with Mama, at least not until some years later, and even then, we were to be in the company of other adults. She could only have supervised visits with us, and Daddy didn't give that responsibility to anyone else until he felt comfortable enough to do so.

Sitting there with us, he watched as we visited with Mama. She had begun to settle in with Grandmother Wilma, and in the beginning, all seemed fine.

After a while, however, tension developed between Mama and Grandmother Wilma. It had really always existed, but the excitement of just having Mama back home initially overshadowed it. It started to build up again and became more and more noticeable. Mama really wanted her own place but would have to wait again for approval to live on her own, with no required supervision.

Chris and I understood that Mama and Daddy would never get back together, and that wasn't something that we wanted anyway. We were satisfied having what seemed like 'two' families—one with Mama and one with Daddy. We were now okay with things being different because that's just how life would have to be.

CHAPTER TEN

EASING INTO TRUSTING AGAIN

Eventually, one of Mama's greatest wishes came true, second only to her desire to see us again. She was granted her independence and would now be allowed to live on her own, although she would have to continue to follow strict guidelines regarding taking her medicine and adhering to therapy requirements.

ON HER OWN

Getting her independence back, Mama loved having her own place and being able to live on her own again. Mama had an extra room so she could eventually get a roommate, but that didn't happen for a while. She found a nice little two-bedroom, wood-framed house nestled among several similar houses near a large, wooded area. The mosquitoes, however, were so terrible that we avoided going outside as much as possible whenever we were over for a visit.

Her place was about a ten-minute drive from Grandmother Wilma's house. Sometimes, Daddy would take us to see Mama, and she would cook us a meal, usually boiled chicken and rice. During other times, we'd just go over to visit and sit and talk.

Daddy was very patient, allowing us to spend quality time with Mama, not interfering with her interaction with us as long as everything was in order, and he definitely kept a close eye on all of Mama's movements. Thankfully, we never had a problem during any of our visits.

In the beginning, Mama seemed nervous, trying to make sure that she did the right thing, said the right thing, and made the right decisions down to the smallest detail. Eventually, after spending so much time with Mama, the time came when we were no longer afraid to be around her by ourselves, trusting she wouldn't do anything to harm us.

I had gotten my driver's license and was permitted to shuttle Chris and myself back and forth. Daddy began permitting us to visit Mama alone for an hour or so, after which we were expected to return home. It actually felt good to be able to visit Mama on our own.

Despite all that had happened, our relationship was starting to feel 'normal'...as normal as 'normal' could be for us.

FEAR

The time came when Mama wanted us to spend the night with her. That was the first time we'd had any kind of issue since we'd been visiting Mama unaccompanied by Daddy. There was mixed communication between Daddy and me that day.

We'd planned to go see Mama, and while talking to her on the phone before we left home, Mama asked if we could spend the night with her. I was a little hesitant to ask Daddy, but I bit the bullet and went into his room, where he was watching football, one of his favorite things to do.

Surprisingly, Daddy gave me the okay. Or, so I thought.

Mama really wanted us to stay the night and have a kind of slumber party. We were going to play cards, watch television, and just hang out. I thought I'd made our desire to spend the night clear when I asked for Daddy's permission. Apparently, he didn't understand that we were staying the 'entire' night because when I called him again to check in and remind him that we'd be home the next morning, he hit the ceiling!

At first, there was a pause on the other end of the line, and then Daddy lashed out at me unlike he'd ever done before.

"What do you mean y'all are spending the night?! We didn't talk about y'all staying overnight, Cheryl!"

Daddy was a reserved man, not generally moved emotionally by anything, but at that moment, I could feel his anger coming through the phone.

"Yes, we did, Daddy," I said nervously, trying to taper his anger and calm him down.

With my voice cracking, I said, "You remember, Daddy? I told you Mama wanted us to stay overnight, and I thought you said it was okay?"

"Cheryl, you know I didn't say it was ok! Why would I ever say it was alright for you to stay with your mama overnight?! You know that doesn't even sound right!" Daddy yelled back, his tone of voice intensifying as it came through the receiver.

He was so loud for a second that I had to put a little distance between my ears and the phone. I began to panic because, at that point, I realized either Daddy hadn't heard me correctly and he'd just responded, or I misunderstood him. We didn't have a long conversation, but there had been a huge breakdown in our communication. I was just silent, not really knowing what to say.

Mama had just walked into the room, and I didn't want her to know how Daddy really felt about us staying. I knew so many already thought so badly of her, and I felt sorry for her.

So I picked up the conversation again, hoping to persuade him to approve the request, "We're only staying tonight, Daddy, and we'll be home early tomorrow afternoon,"

It didn't work. While he allowed us to stay, he didn't approve. He was very upset about the whole situation.

"If anything happens to you all, I'm holding you responsible, Cheryl!" he said, probably hoping that statement alone would cause me to change my mind and decide to not stay overnight.

Daddy wanted me to clearly understand how he felt.

I tried to remind Daddy of our dialogue earlier during the day when he'd given me the 'okay' for us to stay overnight, but it was futile. Not wanting to be disrespectful, I stopped trying to plead my case and just listened.

"Yes sir, I'm sorry," I said, wiping my face so that Mama wouldn't see the tears running down my cheek.

On one hand, I was happy that Mama was happy, but on the other hand, I hated the fact that Daddy was upset with me. This kind of tension between us was very unusual because I had such a great relationship with Daddy and hardly ever stirred him to anger.

Not wanting to disappoint Mama and not wanting to cause Daddy more grief than I already had, I resolved in my mind to stay up all night long and keep watch over me and Chris, making sure nothing bad happened to us. My goal was for us to stay overnight with Mama and return safely home to Daddy the next day. It was a heavy load for a 16-year-old kid, but I guess I brought it on myself. We were 'trying to adapt' to having Mama around again. There were not a lot of spoken rules, but there were plenty of silent ones.

I'm sure it wasn't easy for Mama either. She could only ever have part of her family back, never George, and never Daddy.

In thinking about how angry Daddy had become, I did question myself, 'How could I possibly have thought I'd heard Daddy correctly?' He was right; I should have known better. He'd been so protective of us, even when he'd take us for visits when we were younger. The fact that we were older didn't mean he trusted Mama more; it meant he believed we were old enough to handle ourselves if she did try something. Even still, it was difficult for him, and I understood that. I guess he just thought we were old enough to visit with her for a couple of hours by ourselves but not stay an entire night! That was simply too much of an opportunity for something bad to happen.

"Ok...Cheryl," Daddy said, hanging up the phone, with his 'Goodbye' being barely audible.

In fact, I don't know if he even said 'Goodbye'.

"I've really messed up," I said to myself.

With Mama out of the kitchen, I quickly snatched a knife from the drawer and dashed to the room where Chris and I would sleep, prepared to defend us. I carefully tucked it beneath the mattress of our bed so that we wouldn't accidentally come into contact with it. At that moment, I wished that the day and the night had already passed and that we were on our way back home to Daddy. The drama our staying overnight with Mama had caused just wasn't worth the trouble.

Trying to put our conversation behind me, I prayed to God that all would go well so that we could just move forward and forget it ever happened. I'd never put myself and Chris in this situation again, so I had no doubt that it would never happen again!

Our evening with Mama went fine. She cooked a really good meal—boiled chicken and rice, of course, with a side of string beans.

After finishing supper, Chris and I got ready for bed. We sat together on the sofa in the front room and watched television for the remainder of the night until it was time for us to lay down.

After saying 'Goodnight' to Mama, we settled in the extra bedroom, which was down the hallway from Mama's room. Our door didn't have a lock on it, so we could only close it.

All was uneventful until a little after one o'clock in the morning when I heard knocking and banging noises, seemingly coming from the kitchen.

Getting out of bed, I slowly opened the door and tried to peek out and see what was going on, but I couldn't see anything. Remembering that it was on me to protect myself and Chris, I decided to quietly step towards the living room to see what all the commotion was about. Cautiously walking into the front room area, I saw Mama in her white nightgown and head bonnet, staggering around in the kitchen. Observing her odd behavior, I became very afraid and immediately called out to her, "Mama?"

However, she didn't answer me. Mama was acting very bizarre and had a faraway look on her face as she mumbled something unintelligible. She seemed very confused, and I guessed that maybe she was sleepwalking because she walked aimlessly for no apparent reason.

When she didn't acknowledge me, I hurried back into the room and closed the door. Knowing that the door couldn't lock, I sat up in the bed and stared at it, not taking my eyes off of it. Too scared to sleep, I stayed awake the entire night. Needless to say, morning couldn't come quickly enough.

Several times, I reached down to feel the knife handle, making sure it was easily accessible in case I had to grab it. Bringing it close enough to the edge of the mattress to keep it concealed but close enough for me to be able to grab it in an instant if Mama came barging in, I kept my hand hanging nearby.

Thankfully for everyone, Mama never attempted to come in. Daddy never knew about that night. I also neither mentioned it to Chris nor asked Mama about it the next morning. There was no need to because my mind had already been made up that this would be our first and last time spending the night with Mama.

When morning came, I was a sleepy, nervous wreck but so very grateful to see daybreak. It wouldn't have surprised me if Daddy had stayed up all night, too, worrying about us.

The only other thing that caused me a bit more anxiety was returning the knife to the kitchen drawer without Mama seeing me. How hurtful it would be for her, and very uncomfortable for me, for her to find out just how afraid I still am of her.

The night was an eye-opener for me because I didn't think such fear of Mama still lay within me. As soon as Mama made a trip to the bathroom, I quickly slipped into the kitchen and put the knife back in the drawer. As far as I knew, she never realized it was gone.

We ate the breakfast Mama prepared, and then we left.

We did continue to spend time with Mama, just no more overnight stays. Daddy and I never discussed our stay with Mama beyond my apologizing to him again as soon as we made it home. He forgave me, and he and I moved forward.

GOOD TIMES

Chris had just turned 15 and would soon be applying for his driver's permit. Mama, knowing how badly Chris wanted to learn to drive, asked Daddy if she could take him to vacant lots and teach him how to drive. Daddy was fine with that, so during many of our visits with Mama, she would take us to the parking lot of nearby parks and give Chris the wheel.

Oh my gosh! What a hilarious experience! I'm not sure if Mama realized what she was signing up for because the moment Chris was allowed to move beyond driving in vacant lots and actually driving on the street, Mama's nerves frazzled! I did my best not to laugh, but most of the time, it was an epic failure on my part.

Each time we would drive on the neighborhood streets, Mama would constantly holler, grab the armrest on the door, and yell at Chris, telling him he was too close to the ditch.

Mama would exclaim, "Boy! Don't you get us stuck in the ditch! You too close, Chris!"

To which Chris would snicker and respond, "Mama, I'm nowhere even close to the ditch."

"Yes, you are. I'm going to make you stop if you don't move over!" she'd reply, almost having a meltdown.

"Mama, I'm away from the ditch. I'm not going to run into the ditch. I can see how close I am," Chris would say, trying to calm her down.

Mama would then, without fail, turn to me in the back seat and ask, "Cheryl, isn't he too close?"

I'd respond, trying to keep a straight face, "No, ma'am, I'm looking. He's fine."

That would be good enough for Mama, for just a few minutes, that is, and then she'd start all over again. Chris would actually be no closer to the ditch than the other drivers, as he was a very careful driver.

In the beginning, I believe Mama scared Chris, but after a while, he became accustomed to her overreacting to his driving and would laugh himself, making it very difficult for me not to lay prostrate on the seat, laughing to tears.

We were in no way trying to be disrespectful to Mama, and she knew that because, on occasion, she would even laugh along with us, realizing her reactions at times were a bit 'over the top.'

Sometimes, just to keep Mama calm, Chris would intentionally drive in the middle of the street if no other cars were behind us or approaching from the opposite direction.

Honestly, when spending time with Mama, I looked forward to Chris' driving lessons more than anything else. I have to say I admired Mama for sticking with it because she could have called it quits. She was a trooper and didn't stop the lessons until Chris received his driver's permit a few months later. Those were some of the best times we had with Mama as teenagers.

Our relationship with her did deepen, but because she still suffered from occasional episodes of mental lapses, our relationship was also still hindered to a certain degree. Not understanding Mama's mental health challenges, I would at times become frustrated with her, not knowing how to respond in a way that would help whatever situation had developed.

There were numerous times when she'd call me complaining that someone was eating the food out of her refrigerator, though she lived alone and no one, other than the landlord, had access to the inside of her home. At other times, she would call, frightened, saying that there was a man dragging his leg down her driveway.

Dealing with paranoia was still very challenging for Mama, and it also left my feelings all over the place. In line with her mental illness diagnosis, Mama hallucinated quite a bit, and that hampered us from having the type of 'mother-daughter' relationship I really yearned for. I felt disconnected during those times when she'd become delusional because it was very difficult to communicate with her.

Beyond taking medication, Mama couldn't help or change her sickness, and in spite of it, I was still happy to have her back in my life. I loved her, and nothing had changed that.

Though we never discussed with Mama anything about 'the tragedy,' Mama would often ask Chris and me, "Babies…did Mama ruin your lives?"

Whoa, that was such a loaded question! Remembering the first time she asked us that question, I was completely thrown off and, for a moment, didn't know how to answer.

Do I tell the truth? What is the truth?

Had our lives been completely ruined, or was there still hope?

I believed that George's life had definitely been ruined, cut short, because he was longer living. Did we still have a chance at a decent life despite what our mama had done?

I did hope so, but I had my own times of doubt.

Not wanting to make her feel any worse, we simply responded, "No, ma'am."

Asking earnestly and sincerely, Mama had such a look of regret and sorrow on her face, as if she had already answered the question for us in her own head but was maybe hoping we'd tell her something different.

I don't know if I'd say at that point that she'd ruined our lives, but *what she did* definitely changed our lives and, in some ways, especially in the beginning, made our lives very challenging.

We knew she was sorry for what she'd done because she'd apologized over and over again, though never specifically saying, "I'm sorry for killing George and for wanting to hurt you, Chris, and your daddy."

Her apologies didn't contain any such statements or sentiments, but the fact was we knew why she was sorry, and she didn't have to elaborate.

"I'm sorry" was enough for us because we believed she genuinely meant it.

Though we wouldn't be *discussing* any specifics about *that* day, it became obvious that this question often haunted Mama. Every waking moment of her life, Mama had to deal with the fact that she'd killed George, her son, our brother. I thought about how tormenting even sleep probably was for her sometimes, as I was sure she had to, at times, relive that day in her dreams, not being able to escape from it when she laid down and closed her eyes.

Medications helped Mama cope with life, and we hoped that knowing that we still loved her would help ease the pain. However, more than likely, every time she saw me and Chris, the pain and memory of that day became even more memorable because our presence surely reminded her of George's absence.

That one act that she committed drastically changed all our lives. Mama knew it, and we knew it.

From this point onward, I will share more intimately about my own personal journey.

I can't tell my brother's story; only he can speak from his heart.

CHAPTER ELEVEN

GROWING PAINS

AWKWARDNESS

'Tall, lanky, no hips, no curves,' described me to a 'T' during my preadolescent and adolescent years. It didn't help that I sported a 'Jeri curl,' which caused me to look more like a boy than a girl. I lost count of the number of times I was mistaken for a boy, even by some of my Daddy's co-workers who'd known me since I was a baby. Ugh!!! To be called my Daddy's 'son' instead of 'daughter' made me so self-conscious that I would do whatever I could to make my appearance more feminine, including wearing earrings and even small bows in my hair. It was so bad that, at times, even the earrings and hair bows were missed.

Puberty was a particularly difficult time for me, especially since Mama wasn't living in the same house with me. When I began to menstruate, I was terrified, even embarrassed. Grandmother and Aunt Della did their best to explain to me the changes that my body would go through as I became 'a young woman,' including throwing a few myths in the mix.

Really missing Mama during this time, I wished things in my life had gone 'normally.' I needed her to be the mother I wanted and needed so that I could feel comfortable talking to her about the things I was going through. That desire didn't change the way things were, and I had to accept that.

Though I was close to Grandmother, I felt too uncomfortable telling her when my cycle started and way too 'shamed-faced,' as the older folks would call it, to ask for sanitary napkins. Oh, how I wished my periods would just go away, but of course, that didn't happen! Grandmother had stopped having them a long time ago, and talking to her about it just seemed so awkward to me. I didn't think Grandmother would understand or be able to relate to what I was going through, but honestly, I should have at least given her a chance. Afterall, she had at one time also had periods.

My grandmother was there for me with everything else I went through, including getting me through 'girlhood' crushes that didn't end well. In fact, Grandmother was by far the wisest woman I knew when it came to life and boys.

In elementary, my first crush was on this little boy named Kenneth. Kenneth had the most beautiful hazel-gray eyes, and I daydreamed about him being my boyfriend. We were in the third grade. I found out the hard way that Kenneth didn't feel the same way about me.

In fact, Kenneth liked to tease me, saying I looked like 'Aunt Esther' on the TV show *"Sanford and Son."* Oh man, how that *stung*!

I'd always fire back with a little neck roll, "Oh yeah? Well, you look like Fred Sanford!"

He'd just laugh because that was a good 'comeback,' and I'd laugh along with him, pretending not to be hurt by his words, but they really did hurt.

The last thing I wanted to be called by the boy I had a huge crush on was "Aunt Esther"! Now, as talented as Aunt Esther was, and though I was a fan, I found it downright insulting to be told I looked like a woman who was about 7 to 8 times my age, who wore a black and gray wig and was known for her animated, over-the-top personality.

I wasn't at all flattered, but then again, Kenneth's words weren't meant to be flattering. Kenneth never found out how I actually felt about him, but Grandmother knew because I cried in her lap one day about the things he would say to me. Grandmother, being the loving woman she was, reassured me that I was beautiful and smart and that it was Kenneth's loss.

I'm, however, sure she was okay with my not having a boyfriend, being that I was just in the third grade. I know she was put in a difficult position because I'm almost certain that what she really wanted to tell me was to 'focus' on my studies and not on boys. I'm glad she told me I was 'beautiful and smart,' even though I only felt like the latter was true.

Whenever I was consumed with feelings of unattractiveness, I thought about what Grandmother said, and it helped me feel better about myself. She continually emphasized how important it was for me to concentrate on my schoolwork and do well so that when I grew up, I could be whatever I wanted to be. Boys could be such a distraction if I allowed them to be.

Doing well in elementary school, I made straight A's on all my report cards. My family was very proud that I'd done well as I was on my way to then 'junior' high school. Though nervous, I was ecstatic about my acceptance into a vanguard program that focused on math and science. That was perfect for me because, for as long as I can remember, I wanted to become a doctor so that I could help people fight diseases.

MIDDLE SCHOOL

Leaving elementary school and going to middle school was a sure sign that we were growing up—pre-teenagers on our way to becoming full-fledged teenagers! It helped that our grandparents and Daddy, in particular, took a lead role in our education and stayed active because we had so much to deal with, from bullying to negative peer pressure and so much in between, especially starting in middle school.

So much seemed to be changing as I had to venture out of my comfort zone to make new friends, get acquainted with new teachers, and become accustomed to riding a school bus to a new school, which was quite a ways from my house. Thankfully, my home life was still stable and not much changed as far as our weekend routine was concerned. Daddy still picked Chris and me up on Friday nights.

It was clear that Daddy and Mama wouldn't ever live together as husband and wife, so Daddy began dating other women, of which Mama was aware. Daddy didn't divorce Mama so that she could continue to receive much-needed medical benefits as his spouse.

We, while continuing to spend our weekends with Daddy, also began to share him with his lady friend, Ms. Bettye, and that was fine with us because she was nice. Ms. Bettye became the mainstay in Daddy's life, and she became a part of our family.

Mama moved on with her life too, but she didn't date anyone seriously. She and Daddy got along well for our sake, which made things easier. That was good because puberty was hard enough on its own!

Shortly after entering the seventh grade, I tried out for the girls' basketball team and made it. Putting my height to use, the coach had me playing forward on the junior varsity team. Because my grandparents were getting old and were starting to experience health issues, especially

Granddaddy, my basketball coach would pick me up early every school morning for basketball practice before school started. Without fail, regardless of the weather, my coach would drop by and scoop me up.

Daddy came to every game he could, with his work schedule permitting, and my grandparents hardly missed any of my games, oftentimes with Aunt Della bringing them. Our family was so supportive of everything Chris and I did.

As I began blossoming from a little girl into a young woman, middle school set the stage for me to learn quite a bit about myself and about life, including sexuality. We NEVER discussed sex or anything even closely related to it. It was almost as taboo to talk about it as it was to talk about what Mama did, so the grownups in our family avoided that conversation with us like avoiding the plague.

However, entering middle school made me realize that *some* talk would have better prepared me for what was just ahead. Seventh-grade gym class was an eye-opener for me. Each day following class, the boys would head to the boys' locker room to change their clothes, and of course, the girls would go to the girls' locker room to do the same. Having enrolled in swim class, I was required to shower after class and then get back into the clothes I'd worn to school.

One day, a female student that I'd heard liked other girls seemingly had her eyes *on me*. It was my first year in middle school, and I didn't like anyone, not in that way. Looking 'nerdier' than anything, I didn't know what her attraction to me was. Although I was a decent basketball player, maybe *that* was it: my athleticism? Though I hadn't had a 'real' boyfriend yet, I wasn't looking for a girlfriend. I didn't think the girl was a bad person because I didn't even know her personally. I just knew I didn't want to go there with her, and I also knew the day would eventually come when I'd have to let her know I wasn't interested.

Well, that day arrived sooner than later, and unfortunately for me, things didn't go the way I would have liked. My grandparents never taught us to hate anyone, not because they looked different or acted different, not for any reason. They, in addition to that, taught us that it wasn't acceptable for anyone to bully us and that anyone who did so needed to be dealt with. Grandmother, of course, wasn't with me that day at school, and I soon found myself having to deal with this particular situation all by myself.

After my swimming class ended, I was on my way out of the shower with my towel wrapped around me. I'd already put on my underclothes and was just using the towel to cover myself until I could get back to my locker and put on the rest of my clothes. As soon as I pulled the cloth shower curtain back, there she stood. Taken by surprise, I jumped back a little because she startled me.

At first, I became nervous, realizing she and I were getting ready to have a confrontation. Almost as if on cue, the other girls in the locker room turned to see what was going on between us. I did have a couple of classmates in there that I considered 'good' friends, but they were too afraid or *too curious* to jump in.

Initially, they just watched with the rest of the girls, though towards the end of our altercation, they did move much closer to the shower area, ready to grab the girl if necessary.

The fight, or more like a tussle, didn't last long at all. There were more words exchanged than licks released when the girl realized I wasn't going to allow her to do what she wanted to with me. Though she was a year older than me, from my days of *ole*, I wasn't about to back down, even if it meant getting punched. It was at that very moment that I was so glad I had already put my underwear on. To fight her 'butt-naked' wouldn't have been a good sight.

The girl seemed a little shocked by the fact that I wasn't afraid of her, and when she went to grab me, trying to push me back into the shower, I grabbed her arms first, shoved her into the shower wall, and then began to shout a few 'obscenities' at her. I did know a little something about cursing, having heard other kids curse. How quickly the 'fight' turned in my favor, and just as the other girls began to cheer and make all kinds of noise in the background, our gym coach rushed in, blowing her whistle.

Coach Smith had been around a long time and was now in her mid to late sixties, and she attributed all of her age marks and wrinkles to the students she'd taught and coached over the years. Wearing gold horn-rimmed glasses, Coach Smith was a short, White woman with a frail body frame and thinning, white hair sparsely covering her scalp.

"Hey, what's going on in here?!" she yelled, shouting at the top of her lungs, blowing her whistle so loudly that some of the girls covered their ears.

At first, no one responded, being frightened by her tone alone, and then one of the girls in the locker room pointed and told the coach how the girl, now frowning and standing somewhat damp outside the shower, tried to touch me.

The coach looked at me with a stern, disgusted face and asked, "Is that true?!" causing me to jump a little as she sprayed my face with some of her spit.

Nervously, I softly replied, "Yes, ma'am".

The coach, though petite, was intimidating looking because her thick lenses magnified her eyes, and that, along with her loud, raspy voice, gave her a very 'threatening' appearance. Walking over and standing in front of the girl, the coach interrogated her, asking, "What do you have to say about it? Did you do that?"

The girl didn't answer.

"I asked you a question!" The coach shouted at the girl. "You answer me!"

"Did you try to touch her?!" Coach Smith asked again, moving even closer to the girl.

"Why are you in my face?" The girl spouted back very disrespectfully and with plenty of attitude.

Oh no, she didn't just say that to the coach!

"You come with me!" The coach said, grabbing the girl by the arm and taking her out of the locker room as the other girls cheered and laughed.

I don't know what happened to that girl, but that was the last time I saw her. That little incident bumped my 'popularity' ratings up a little bit, and after that day, I had a few more friends, though I still wasn't quite the girl all the 'cute' boys wanted to sit next to at lunch. I was okay with that, though and didn't let that bother me since there wasn't anyone in particular, at least not a really smart boy, that had caught my attention.

Doing as my grandmother had taught me to do, I continued focusing on my studies and not so much on boys. Really, after witnessing all the drama that having a 'boyfriend brought my friends, I concluded that my life was actually okay without one.

My first boyfriend didn't come along until I was a junior in high school, and by then, I was slated to graduate at the top of my class, so I was glad I was able to remain focused. Listening to Grandmother did pay off. Seventh grade, with all the bumps and the bruises, turned out to not be so frightening after all.

Sadly, towards the end of my seventh-grade year in May of 1980, our Grandmother Wilma passed. It was heartbreaking, especially since we'd spent quite a bit of time at her house after Mama's release and had grown closer to her. Many times, we'd sit on her bed as she lay there and comb through and brush her hair. That really relaxed her and sometimes actually put her to sleep.

Surrounding by family who loved her, Grandmother Wilma was young when she died, passing at the age of 57 from complications stemming from diabetes. Towards the latter end of her life, one of her legs had been amputated, and she was nearly blind. Grandmother at least had been able to see her daughter, our mother, return home.

The summer of 1980, following Grandmother Wilma's death, came and went fairly quickly. Most of the days were hot and long, as we spent the entire summer splitting our time between Daddy, Mama, and our grandparents. Our summer months were uneventful, for which we were grateful. August rolled around, and it was time again for us to get ready for the upcoming school year.

We always looked forward to the couple of weeks just prior to the start of school because Daddy would take us on a big shopping spree and buy us new clothes and shoes and a lot of school supplies. This would be Chris' first year in junior high school.

Having to get used to switching classes, we had to learn how to not stop and talk with friends but instead move quickly from one class to the next. Enjoying much more independence in middle school, we no longer had to be lined up by our teachers to go to the bathroom, the lunchroom, or outside. Now, we were responsible for doing those things on our own, in a timely fashion, and also making sure that we had all of our things for each class. Being called out by the teachers for being late quickly taught us to be on time and avoid being embarrassed.

By the beginning of my eighth-grade year in middle school, I was known as one of the smartest girls on campus, and much of the teasing

I'd endured early in the seventh grade like being called 'nerdy' or 'a geek,' had for the most part subsided, though occasionally, an insult would come flying my way. By then, being content with who I was, I didn't allow what other kids said about me to discourage me. Knowing that Daddy and my grandparents loved me, were proud of me, and believed in me kept me striving to do my best.

One year had brought about a change, and I wasn't the same quiet, soft-spoken girl I was when I entered seventh grade. Becoming more confident, I learned how to stand up for myself, and even, on occasion, took on the role of fighting for the 'underdogs' (other kids who were being bullied or teased). In fact, it was because of that that I ended up in the principal's office, in trouble, for the very first time one school afternoon.

I was in Math Class, and my eighth-grade teacher, Mr. Woods, a very tall Black man who looked so much like the actor Lawrence Fishburne, was doing his best to overlook what started out as a minor spat. Soon, however, our spat turned into a 'cat fight.' There was no physical exchange or altercation, but there was plenty of intense, heated verbal exchange. One of my classmates would constantly taunt and tease another girl in our class. I just got sick of it because the girl being teased was very shy and would not stand up for herself. More days than not, she'd end up crying because of the bullying. She reminded me of myself at the beginning of my first year in middle school.

Turning to the girl doing the teasing, I just 'went off' and told her to leave the other girl alone. "Hey, why don't you stop messing with her? She's not doing anything to you!" I said, frowning at the girl doing the bullying, tired of hearing her mouth.

"Who's talking to you, Cheryl...*Ms. Olive Oyl?*" She quickly rebutted.

I was so sick of being compared to the cartoon character Olive Oyl, Popeye's tall and lanky girlfriend. However, calling me names didn't get to me like they used to, and it didn't shut me up either.

"I'm talking to you. Leave her alone. That makes you feel better about yourself, picking on her?" I shot back quickly, looking directly into her eyes.

"What you going to do about it? You need to mind your own business, Cheryl Battle. I *didn't* call your name, so I wasn't talking to you!" She said back, rolling her eyes long and hard at me and moving her neck.

Of course, she didn't take too well to my interference and was really beginning to tear into me verbally when our teacher stopped the class to reprimand both of us for being a disruption.

"Hey, hey, hey! What's going on?" Mr. Woods asked, very irritated while tapping the chalk on the chalkboard.

He looked at us and said, "You two ladies have a problem? Close your mouths right now!"

The teacher sternly stared at us for a couple of seconds as the rest of the class looked on, stunned. He then turned back around and continued to write on the board.

My anger got the best of me that day because even after the teacher told both of us to be quiet, I continued to go back and forth with the girl, first softly and then louder, as the volume of our voices increased and carried. My classmate was so angry that I had gotten 'in her business' that she wouldn't leave me alone and kept calling me names, and I, letting her push my buttons, wasn't about to ignore her. We were both then put out of class by Mr. Woods and sent to the principal's office.

"Get up! Get up! And get out of my class! Go to the principal's office right now! I will not tolerate your rude and disrespectful behavior!" Mr. Woods screamed at both of us.

You could hear the other kids go, "Ooooh," with their mouths hanging open.

My teacher looked particularly puzzled at me. My behavior was very unbecoming of the student everyone, including the teachers, knew me to be.

"Everybody be quiet, or else you'll be going with them!" He shouted at the class and watched us as we stood up from our chairs and headed out of the door for the principal's office.

I'd never had a teacher yell at me like that or become *that* upset with me. Always known as the quiet, attentive kid, that day, I wrecked my reputation for a moment, though I was trying to do the right thing regarding the girl being bullied. Honestly, I surprised myself. What in the world would Daddy and my grandparents say?

No surprise, however, this wasn't the other girl's first time getting into trouble, because though she was very smart, she had a real 'potty' mouth and would insult, curse, and 'tell off' others in an instant, earning her multiple trips to the principal's office.

I wasn't nearly as clever or quick with my tongue as she was, but I did have a 'fight' in me that day, believing I was standing up for what was right, though I definitely went about it the wrong way.

Because the vanguard program at our school was housed in a separate, two-story building from the main building, we had to walk downstairs, outside, and then enter the main building and walk down a long hallway that led to the Main Office. My classmate and I walked together slowly down the hallway, dreading what was coming.

As soon as we walked through the door, the school secretary gave us a look and told us to have a seat. Apparently, Mr. Woods had already called the office because they were expecting us. I wasn't used to getting into trouble and didn't like it one bit.

As I sat there, I thought about what I'd done. I'd been very disrespectful to my teacher and my classmates, though I felt justified in the beginning for doing what I did. In my head, I could hear Grandmother talking to me about this very thing, about not being disrespectful and about paying attention. Would I get a little break, at least for trying to stand up for someone else? Time would tell.

Realizing how wrong I was in not handling the situation the right way, I looked at my classmate, who had actually been my friend in the past, and apologized. She apologized back to me.

Then I thought to myself, 'Maybe we can get out of a paddling by letting the principal know that we realize how wrong we were for what we had done and that we wanted to make it right by apologizing to our teacher and class.' We could tell her how we'd even just now apologized to each other.

Sitting next to my classmate, I told her what I was thinking, and she agreed, thinking it was a good idea. In fact, her entire countenance changed, and she perked right up. I began to feel so much better too. I thought to myself, 'The principal will listen, at least to me. I'd never been in her office and had never gotten into trouble before. Yeah, she'll give us a break. I was hopeful, even confident, thinking my plan would work. Neither one of us wanted to get paddled.

'Whew, we'll be okay,' I thought again to myself.

The principal, standing inside her office, opened her office door and called both of us in. We went right on in, greeting her as we passed by.

Unlike my friend, who kept her head down as she walked in, I quickly glanced at the principal's face to see if she looked like she was in the mood for talking. She wasn't smiling, and I knew then we were really in trouble.

Our principal was a short, stocky, middle-aged Black lady who was known for being strict and having a mean swing with the paddle.

All of a sudden, I got nervous, really nervous all over again. Closing the door behind us, she walked over to her desk and sat down while we continued to stand. Looking sternly at us and folding her hands together on her desk, she told us to have a seat in the two chairs facing her desk. We sat down and looked at her as she stared at both of us for a moment, looking at the other girl first and then at me.

"So why are y'all in my office?" She asked with a grimace on her face, appearing as though she was in some sort of pain.

We nervously explained to her what happened, including letting her know that we'd seen the 'err of our ways,' and had apologized to each other, and wanted to apologize to our teacher and classmates.

Obviously, we weren't the first to get this great revelation of making amends for wrongdoing because she didn't look at all impressed. We did follow that up with an attempt to convince her that we would do better.

It didn't work!

After hearing from both of us, she still said, "OK, stand up."

What?!!! Wait a minute. What did she mean by that?! Had she heard anything we said?!

Too little, *too* late.

Whack! Whack! Whack!

The paddle caused our behinds to move with each pop, and the hard licks left our backsides stinging. She gave both of us three pops a piece! Since this was my first time in the principal's office, why didn't I get some kind of leniency?

Thinking back, I guess the leniency, or mercy, came when our teacher told us to be quiet the first time before actually sending us to the principal's office. We completely disregarded what he'd said, earning us a painful, one-on-one session with the principal.

The other girl and I both stood there, balling our eyes out. The principal then looked directly at us and shouted, "Now get back to class and stop acting like fools!"

That was the first and last time I'd done anything warranting a trip to the principal's office. Although I didn't regret standing up for my classmate, I did regret the way I did it. That paddling gave me a quick lesson in self-discipline.

The school had already called my grandparents and informed them of my in-school discipline, so when I got home, I got more scolding, this time from Grandmother. After a good talking-to by her, I apologized again, wiped the tears from my face, and we put it behind us. I learned to appreciate that neither our grandparents nor our daddy harped too long on any incident that happened. After they addressed it, it was over, and we moved forward.

The rest of my time in eighth grade came and went without any significant problems, and soon, I entered my final year of junior high school—ninth grade! So much was going on as my friends and I were preparing to graduate. We had to order our caps and gowns and ready ourselves for that big day.

Elementary school graduation was very subtle compared to junior high school graduation. Discussions about where we wanted to attend high school began to monopolize most of our conversations. This time, unlike with junior high school, I had a full say as to where I wanted to attend high school.

Still wanting to become a doctor, my mind was made up to attend a high school specializing in the medical field, which was 'The High School for Health Professions,' later changed to 'Michael E. DeBakey High School for Health Professions.' Because I wasn't zoned to the school, we had to apply to the high school, and I had to meet certain grade criteria. And thankfully, because I'd stayed focused on my studies, I had no problem getting in.

The day my acceptance letter arrived was one of the happiest days of my life!

We'd been through so much, but I finally was beginning to feel like my life was 'on track' and moving in the right direction. Very encouraged about my future, I was thrilled about possibly one day becoming a doctor! Pondering a career in Family Medicine or Internal Medicine, I was just so happy to be on a good path, headed towards seeing my dreams one day come true.

High School

Entering The High School for Health Professions in the tenth grade (back in the day, junior high ran from the seventh grade to the ninth grade), I soon realized what a melting pot my new school was, having a dynamic makeup of Whites, Blacks, Native-American, Hispanics, and Asians.

My middle school hadn't offered that kind of diversity, and it was exciting and different, being able to go to school with kids who didn't look like me and who were from different backgrounds and cultures.

Though different in many ways, we all got along fairly well because the things that we shared, an interest in the health and science field, connected us all.

My love for science, in particular Biology, increased over the span of my high school years. One thing that was unique about our campus was the opportunity we had as students to work as interns in local hospitals and medical laboratories, including Baylor College of Medicine. I couldn't wait for my chance to roll around!

As to be expected, the academics were much harder in high school than in junior high school, and having good study habits was absolutely necessary for success. Because I also enjoyed math, I was encouraged by my math teacher to check out our high school's Math Club.

Manipulating numbers and using formulas to find answers to problems had always intrigued me, so I was eager to join the group after attending just one of their meetings. Those of us in the group would compete in what was known as 'Number Sense Competitions.'

While being able to proudly take trophies, medals, and certificates back to our school after winning competitions was something we looked forward to, we also just enjoyed hanging out after school and practicing for upcoming competitions.

Our math coach, also our math teacher, was Kim Vernon, a young educator in her early twenties. It was so cool that she wasn't very much older than us and that she actually liked being around us.

In no time, those of us in the Math Club developed a close bond, which led to our hanging out together on the weekends. Most of the time, with Ms. Vernon behind the wheel, we'd attend various fun events together. Though there were boys and girls in the Math Club, none of us became romantically involved with each other. That seemed to help keep our friendships strong and our Math Club intact.

Ms. Vernon came up with a good idea, suggesting that we all go out on a Saturday morning and play softball. Soon, playing softball became an almost every weekend activity for us, from which I received my infamous nickname, 'Bear.'

During high school, several more inches added to my height, making me taller but still not curvaceous at all. There was a period of time when I did my best to gain weight but just couldn't. After a while, I just accepted the fact that I was skinny and that there was nothing I could do about it.

My real friends neither teased me about it nor cared that I was skinny, so I settled into just being who I was. By the time we'd begun playing softball on a regular basis, my arms and legs, though still lean, started to develop more of an athletic build, but that wasn't the reason I was nicknamed 'Bear.' I was given that name because, during my first time at bat, I approached the home plate getting ready to bat, held the bat firmly in my hands and then, in slow motion, leaned back with the bat with a serious look, and hit the ball harder than anyone expected me to! This tall, skinny girl was at bat, but a 'fierce' bear emerged and put the outfielders to work!

After playing softball that first weekend, the next time I approached the plate, one of my buddies yelled out, "Go Bear, hit that ball!" and from that moment on, I was pegged with the name "Bear."

I loved my nickname, and so did my friends, so much so that one day, a few years later, while walking down a hallway during my college years, I heard a voice out in the distance yell out, "Bear!" While I was very amused, I wondered who in the world was calling me 'Bear' in college.

Sure enough, it was one of my old Math Club buddies from high school! It had been at least three years since I'd last seen him, but that didn't keep him from immediately calling me 'Bear.' More than embarrassing me, it made me smile.

Continuing to do well in my studies and forming some great friendships, I enjoyed my first year of high school. No additional motivation was needed as every day, I looked forward to going to school.

The teachers, mostly women, were like 'mamas away from home' for most of us. Though we were growing up quickly, we still, from time to time, needed that motherly 'wisdom' and even instruction to keep us on the right track while at school. They did so much more than teach us the fundamentals of different academic subjects; they taught us the fundamentals of life! My life was headed for even more major changes, and what a significant impact my teachers would have on my survival.

There wasn't anything I disliked about high school; the teachers were great, and the curriculum was very good. The one thing I did miss, however, was being involved in organized sports like basketball. Our school's focus was solely on academics, and as such, it didn't offer any kind of extracurricular sports activities.

While we didn't have basketball, baseball, football, cheerleading, or any of the typical sports you'd find at most high schools, we did have 'Talent Night,' which all of the students, and even the staff, looked forward to. One of the highlights of my freshman year was actually being a part of the talent show.

I liked to dance, so along with three of my friends, I entered the talent show. We all enjoyed dancing and, with ease, learned how to execute all of the latest dance moves- like 'the *Whopp*' and 'the *Popeye*.'

The show was being held in our school cafeteria on a Friday night, and my friends and I practiced after school for about four weeks in preparation for the event. Our dance routine required us to partner up, and we each had input in choreographing about a five-minute dance routine.

Somewhat shy, I was as nervous as I was excited to display my dancing skills in front of a large audience. Daddy, Chris, Aunt Della, and my grandparents would be there. Mama, however, would not be able to come.

She lived across town, and because of her nervous condition, she neither drove on the freeways nor at night and that unfortunately caused her to miss many of Chris' and my school functions.

Mama actually had gotten a job at a diner close to her house, and that kept her busy, which was good because we didn't see her as often as before because of all the different things we were involved in. She was very happy being able to work for the first time in many years. While Mama was doing very well, living on her own, managing her mental health issues, and keeping her appointments without Grandmother Wilma, she unfortunately began to wrestle with other chronic illnesses.

Surrounding herself with more support, Mama joined a church, and the sisters, though knowing about her past, welcomed her in with loving arms. Not before too long, Mama had developed close friendships with several of the sisters in the church. One such sister, Sister Gatlin, a very large woman with an even larger heart, became Mama's best friend.

How amusing it was that most times Mama and her small circle of lady friends called each other by their last names instead of by their first names, so Mama was called 'Battle' instead of 'Alice.'

Of course, there were those who wanted nothing to do with Mama, also having knowledge of her past, but Mama was still so grateful just to be a part of a church family and to have a few friends who loved her unconditionally.

Mama wouldn't be at the talent show Friday night, but she had already sent her best wishes and her regrets about not being able to attend.

There were plenty of acts lined up for the talent show, and many tickets had been sold, so my group and I had to get ourselves mentally prepared for all the people coming. Because we'd practiced long and hard and had our dance moves down, we were very hopeful about taking home the first-place trophy. We'd already checked out the competition, and while they were good, we thought our act would pull out the win.

The night of the talent show came, and it was really nerve-racking! Dressed in matching black tops with white, starched slacks, we made sure all of the last-minute details had been taken care of, including making sure our music was ready to go with the push of a button. Dancing with strobe lights, we tested them to make sure they were working right because they would give our dance moves a robotic appearance. Aww, man, we were ready!

Peeking from behind the thick stage curtain, I spotted my family.

"The show will be starting in fifteen minutes," came the announcement over the loudspeaker.

"Fifteen minutes? Where's Joann?" I asked, worried because she hadn't shown up yet.

She was my partner, and we all had been looking forward to the dance for about a month. In fact, we talked more about the talent show than about anything else. It consumed our thoughts outside of class, even leading us to practice on our own at home. Hoping Joann was in the building somewhere, the three of us separated to go and see if we could find her.

Ten more minutes passed, and the announcer for the evening began telling everyone in the audience to take their seats because we were preparing to begin.

"Man…where is Joann?" Micheala asked as the three of us stood in a semi-circle, now worried that our fourth dancer wouldn't show up.

"She told me after school that she would be here early. Where is she?" Wanda said, visibly nervous.

All of a sudden, I started feeling queasy in the pit of my stomach.

"Shoot…she'd better get here, like now, because she's my partner! We are dancing together. I can't dance by myself!" I said angrily.

"Well, we don't go on first, so she still has a little time to make it. I'm going to call her house again," said Micheala.

Wanda and I just stood backstage and watched the other acts line up to go on while Micheala went to the office to call Joann. Michaela, getting no answer at Joann's house, made it back within five minutes, just as the first act finished their performances. The three of us just stood there.

"What are we going to do? It's not going to look right without Joann." I said, on the verge of a meltdown.

"We are just going to have to dance without her if she doesn't make it in time," Micheala said, shrugging her shoulders, trying to ease my fears.

No one knew how I was feeling at that moment. It would be me, more than them, who looked strange doing a dance by myself that was meant for two people.

Where in the world was she?! She knew we were depending on her. I just couldn't believe she hadn't shown up.

At that moment, all of a sudden, I didn't care about winning first place. I just wanted her to show up. I was going to be so embarrassed if I had to dance by myself.

After a couple of more acts, it was time for us to take the stage. Joann never showed. She never called or sent any word, and I unfortunately did end up dancing by myself. Feeling absolutely foolish, I did my best to control my anxiety and disappointment, but the truth is I was *mortified.* Managing to make it through the entire five minutes of our routine without breaking down, I waited for the curtain to close again and then ran out the back of the stage, crying.

As I ran, I could hear the applause for us on the other side of the curtains. Breaking down, I was in major sobs and tears. Micheala and Wanda were upset too, but I was in full meltdown mode because I thought I looked like such a fool!

The teachers and sponsors backstage did their best to console me, but the sting of defeat felt so terrible. At that moment, nothing else in life mattered to me, and I just wanted to go home.

All throughout school, from elementary through high school, I'd won all kinds of medals and certificates of achievements, always being at the top of my class. Even though in junior high school, my junior varsity basketball team did lose some games, we also won some, so I never felt totally defeated. When we lost games, we would just work harder to win the next time.

But what could I do about what just happened at the talent show? Even more than feeling like a failure, I was so annoyed about Joann letting us down.

'How could she do that to us?' I kept thinking over and over again in my head.

We'd practiced a whole lot. Trying to find matching outfits, we went to the mall together. Our music was just right and prepared on tape, and the strobe lights were working! Everything was in place, and all we had to do was show up and dance!

After exiting the stage, my family greeted me with high praises and hugs, but I could only greet them with tears.

"Cheryl, what's wrong, baby? Why are you crying?" Grandmother asked, becoming very concerned and grabbing and rubbing my hand.

Everyone else moved in, looking confused and trying to find out what was going on. There was so much noise in the cafeteria that it was hard to hear anyone clearly.

"Joann didn't show up, and I had to dance by myself!" I said, somewhat shouting and then breaking down in tears again.

"We couldn't tell there was a problem. Y'all did a good job," Daddy said sincerely, putting his hand on my shoulder, trying to encourage me.

"Cheryl, your friend didn't show up, but you see, you still danced and did a great job. We are so proud of you," Grandmother said, hugging me.

"Oh, don't cry. Grandmother thinks y'all did well!" She said again, wiping my tears off my face.

"You should be proud of yourself, baby. Most people wouldn't have gone on stage at all, but you did, and I'm telling you, y'all did a wonderful job!" Grandmother said, moving her shoulders and trying to snap her fingers. "I tell you what, I wish I could move like you, girl."

Grandmother's *mad* dance moves made me smile, and everyone else laugh.

Although I was very disappointed about the way things had gone that evening, something significant happened that Friday night at the Talent Show as Grandmother taught me about the courage it takes to not give up when things aren't going my way.

She'd say, "As long as another day comes along, that's another opportunity for things to get better."

It took me some time to fully grasp what Grandmother was really saying, but eventually, I got it, and what a difference it would make.

CHAPTER TWELVE

ALMOST TOO MUCH TO BEAR

Well up in age now, our grandparents were in their mid-seventies, I was in high school, and Chris was in junior high.

As time passed, it became increasingly harder for them to get around, even to our school events, though they always made a genuine effort. Slowly, things began to change, and I didn't like the change.

Our grandparents, especially Granddaddy, began to have more and more health problems. It's not that I hated what was happening to them because it prevented them from coming to support us. I didn't like the fact that they were having health issues because I loved them; they were my second parents, and I didn't like seeing them suffering and in pain. Most importantly, I didn't want to lose them.

Eventually, the day came when Granddaddy could no longer drive, and Grandmother, never having learned how to drive, now had to depend on others to get around. Granddaddy's health deteriorated quickly, as he suffered from kidney problems, and within just a few months, he was requiring weekly dialysis treatment. Near the end of my freshman year, he developed gangrene in one of his legs, leading to its amputation. It was a very sad time for our family.

Granddaddy had lived a long life and had been a fixture in our lives for as long as I could remember. Though he certainly had his 'cranky' moments, I wouldn't have traded him for any other grandfather in the world! I appreciated everything he did for us because he 'moved over' and made room for me and Chris, sharing his and Grandmother's life with us when Daddy needed them the most.

Telling our family that there was nothing else they could do for Granddaddy, the doctors switched their care to just making sure he was comfortable. Because his heart was too weak for any additional major medical treatments or interventions, Granddaddy was sent home to die.

Now completely bedridden, he couldn't even get around in a wheelchair. Taking care of him, which we all lent a hand in doing, took its toll physically and emotionally, especially on Grandmother. Most days, she looked so weary, but she continued taking care of Granddaddy, not opting to put him in a nursing home.

The summer Granddaddy's health turned for the worse, I got my first job. Just a couple of months shy of my sixteenth birthday, I began working on a special two-week program for the Texas Employment Commission. My uncle, Uncle Charles, helped me get the position, and it felt good working on an actual job and making money.

Uncle Charles was like one of those 'quiet angels' who was there for Mama and continually helped her out, especially following her release from the mental hospital.

For the remainder of the summer, Chris and I hung around the house, helping Grandmother out with Granddaddy. Daddy continued to drop by to see us during the week as often as he could. Anything Grandmother needed to be done, Daddy or Uncle Irving would do it now that Granddaddy was unable to.

Much like Daddy, Uncle Irving worked quite a bit, so we didn't see him nearly as much as we would see Aunt Della. Though a nice man, Uncle Irving wasn't overly sociable. He was more of a 'homebody' and would rather recline at home in his favorite chair, watching his television, than be out fraternizing. Aunt Della didn't seem to mind. Rarely openly complaining, she'd just leave him at home in his chair and come around to our house and stay many days for hours at a time. Once Granddaddy became confined to the bed, we saw her even more often, which was a great help to Grandmother.

Ms. Mandy was also a huge help to Grandmother. However, the jealousy that had been there for some years on Aunt Della's part began to grow even more and become noticeable as Grandmother also became more dependent upon Ms. Mandy. Grandmother could call on Ms. Mandy day or night, and she'd come without hesitation if she was near.

There were times when Grandmother needed help with Granddaddy, and Aunt Della would be out shopping, which seemed to be almost an addiction, and Grandmother would have to call Ms. Mandy instead to come and help.

If, during such a time, Aunt Della stopped by and found Ms. Mandy at our house assisting Grandmother, she would become irritated, wanting Ms. Mandy to stop doing whatever she was doing so that she could take over. Most times, Ms. Mandy just kind of blew Aunt Della off and, with Grandmother's permission, would continue helping with Granddaddy. Though that caused tension between Aunt Della and Ms. Mandy, Grandmother didn't allow that to keep her from calling on Ms. Mandy whenever she needed her.

Knowing that Granddaddy wouldn't be with us much longer didn't make the *inevitable* easier to accept. Though we didn't want him to be in pain any longer, the thought of him losing him hurt to the soul.

Grandmother was handling it all as best she could and still being a strength for all of us. They'd built a life together, having been married over 50 years, longer than they'd ever been apart from each other.

Summer 1982

The summer months were very busy and very long for us. Though Granddaddy continued to hold on, we knew he was near the end of his life because his mind began to come and go, and he would hallucinate. We were on an 'around the clock' watch.

One evening in early August, I went into Granddaddy's room to check on him. Oddly, he was smiling, showing all his teeth, and moving his head repeatedly to the left and then to the right while staring up at the ceiling.

What was he looking at?

Gazing so intently and smiling, though no sound came from his mouth, he caused me to look up at the ceiling too, in an effort to try to see what he was seeing. I saw nothing.

Stepping out of his room and into the hallway, I called for Grandmother. Both she and Chris came right away.

"Grandmother," I said, "Granddaddy is staring at the ceiling, moving his head from side to side, and smiling. What's he looking at?"

"Hum…I don't know, but he's looking at something, isn't he?" Grandmother said, looking at Granddaddy glaring at the ceiling.

Shrugging her shoulders, she looked at us with a small grin and then started to walk out of the room. Briefly, she looked back at Granddaddy and then continued out the door. Grandmother went to the living room, grabbed the phone, called Aunt Della, and asked her to come. Grandmother must have sensed something was getting ready to happen.

Chris also walked out of the room, following Grandmother to the living room. I'd gone to my bedroom to grab another book and then went back into Granddaddy's room, taking my seat again in the chair next to his bed. It was difficult to focus on my reading, however, because I kept seeing Granddaddy's head moving out of my peripheral vision. I put the book down and just watched him, somewhat amused by the facial expressions he was making. How very peculiar it was that not a sound was coming from him other than the slight 'mushing' sound of his head moving back and forth on top of the pillow.

Suddenly, he stopped moving his head and stopped smiling but continued to stare at the ceiling. I sat up from my reclined position because the abrupt change in his movement kind of scared me. Jumping up from my chair, I was getting ready to get Grandmother again when all of a sudden, Granddaddy let out a big, deep breath, the only sound he'd made all the while I'd been sitting there with him. His face then turned towards my chair.

With my heart racing, I hurried to get Grandmother. She quickly went in to check on Granddaddy, entering the room first, with Chris and I following closely behind her. Hovering over him, she looked into his eyes, which just stared straight ahead, and placed her hands on his chest. Grandmother turned around back to us, and we could see tears in her eyes. We moved closer to her as she began to cry quietly.

"Is he dead?" I asked, reaching and putting my arms around her as the tears started.

I knew he'd taken his last breath.

"Yeah baby, he's gone," Grandmother said with her voice cracking.

Chris hugged her too, as the three of us stood there weeping.

"Y'all, come on. Let me call Mandy," she said, leading us out of the room.

It seemed so strange how one moment Granddaddy was still with us, and the next, he was gone, forever, just like that. I'm glad I was with him and that he didn't die alone in the room. Because I'd seen death before, I wasn't terribly afraid at that moment.

There was no drama, no horrific scene. Granddaddy went so peacefully; no more suffering, no more pain. He could finally rest.

Ms. Mandy rushed over and went in with Grandmother to check on Granddaddy while Chris and I stood outside the bedroom door. Daddy had been called and was en route to the house.

Within a couple of minutes, Aunt Della and Uncle Irving arrived. Aunt Della rushed to Granddaddy's room, where Grandmother and Ms. Mandy were, as Uncle Irving waited just outside the door with me and Chris.

Right away, we heard Aunt Della crying out loud, "Oh Daddy… my daddy's gone! Oh, I'm going to miss you, Daddy." She continued on, sobbing very loudly.

Uncle Irving then walked into the room, gave Grandmother a hug, grabbed Ms. Mandy's hand and squeezed it, and then proceeded to reach for Aunt Della and hold her, trying to console her.

A few minutes later, Daddy was letting himself in with the key Grandmother had given him. Chris and I, hearing the door, went to the living room. What a relief it was to see him, and we let him know that as we hurried over to him before he was even in the doorway.

"Hey, Daddy!" we said, greeting him with tears and a hug as he hugged us back.

Granddaddy's death made both of us anxious to see our daddy.

He hugged us for a moment and then, looking around the empty room, asked, "Where is everybody? In the back?"

"Yes sir," we replied.

"They're all back there, and so is Ms. Mandy," I said.

Daddy closed and locked the front door, and as soon as he began to make steps toward the back room, he heard Aunt Della crying out again. Uncle Irving had been able to quiet her down a little bit, but then she started talking and sobbing at the same time again.

"Y'all sit still. I'll be back." Daddy said, leaving us alone in the living room.

I decided that I wasn't going to sit there while everyone else was in the back of the house, so I got up, with Chris following me, and went and stood against the wall in the hallway so that at least we could still be near everybody.

Soon, neighbors began filing into our house as word spread that Granddaddy had passed. Daddy's girlfriend, Ms. Bettye, also came over to be with us.

Though we knew this day was looming, it still hurt. Granddaddy was the closest person to us that had died since George. Almost ten years separated their deaths, as Granddaddy passed on August 7, 1982, at the age of 78.

We held a wake and funeral for Granddaddy, which was attended by many. Granddaddy had been a deacon in the church for a number of years and was well-known and respected by family, friends, and church members.

Grandmother and Granddaddy had purchased a family burial plot years earlier, and that's where Granddaddy was laid to rest alongside Uncle De'Walter.

1982 - HIGH SCHOOL SOPHOMORE YEAR

The school year began, and I entered the tenth grade while Chris entered the ninth grade. Not having Granddaddy around took some getting used to. Grandmother was a very strong woman as she continued to go on with life, now without Granddaddy. Daddy came over more often now that Granddaddy was gone, making sure he was there for Grandmother and us. Sometimes, wearing himself out after a long day on the job, he didn't let weariness keep him from tending to us. Even when Grandmother didn't need anything in particular done, Daddy would still come and just sit with us.

Grandmother was a woman of faith, and though we'd missed quite a bit of church during the final year of Granddaddy's sickness, Grandmother never stopped praying or reading her bible. The month following Granddaddy's death, we began attending church on a regular basis again, going back to our old church. Continuing on as before, we rode the bus to church unless Daddy or Aunt Della dropped us off. Also, just like before, because Grandmother was such a sweet lady, the bus driver was more than willing to drop us off right in front of our home.

The majority of our neighbors were elderly, like our grandparents, and many of them suffered from health issues and began to pass away too. I'd become so attached to the neighbors around us, to the life we were living, and I didn't want things to change, but I had absolutely no control over what was happening.

I did my best to stay focused on school as the school year seemed to fly by. Nearing the end of my sophomore year, I had already taken the SAT, scoring well, in preparation for admission to college in a couple of years. My plan included obtaining an undergraduate degree in Biology from a 4-year college and then attending medical school at a school like Baylor College of Medicine or The University of Texas. I still had a couple of years to finalize my plans.

At the beginning of the summer following my Sophomore year, I got my first full-time job at Astroworld, an amusement park, working in the games section. What a fun job it was! It was great actually getting paid to do something I enjoyed. Working four and five-day work weeks, I liked having my own money and being able to buy my own clothes and other things I wanted or needed.

Though I worked full-time in June and July to get ready for school again, I scaled my hours back beginning the first week of August. Besides that, Grandmother needed me at home. She'd been the picture of health but had begun to feel unusually tired.

After an initial visit with her doctor, it was suggested that she go into the hospital for a very short stay to have some routine tests run, just to make sure everything was okay. It certainly had been a rough year for Grandmother and a year of adjusting to not having Granddaddy around. She never complained, though, about pain of any kind, so the fact that she needed to go to the hospital alarmed all of us. She tried to put everyone's fears to rest, saying she hadn't had a checkup in some years and thought it would be good to get one, just to be on the safe side. Jokingly, she'd assured us that her intention was to stay around as long as possible, and being our second mom, we definitely wanted that.

As planned, Grandmother went into the hospital and began having a series of tests performed. Her plan was to go ahead and get it done before school started for us again. All came back good, and the doctors gave her a clean bill of health.

Whew!!! We all breathed a sigh of relief.

"You'll be the woman of the house until Grandmother gets back," she said, smiling at me, just prior to walking out the door with Daddy on her way to the hospital.

"Yes, ma'am," was my quick response.

It was not a problem at all for me to temporarily fill in for Grandmother until she came back home. Doing whatever I needed to do, I didn't want her to worry about a thing. I just wanted her to hurry up and come back home. I tried my best to do what Grandmother did at home, though I certainly was no replacement for her.

Grandmother would be coming home the next day after three days in the hospital. Waking up early the next morning, I was thrilled about Grandmother being released from the hospital and returning home in just a few hours. Making sure the house was clean and neat, I paid careful attention to everything being put in its place, just like Grandmother taught me.

Daddy had come each night to stay with me and Chris while Grandmother was in the hospital. Still working at the steel mill, he'd leave us during the day and return in the evening.

Because I needed to be at home with Chris, I temporarily stopped working at Astroworld.

Grandmother called the house early in the afternoon, and Chris answered the phone.

"Hello," Chris said.

"Hey, Chris, I'm ready to come home. The doctors have released me, so tell your daddy I'm ready for y'all to come and get me," Grandmother said.

"Ok, yes, ma'am, I'll tell Daddy," Chris said excitedly.

"Alright, I'll see y'all in a little bit. Bye-bye." Grandmother said, hanging up the phone.

"Bye, Grandmother," Chris said, hanging up his end.

After telling me what Grandmother had said, he rushed to tell Daddy.

Knowing that Grandmother was being released from the hospital sometime during the day, Daddy took the day off from work.

"Yes!" I rejoiced, "Grandmother's coming home!"

I could hardly contain myself, as I even pumped my fists as if I'd won something. Grandmother's coming home was like Christmas in August! The only other times we'd been separated from her for that long since we'd begun living with our grandparents was when we'd go with Daddy.

The three of us- Daddy, Chris, and I got into the car and headed to the hospital. After pulling into the parking lot, we all got out and started walking towards the hospital's entrance, and Chris and I followed Daddy inside as he went directly to the receptionist at the front desk. Letting her know why we were there, we stood at the front patiently waiting as the lady made a phone call to the wing where Grandmother's room was. After a pause on the phone, she told us to wait in the nearby waiting room, which she led us to after getting up from her seat.

I'd guessed Grandmother was being brought down in a wheelchair. Sometimes, hospitals do that with their patients. Within a couple of minutes, one of Grandmother's doctors appeared in the doorway and walked over to Daddy, knowing who he was from Daddy's hospital visits with Grandmother.

"Mr. Battle, hi…may I talk to you?" the doctor asked, glancing at me and Chris, reclined on the sofa.

"Oh yeah, okay," Daddy said, standing to his feet with a curious look on his face.

"You'll wait here. Let me talk to the doctor," Daddy said, following the doctor down a long corridor.

We didn't know what was going on.

Daddy came back in less than five minutes, and he was crying, wiping his face with his hand.

'Oh no!' I thought to myself, my heart beginning to beat rapidly.

"No! Please! No!" I prayed under my breath.

"Please! No!" I continued to say as Daddy walked over to us.

I knew something was wrong. Something was wrong with Grandmother. She wasn't walking beside him.

"Where's Grandmother?" I asked, beginning to cry, along with Chris, who also sensed that something was not right.

"She's gone," Daddy said, trying to pull himself together, wiping his face with his hand again.

He breathed deeply and said, "I'm sorry you'll, Grandmother's gone."

"Huh? What do you mean she's gone?! No! She can't be gone, Daddy! We came to pick her up!" I said, raising my voice, devastated and angry.

"No, Daddy, she can't be gone, Oh no...Grandmother," I said, crying and burying my face in Daddy's shirt, soaking it with my tears.

"Grandmother!" I cried even louder as Chris joined in, sobbing loudly too.

Chris and I stood there, holding on to Daddy, just crying because this wasn't fair! The doctors had said she was fine, that she could come home! What had happened from the time Chris hung up the phone to the time we walked through the hospital door?!

Then I thought to myself, "The hospital has made a mistake...they have the wrong woman! Grandmother wasn't dead! There was no way she could be gone! They had to have made a mistake!"

I didn't believe them and told Daddy that they had the wrong person.

"No Cheryl, she passed on our way here," Daddy said, holding my shoulders and looking at me with his blood shot eyes. I wasn't convinced, and my daddy knew that.

However, wanting to deny the truth didn't change the truth.

"Come on," he said, taking both Chris and me by the hand and leading us to a hospital room down the corridor and around the corner from the waiting room.

We all wept as we walked down the hallway. Slowly entering a hospital room, Daddy led us over to the bed, and sure enough, there our grandmother lay, covered up to her chest with the bed sheet.

My heart sank, and I couldn't control the tears that steadily streamed down my face. Chris sobbed uncontrollably, covering his face with his hands. Letting go of Daddy's hand, I stood right next to the bed and leaned over to get a closer look at Grandmother, just hoping she would wake up. Tears and snot ran down my face and hit her face.

Chris came and stood next to me, and we both stared at Grandmother and just cried as we held each other.

Her wig was on, her make-up and even her shoes were on. She had indeed been waiting for us to pick her up because she was completely dressed to go. The doctor told Daddy that he and the entire staff were completely stunned, bewildered because he'd just gone in to sign her release papers, and she was talking and didn't have any complaints or concerns other than wanting to return home. He had no explanation for Daddy. His best guess was that her heart simply stopped beating.

An autopsy would later show that that's exactly what happened.

Exactly one year and one day after Granddaddy died, Grandmother passed. It was almost too much for us to bear.

Several people remarked that it wasn't unusual, given how long our grandparents had been married, that she wouldn't live much longer after he'd passed. We were devastated.

Daddy had the very difficult task of calling Aunt Della, who was at home busy cooking for us and telling her what had happened. Aunt Della had always been very close to Grandmother, still seeing herself as 'Grandmother's little girl,' sometimes even saying those words in a babyish, whiny voice. We understood Aunt Della's great love for Grandmother because if God sent angels to earth, our grandmother was definitely one.

As the matriarch of the family, Grandmother was the backbone, 'the glue,' that held us together. After George's death, we were able to pick up the pieces and move forward because of the strength we had in Grandmother. I couldn't even fathom being able to move on now without her.

Upset and very distraught, Aunt Della arrived at the hospital with Uncle Irving in tow, and things all of a sudden went from being very sad to purely chaotic as she, along with emotionally breaking down, began ranting and raving about the doctor's having done something wrong to cause Grandmother's death. A few neighbors, including Ms. Mandy, also came to the hospital, and it took them, Uncle Irving, Daddy, *and* some of the hospital staff to get Aunt Della to calm down. She was screaming, moving, and acting erratically, like she was getting ready to run down the hallway. All of them had to form a circle around her to prevent her from hurting herself or anyone else, as she completely lost it.

Then, shocking all of us, Aunt Della announced in the midst of her ranting that she didn't want any of the neighbors in her mama's house!

Ms. Mandy was probably the main target of Aunt Della's assault. Still, we could tell the neighbors who'd come to comfort and console us as they grieved with us were visibly offended, though they continued to try to be compassionate towards Aunt Della. She was understandably devastated beyond words by Grandmother's death; we all were. Her statement, however, was not only hurtful but, from that day forward, caused a rift in her relationship with the neighbors.

It was one of the worst days of our lives *again*. I was *angry* at God because He took Grandmother. He had Granddaddy. Why would He come so soon for Grandmother? Didn't He know we needed her? It seemed heartless, as if God was angry at us, at our family.

Though in advanced years, our grandparents stepped in and helped Daddy raise us. They both changed their lives for us. Grandmother was our second Mama. In fact, she was like our only mama in many ways, doing for us what our biological mother could no longer do. Grandmother became what we needed, and she, like Granddaddy, was no longer a part of our lives either.

With Granddaddy, we'd been put on alert and had some time to prepare ourselves, but we had no such warning with Grandmother. It wasn't fair, and life sucked!!!

It felt like Deja vu like when Mama was taken from us, except this time, it happened for a different reason. Now, there were just three of us again- me, Daddy, and Chris.

Chris and I both became depressed, not wanting to eat or do anything. We were at a difficult place in life that called for more adjustment, and I just didn't know how we were going to do it.

Disconnected from reality during Grandmother's wake and funeral, I found it hard to even cry. Grandmother meant the world to me, and not just to me, to all of us. I ended up in the hospital for a week because I'd stopped eating. I needed help; I wanted my Grandmother.

After being diagnosed with hypoglycemia, I was released into Daddy's care from the hospital with strict diet instructions to follow to help get me back on my feet and healthy again. Part of my getting healthy again meant I had to come to terms with Grandmother's death. That was so hard to do.

Though our biological mama was still very much a part of our lives, and we'd still visit her on some weekends, the void we felt because of Grandmother's death couldn't be filled.

As with all the other times our family was in crisis, people came from all over to help and support us. So touched by the outpouring of love we received, especially from our church, Chris and I continued to go to church across town, as we had before, but now without Grandmother. It was what we'd become accustomed to doing because Grandmother insisted, when we were very young, that we go to church. Chris and I continued to do what Grandmother had taught us to do and what we knew she would want us to do. We still rode the bus to church whenever we didn't get dropped off by Daddy or Aunt Della.

Immediately following Grandmother's death, things between Daddy and Aunt Della deteriorated, and she stopped offering to take us to church. Daddy continued to work most Sundays, not going to church with us or to any church for that matter. He was overwhelmed and stressed, and after so many years, it was now showing. He smiled less and drank more, though not to the point of becoming drunk. Maybe he asked the same thing Chris and I asked, "When is all the bad stuff going to stop?"

1983, JUNIOR YEAR

Less than a month after we'd buried Grandmother, school started again. Staying very busy with my courses at school and my chores at home helped prevent me from slipping into an even deeper depression.

Grandmother would often say, "An idle mind is the devil's workshop."

Remembering that, I did whatever I could to stay focused on graduating from high school with honors, and I still wanted to go to college and then to medical school. During my junior year at Health Professions, my time to participate in medical rotations as a part of our school curriculum arrived.

Chris, meanwhile, was preoccupied with doing well in his first year in high school. He attended the high school in our neighborhood and joined the school's band. The saxophone was his musical instrument of choice, so Daddy bought him the nicest, shiniest saxophone I'd ever seen. I didn't personally know anyone who played musical instruments, so it was different having a musician in the house. Chris would blow that sax in the house, outside the house, in the morning, and in the evening, and he was actually starting to sound pretty good. Daddy was so proud of Chris as he continued to excel in the band.

Daddy and I would go to many of Chris' school's football games, at which the band would play and perform. Because I already knew what to expect, I looked forward to watching Chris *get his groove on* with his bandmates as they performed a medley of songs and dances.

Having a very busy schedule, it was necessary for me to get my driver's license to help Daddy with getting me and Chris around. Ms. Bettye took me to the DPS office so that I could take my test. The morning of my driving test, I drove one of Daddy's cars, a pale yellow Buick Regal, for the road exercise. Daddy had owned this particular car for a while, and it had a few minor cosmetic issues, one being a small hole in the right back passenger floor.

Once I got my license, I would, from time to time, drop a couple of my friends off at home, and that hole was always such a funny subject of conversation. However, my friends were just happy to be catching a ride with me and weren't at all bothered by my car's defects. They didn't act snobbish at all.

Daddy had to work even harder, now having to maintain two households, our grandparent's home and our family home on the north side of town. He traveled back and forth quite a bit, staying with us each night and also going to our other home some evenings and on the weekends.

Though things had changed and we were getting older, Chris and I still looked forward to spending time with Daddy on the weekends, which included going over to his girlfriend's house with him just about every Friday night.

We did continue to see Mama when we could, though our visits with her were dropping off considerably because we had so much going on.

The steel mill, Daddy's job for many years, fell into a financial crisis because of the economy. Many people were losing their jobs, which, for most, was their primary source of income. Many of the guys Daddy had worked with over the years had already been laid off, and Daddy was expecting his pink slip any day now.

Still hopeful about college, I began filling out applications for college scholarships. I knew with our financial situation, there was no way Daddy could afford to send me to college without assistance. Because my GPA was greater than 4.0, there was a good chance that I'd be awarded scholarships. Daddy, Chris, and I did our best to keep moving forward.

Aunt Della, however, wasn't the same after Grandmother died. Becoming a woman we didn't care to be around, she would soon be at the center of a lot of our heartache and pain.

Going back to the day Grandmother passed, we'd gotten a glimpse of this 'other side' of her. She turned and changed for the worse. Unfortunately, the tension between her and Daddy only grew. Aunt Della thought she was within her rights to tell Daddy how to run our home, including who to allow in and who to keep out.

Daddy, while trying not to worsen their already deteriorating relationship, let it be known to her that 'he was grown and well able to run our house the way it needed to be run.' Not a bit surprising, of course, Aunt Della didn't at all like Daddy's response, and that set the stage for an all-out war, one that, unfortunately, Chris and I would eventually be pulled into.

While doing his best to deal with Aunt Della cordially, Daddy didn't seem to see a peaceful resolution in sight. Daddy and Aunt Della's relationship went from being tense to becoming estranged after escalating into a physical confrontation:

One afternoon, following numerous unannounced visits by Aunt Della, Daddy decided to change the locks on the doors. He'd had enough. Aunt Della would, sometimes even late at night, use her personal house key, which Grandmother had given her, to gain entry into our home. She would just come in without warning and walk around the house as if she were inspecting it. Sometimes, we'd actually be preparing for bed when she would come through the front door. We'd watch her as she'd go from room to room. She had to have been losing her mind!

Daddy, trying not to be confrontational, initially asked her to call before coming over. He wanted her to respect our home and our privacy. We still lived there.

Daddy had to change the locks on the door because after he initially told Aunt Della to stop dropping by whenever she felt like it and instead call first, she became so incensed that not only did she begin dropping by even more often, but she began doing so later at night, around 11 pm, and even midnight at times.

Daddy said, "That's it!" and he changed the locks on all the doors, denying her free access to our home.

The day she realized Daddy had changed the locks on the door, she had a fit, drawing attention to herself from our neighbors.

Banging on the door, she shouted, "Open this door, Rudy! Rudy, you hear me?! Open this door right now!"

Daddy didn't allow her to bang on the front door more than a couple of times before he got up from where he was sitting and went over and opened the door. Standing in the doorway to prevent Aunt Della from just walking on in, he looked at her, trying to hold back his anger.

"Who do you think you are, changing the locks on this door?!" She shouted in his face.

"This is my house too!"

Getting up from where I was sitting, I walked over and stood behind Daddy, leaning to the side a little so that I could see Aunt Della.

I'd never seen her so angry. She was furious, screaming so loudly with such force that drops of her spit hit Daddy's face. Laying claim to her territory, Aunt Della let it be known that she too, was part owner of our house. Unfortunately, neither Granddaddy nor Grandmother left a will.

Ironically, Grandmother's pastor said that during his very last visit with Grandmother in the hospital, she told him that 'the first thing' she wanted to do when she got back home was get her will together because, in her own words, "If anything happens to me, Della won't be fair with Rudy and the kids. I want them to have the house."

Grandmother was right. Daddy didn't try to underhand Aunt Della or exclude her from whatever she was entitled to. He just wanted her to be more considerate. For almost nine years, it had been the place Chris and I called home.

That day, the argument between her and Daddy became so heated that Aunt Della attempted to barge her way into our home, even though Daddy was standing in the doorway, and she ended up bouncing off Daddy and onto the cement sidewalk because he wouldn't budge. Getting up crying, she threatened Daddy, pointing her finger at him, telling him he'd be sorry for what he did, though *she caused* herself to fall.

Storming off and getting into her car, she backed out and sped off quickly while Daddy, visibly upset, watched from the front door. The look on his face showed he was sorry all of that had happened, only wanting Aunt Della to leave us alone. However, it was too late to change it, and now we had to let things run their course.

Furious because she'd come against my daddy and threatened him, I yelled outside the door, "O fat pig!" referring to her large size.

Immediately, Daddy chastised me for what I'd said.

"No, Cheryl! I don't ever want to hear you talk like that. You hear me?"

"Yes, sir," I quickly responded, surprised and embarrassed that Daddy was disciplining me.

"That's *still* your aunt; she's *still* an adult, and you will respect her. Do you hear me?" Daddy said angrily.

I hadn't actually said what I said to her face, but because Daddy heard it, he let me know he wouldn't tolerate it.

Starting to tear up and feeling misunderstood, I thought to myself, 'Why am I being fussed at? I'm just trying to let him know that I'm on his side.'

Daddy could tell I was stunned by his response. Chris got up from the sofa and came closer to see if I was crying after witnessing Daddy rebuke me. Daddy knew I was only trying to show support for him, but he didn't like the way I did it.

He then said, trying to bring calm to the entire situation, "You and Chris need to understand that your Aunt Della is sick. She hasn't been the same since Grandmother died. Y'all can tell that, right?"

We both just nodded.

Grandmother meant the world to all of us, but instead of our family healing together, we were growing further and further apart.

Daddy closed the door, and we all went and sat on the sofa in front of the television. With all the drama that had just unfolded, we weren't watching the television; it was watching us.

I knew Daddy was right. Aunt Della was my elder, and my daddy didn't need me helping him fight his battles. It was a 'grown-up issue,' and though we were definitely involved, it was Daddy's job to fix it. We sat there waiting for Aunt Della to return because we knew she was coming back.

Aunt Della did indeed come back, but thankfully with Uncle Irving instead of a gun. We heard their car pull into the driveway.

Daddy rose from sitting and looked out of the peephole of the front door. Seeing Uncle Irving getting out of his car, Daddy opened the door, stepped out onto the porch, and waited. Aunt Della remained in the car, likely at Uncle Irving's insistence. The two of them greeted each other with their usual "How you doing?" and then Uncle Irving began to talk.

"Rudy, I don't appreciate what you did to my wife today," he said, frowning a bit.

"Listen, Irving, I didn't want it to happen, and I never raised my hand to Della. She was trying to move me out the way so she could come in, and she lost her balance."

Uncle Irving just listened as Daddy talked.

"Della is my sister, and I wasn't trying to hurt her. I just wanted her to listen to me.

Me and these kids are staying here, and I've asked Della to stop just barging her way into the house. We live here, Irving. This is our home. Della wouldn't want anyone just walking into her house unannounced who didn't stay there, and all I asked her to do is show us that same respect. Mother's gone, and it's hard on all of us, not just Della, not just on me, but on these kids too. I'm trying to keep things together, and when I told her I didn't want her walking through the door whenever she felt like it, that's what I meant. So I changed the locks on the door, and she's *not* getting a key. I don't want to fight with Della, but I'm not going to let her continue to do what she's been doing."

Daddy was adamant as he talked to Uncle Irving and didn't flinch.

"Well," Uncle Irving began, not quite knowing what to say, "…uh, okay, Rudy. Well, you'll need to work something out. I know Mr. and Mrs. Battle didn't leave a will, so you'll need to get something worked out. Della just doesn't want to be left out. She misses Mrs. Battle, Rudy. You know how close she was to her."

Uncle Irving always referred to Grandmother as 'Mrs. Battle' and Granddaddy as 'Mr. Battle', never calling them 'Mother' or 'Dad' as some do their mother and father-in-law.

"Yeah, Irving, I know," Daddy told Uncle Irving, looking directly at him.

"Well, okay, Rudy, that's all I really wanted to say. I hope you and Della get this worked out somehow so there can be peace," Uncle Irving said, preparing to turn to step down off the porch.

"That's what I want too, Irving—peace," Daddy said, stopping Uncle Irving. "I don't want to fight Della, but I'm not going to allow her to disrupt this house."

"Ok, Rudy," Uncle Irving said, "I'll talk to her. Okay then," he nodded at Daddy and then continued on, walking to their car.

"Okay, Irving," Daddy said, stepping inside our house and closing the door.

Walking over to where Chris and I had remained seated during his conversation with Uncle Irving, he stood there for a moment and then glanced at his watch. With all of the drama, time had flown quickly, and it was now time for him to start dinner.

He didn't say much the rest of the evening.

The argument for the moment was over, but the fight was far from over. For the next few months, the only time we saw Aunt Della was as she passed our home on her way, either home or somewhere else. Treating us like strangers, she wouldn't wave or even blow her horn if we happened to be outside. It was hard to accept the way she was now treating us, especially since we had been so close to her at one point. Chris and I would talk about her when we were out of Daddy's presence.

Time passed, and we, starting to grow up, were being given more and more responsibility. I did my part, trying not to complain and hoping that Grandmother could see us, even from Heaven. I wanted her to be proud of me because she'd taught me well. Having no say in the matter, I had become the woman of the house.

CHAPTER THIRTEEN

TIRED OF BEING STRONG!

FALL 1984, SENIOR YEAR

Having just turned 18, I was now a senior in high school, and Chris had begun his junior year of high school. School had been in session for close to three months, and we were all looking forward to the upcoming Thanksgiving break.

We stopped sitting on the hood of the car with Daddy. Now he'd sit alone on the bed in his room, which used to be Grandmother's bedroom, drink and listen to the radio by himself.

The steel mill finally caved in and closed down. After years of dedication to his job, Daddy was now unemployed. He'd been one of very few people still employed there, working in whatever capacity he could to hold on to his job. The day he received his pink slip was sad but not surprising.

Already in his early fifties, Daddy had limited education and training and had known only one profession for most of his adult life, and that was working with steel. The steel industry as a whole was suffering, so chances were very slim that he'd be able to secure a similar position with another company.

Unemployment benefits did supply some income but at a drastically reduced amount. He'd have to find some kind of job to help supplement his income.

I'd worked at Astroworld again that summer and was able to help out, especially with buying things for myself and Chris, though Daddy never asked me to help him support our family. Seeing how hard Daddy was trying to keep things going, Chris and I did whatever we could to help take some of the load off, doing things like helping to keep the house clean, washing the car, and helping with the laundry. We didn't do any serious cooking other than making sandwiches for ourselves, but Daddy's girlfriend would often cook, as we'd go over to her house frequently for visits.

Daddy, after months of searching, finally got a job working in a parking garage moving cars. It wasn't the best pay, but it did help Daddy take care of the two households. Daddy tried his absolute best to provide for us. We still had each other, we never went hungry, and our utilities were never turned off.

I felt sorry for Daddy because he worked so hard for less pay. He would wake up early in the morning so he could be at the parking garage at 5:30 a.m. Working most of the day, he wouldn't make it home until late in the evening. Our lives were busy.

With Daddy's permission, I began to date. One of my best friends introduced me to her cousin. Infatuated with him because he was a couple of years older than me and had been a football player at the high school in his hometown, I was beside myself when he actually showed me some attention. Giving me his football jersey, he was winning me over, and I really began to fall for him.

Grandmother was gone, and I dared not mention a boy to Mama because she'd fall all to pieces, believing I was going to get pregnant, drop out of school, and never make it to college. She'd always tell me this same story about this girl named 'Peggy' who she'd say was very smart like I was and who began dating a guy. Soon, Peggy found herself pregnant. Also, like me, Peggy wanted to become a doctor, but once she had her baby, she had to drop out of school to work and take care of the baby after the father of the baby hit the road.

I got so sick and tired of hearing the 'Peggy Story.' I'd get angry with her because I wasn't even having sex, and though I was curious, I wasn't curious enough to start. My friends would share details of their sexual escapades, but that didn't make me want to follow suit. In fact, a young lady I knew had become pregnant during her senior year, and I knew that was not something I wanted for myself, so I actually became too afraid to have sex.

Maybe Mama's paranoia and 'the Peggy story' rubbed off on me. I think that, in some ways, Mama identified with 'Peggy' herself but didn't want to admit that to me. Maybe Mama had aspired to do something other than become a wife and a mother and believed that her life had less value because she didn't become what she aspired to be.

My goal was to go to college and then on to medical school, and I didn't want anything interfering with my plans. Graduating in the top 5% of my class, I could go wherever I wanted to as far as college was concerned, as long as I had the financial means in place to do so. I'd already received my acceptance letter from the University of Texas, my first school of choice, and with Daddy's help, I was eagerly filling out the paperwork regarding housing. I was so ecstatic!

Grandmother's and Granddaddy's deaths had taken their toll, and my childhood had left its scars, but now, finally, one of the things I wanted most in life was getting closer and closer to becoming a reality for me. I was ready for the hard classes and the exams I'd been told I'd have to master to get through college and medical school. Not at all a party animal, and having developed decent study habits, I was ready for the challenges and the next stage of my life.

Having a great example before me, I looked up to Daddy because every time a challenge was thrown his way, he somehow was able to make the adjustment and keep it moving. Wanting to do well in school, I was determined to be successful so that I could help my daddy and even take care of him for a change. He'd worked so hard for us for as long as I could remember. He deserved that—to be relieved of financial stress, to be taken care of, and so much more.

It Just Won't Stop

Daddy and I finished up the college paperwork we'd been working on, sealed it, and prepared it to be dropped in the mail the following day. Tired, we went to our bedrooms and fell asleep.

Being awakened by the alarm clock in Daddy's room going off, I put my blanket over my head in an effort to drown out the sound until he turned it off. He didn't turn it off, and though I didn't know how long it had been beeping, the irritating sound seemed to get louder and louder.

Chris and I still slept in the same room, and he, sound asleep, didn't move a muscle. I, a light sleeper, now couldn't go back to sleep. Annoyed, I threw my blanket and sheet back and jumped to my feet, heading towards Daddy's room. Walking into the room to turn off the alarm and wake Daddy up, I was guided by the red light emitting from the clock. I hit the snooze button.

It seemed like Daddy was still in bed, though I wasn't sure if I was looking at him or at his sheet and thick comforter. I called out to him, telling him that his alarm had gone off.

"Daddy, your alarm went off," I said, rubbing my eyes with my hand.

He didn't respond. Repeating it, I began thinking to myself, 'he must really be tired because he didn't hear the alarm, and he didn't hear me.'

Still no movement.

Certainly, if he had been in the house, he would have heard the alarm and turned it off. Daddy tried not to make any noise that would wake us up on the mornings he had to get up so early. We still had a couple hours of sleep before we had to get up and get ready for school. I then concluded that he wasn't still home. He was probably already outside doing something or getting something out of the car, or maybe he'd gone outside to warm up his car.

It was November, and the temperatures outside had turned cold. Just to be sure, I took one more step closer and repeated, "Daddy, your alarm went off."

I stumbled towards the light switch and turned it on, and was shocked to see that Daddy was still lying in bed!

'Man, was he sleeping hard!' I thought to myself.

Walking over to him, I lightly shook him, and he didn't respond. Immediately becoming afraid, I stepped back and noticed that he was lying on his stomach, with his face buried in his pillow. Daddy generally only slept in his bottoms, so he didn't have a t-shirt on. Both of his hands were clenched, both balled up tightly in fists and were resting on top of the very long pillow he lay on every night. His body was warm to the touch.

I knew something was wrong, but I needed at that moment for what I was feeling to 'not' be true!

Shaking Daddy again, this time much harder, and leaning over to try to see his face, I continued to call his name, "Daddy, Daddy!"

I couldn't see anything except the upper half of his head because his face was hidden by the pillow. He never turned over.

The same fear that came over me when I saw George lying on the floor was the same fear I began to feel, but this time, I was able to move, and I did so quickly!

Jumping to my feet from the bed, I ran to the room to wake up Chris. I wasn't about to leave him this time.

"Chris, wake up! Come on, get up! Something's wrong with Daddy!" I said, forcefully, shaking him.

He woke up completely confused. Barely giving him time to respond, I grabbed his hand and almost dragged him as we ran to the front door.

Nervous and scared, I could barely wrap my hand around the knob.

"Come on," I said to Chris, getting the door open, "…we have to go get Ms. Mandy!"

He stumbled along with me, moving more quickly as he began to wake up and see the panic in my face.

Running next door to Ms. Mandy's house, we bang really hard on the door. It was not even 5 a.m. yet. I knew she'd be able to help us with Daddy. I banged on her front door as hard as I could again while Chris stood very close to me, shaking.

Ms. Mandy, slow in coming to the door, peeked out through the hole in the door and asked, "Who is it?"

I responded anxiously, "It's Cheryl and Chris from next door."

She immediately opened the door, and as soon as I saw her face, I told her, beginning to cry, "Ms. Mandy, something's wrong with Daddy! I tried to wake him up, but he won't wake up!"

At first, she said nothing. She just sighed deeply as if she was trying to catch her breath. She was dazed, in disbelief from what I'd said.

Gathering herself, she said, "OK y'all, let me grab my house coat. Y'all come in for a moment".

Quickly, she ran to her room to grab her coat. We all went out together as she closed her front door behind us.

Taking both of us by the hand, she said, "Come on," and the three of us hurried back to our house. We all ran into our house and into Daddy's room, with me leading us.

Ms. Mandy saw Daddy lying there and immediately called out to him as she shook him.

"Mr. Rudy!"

"Rudy!" She shouted again, trying to wake him.

He didn't respond to her either. That's when reality started to set in with me. I begin to cry, wailing loudly.

"Noooooo! Oh No!" I belted out as loud as I could, bending over to my knees.

"Daddy!!!" Chris began screaming.

"Wait y'all, wait, wait! He's okay! Come on, let's go call for some help," Ms. Mandy said, trying to catch her breath.

"We just need to get an ambulance. He's going to be alright," she said. "…he'll be alright. O God," she started saying over and over again, with her voice cracking.

I wanted to believe her, but I needed a sign that he really was okay. She was just trying to get us to calm down.

I asked her, "Is he dead?! Is Daddy dead?!"

Almost crying herself, she shouted back, "No, Cheryl! No, he's not dead. Come on, let me call for help".

"He's going to be okay," she said anxiously again, hurrying us back next door.

We ran back next door, and she made several phone calls, calling the paramedics first. Within minutes, our neighbors across the street and also on the other side of us came rushing over to her house. Aunt Della and Uncle Irving came, as did Ms. Bettye.

By the time they all arrived, we went back to the house. The ambulance was very slow in coming. It felt like an hour passed before it finally showed up, and as they pulled up, they parked adjacent to our driveway. They got out of the ambulance and rushed into our house.

Though it seemed like an eternity for EMS to show up, their stay was very brief. After initially hurrying into Daddy's room and checking him out, they exited the room without doing anything else. Speaking briefly with Ms. Mandy, Aunt Della, and Ms. Bettye in the hallway, they picked up their bags and headed back toward our front door.

I heard crying as the words "I'm sorry" came from one of the paramedics.

My worst fears had been confirmed. He was gone! Daddy was dead! That was enough for me!

First Granddaddy, two years ago, then Grandmother just last year, and now Daddy, this year! We'd lost someone very important to us each year over less than a three-year span.

What was really going on?! I was convinced that our lives had been cursed.

There'd been no bad medical report, not even a cold in recent weeks. He looked healthy and didn't complain about anything being wrong. What happened!? How could he be gone?!

Was it the stress of losing his job? Too much stress trying to take care of two households?

It didn't matter to me anymore. I wanted to die too.

Chris, Ms. Bettye, and I all entered the room where Daddy's now cool body lay. He had been turned over onto his back by the paramedics and now appeared to be sleeping, just like Grandmother did when she passed, just like George looked at his funeral. His eyes were closed, and the men had placed his arms, one folded over the other, on top of his chest.

That was it. There couldn't be any more hope for me and Chris. The three of us cried together, clinging to Daddy.

"I loved him too," said Ms. Bettye, sobbing.

No other day, not George's death, not even when Grandmother passed, compared to this one.

I ran from the bedroom and into the living room, where the rest of the neighbors and friends had gathered. More than being sad, they were in shock, absolutely stumped. It was the lowest point in my life.

I didn't know anything about committing suicide, but I wanted my heart to just stop beating right then and there; I wanted my breaths to stop so that life for me would end too.

Attempting to run outside, I was grabbed and held by one of our neighbors, who would only allow me to go to a nearby corner and cry.

"They'd better watch Cheryl. She might try to hurt herself," someone in the room said.

As I buried my face into my hands, I cried hard, so hard that my chest hurt.

"God, what are you doing?!" I lashed out inside my head. "It's not fair! Everyone we needed, you have taken away from us!"

Chris, by now, had also left the room and was still crying. When I heard him in the living room, I stood up, wiped my face, and went over to him as the other people in the room were consoling him. Taking him in my arms, I hugged him, and we clung to each other while those around us patted our backs and shed tears too.

Seeing my brother, the only close person I felt like I still had, crying at that moment, made me realize that I couldn't die. If I died, he'd be alone. I knew what that felt like; we both did. If for no other reason, I had to continue to live to be there for Chris. I had to live, but I needed to want to live. We were all each other had to depend on.

Mama was still living, but she was too sick mentally to take care of us. She managed to take care of herself, but there was absolutely no way she could take care of us too, and we, still harboring fears from the past, wouldn't want to stay with her anyway.

Life had become unbelievable, unbearable. Not one of us was prepared for Daddy's death. Daddy was only 52 when a massive heart attack ended his life. He'd been under so much pressure, so much stress, but he wasn't supposed to leave us because everyone else already had.

The hours passed so slowly the rest of the day.

A couple of days passed, and in preparing to make plans to bury Daddy, we discovered that his money in a savings account with the steel mill's credit union was tied up. Apparently, Daddy had cosigned a loan for a co-worker, and that coworker defaulted on the loan, making Daddy responsible for the loan.

Additionally, because Daddy was separated from Mama but had never actually divorced her, there was confusion as to whether she was entitled to the insurance money or if their separation meant it would go directly to me and Chris. The last thing we needed was a shortage of money to bury Daddy.

Family members, including Ms. Bettye, had to pool money together to bury Daddy until all the other financial issues could be settled.

Mama did what she could to help ease the burden and not compound matters.

Getting through Daddy's wake and funeral would be by far the toughest, most emotionally challenging time for me *ever* in life.

THE WAKE — SO SURREAL

On a very cool Friday evening in mid-November, we held Daddy's wake. With Ms. Bettye's help, in two days, we'd gotten the services for Daddy together. The large chapel room was filled with people of all different ages, including family, neighbors, friends, former coworkers, and church members.

On the way to the wake, I sat almost numb in the stretch limousine carrying us from home to the funeral parlor.

Just last year, we'd taken a similar drive on our way to Grandmother's wake. I just couldn't believe Daddy was gone and that I'd only see him two more times in this life, at the services, and then that would be it. I thought about all the memories: the vacations, the fried bologna and cheese sandwiches, the times sitting on the hood of the car.

Being such a daddy's girl, I just enjoyed being around him, period, because I admired him so much.

When Daddy got laid off from the steel factory, he was trying to secure a contract with a local hardware store, building sawhorses for them. You could see the excitement, though subtle, in Daddy's face when he was told the store wanted him to do work for them. Things had been tough financially, and a contract doing something he had a passion for would not only ease our financial woes but also really give Daddy a sense of accomplishment. His death cut that opportunity short.

Although life was challenging, Daddy didn't throw in the towel. He had a family to take care of, and he did whatever he could to make sure we were taken care of. I guess that's one of many reasons why I looked up to him.

After Mama was sent away, Daddy didn't just give us to someone else to raise us while he walked away.

Reflecting on the man he was, my daddy was my hero.

Some might say Daddy did nothing special and that he did what he was supposed to do as a father. Daddy did do what he was supposed to do and so much more. I appreciate the fact that he didn't hide or abandon us but 'stepped up to the plate,' rearranging his and our lives for our best interests without murmuring or complaining about it.

As the family car pulled up to the front of the funeral home, my heart felt like it had dropped into my stomach. We stepped out of the car, along with Aunt Della, Uncle Irving, Ms. Bettye, and our cousin Goldie from Seguin, Texas, all of whom rode with us.

Daddy's death brought family and friends from all over. His sudden death even seemed to cause Aunt Della to have a change of heart towards us, and she became very loving, keeping us close at her side as we entered the funeral home.

We were kissed and hugged by so many people we didn't know or recognize. As we moved further inside, I began to see some familiar faces.

We were nearing the entrance of the chapel room where Daddy's body lay. Slowly, we walked towards his casket, and soon, I was able to see Daddy's face. His hair was perfectly cut, his skin so smooth looking. The gray suit he wore matched his tie.

The more I stared at him, what felt like a lump began to form in my throat, and I broke down in tears. I couldn't take it. It was too much. Standing directly in front of him, I started sobbing so uncontrollably that I was having a hard time breathing. My cries were so deep I gasped for oxygen. A brown bag was placed over my mouth to stop my hyperventilating.

Reality sat in as I looked at Daddy's still body in that casket, and the pain of losing him hurt me to the core of my soul. All of a sudden, everything went blurry. As I began to fall, someone caught me and prevented my head from hitting the floor.

I could see Chris crying just a few feet away from me, and folks were coming from all directions to help both of us. Someone, I'm not sure who, lifted me off the floor and carried me out to the foyer. Chris was brought out behind me. Hands were rubbing my forehead, patting my back, and stroking my arms. I cried loudly, unable to contain my sorrows.

Finally, both Chris and I were taken to the outside of the funeral home and placed in the limousine. People were talking, trying to console us, but at that moment, the only thing that would soothe me would be for our daddy to miraculously wake up and come back to us.

I don't remember ever going back inside the chapel, though I know we did. For the remainder of the night, I was in an emotional stupor - wanting it all to be a very bad dream from which I would soon awake.

How in the world were we going to make it without Daddy??? We depended on him more than anyone else for everything, and now he, just like Grandmother, was gone.

THE FUNERAL

We woke up early the next morning and got dressed for the funeral. Throughout most of the service, I sat motionless next to Aunt Della as she kept her arm around me and Chris, hugged us, and rubbed our arms up and down, trying to console us.

The phrase others repeatedly told Chris and me was, "Be strong, baby."

I didn't want anyone else telling me to "Be strong" because I had been strong through George's death, Mama's separation from us, and Grandmother and Granddaddy's deaths. I had been strong!

"Everything's going to be alright." That's what they'd say, but how could they even think that way, given all we'd been through?

Things were not alright, and I was angry at God. I wanted the world to know how angry I was. Because of what Grandmother had taught me, I feared cursing God, but I absolutely was cursing about my life! All kinds of expletives went through my head, and I wanted to curse out loud so God and everyone could hear me.

"What the hell is going on?!" I said in my head.

"Why are we being put through so much?"

"What did we do to deserve so much pain?"

I thought back to that Sunday in August. If only Mama hadn't done what she did, our lives would have been 'normal,' and we wouldn't have had to deal with so much sorrow. And when sad things happened, we would have had somewhere to go, someone to cling to, and someone to continue to be there for us.

As it was, however, Mama could not fill Daddy's shoes. No one could.

I went from looking forward to my future to living through the moment. I needed help to make it from one minute to the next.

The time came for the funeral directors to lower the casket's cover until it was closed completely. There was nothing to see anymore except a huge cream-colored floral arrangement that draped the bronze casket.

As the tears flowed down my face, I remained still. It hurt too much to breathe in and out. It hurt too much to move.

Many stories and expressions were shared by those who loved Daddy and us. They reminded me how much Daddy loved us and that he would want us to continue on and make him proud.

"He'll always be with you," they said.

"He's in Heaven watching over you right now, Cheryl and Chris."

"It'll be alright. Y'all going to be alright. You're surrounded by people who love you, and God will take care of y'all."

The sentiments kept coming, but none of it made me feel any better about life.

Throughout much of the funeral, I just sat and stared at Daddy's casket, not paying much attention to what was going on.

The service came to an end, and it was time to load up and go to the cemetery. It was a long ride across town.

As the limousine carried us to the grave site, I watched the motorcycle police weaving in and out of traffic, escorting our motorcade. They would make other commuters stop or pull over as our family car, the hearse carrying Daddy's body, and our motorcade passed.

It was as if someone very important was passing by. To me, that was exactly the case because my daddy had been the most important person in my life.

Although Daddy had served in the armed forces, we decided, instead of burying him in the Veterans National Cemetery, that we'd bury him in the same cemetery where Grandmother, Granddaddy, and Uncle

De'Walter were buried. The cemetery was also located right across the street from a different cemetery (the one in which George was buried).

After the last scripture was read and the final prayer given, we stood to return to our vehicles. It was time to go.

Motionless, I continued to stare at Daddy's casket, which now rested on the belts that would be used to lower it into the grave. I wasn't ready to leave. Leaving Daddy there was the most difficult thing I'd ever had to do. The tears started up, and I broke down, weeping loudly for my daddy.

Once again, like the previous night, I was picked up and carried back to the limousine. Chris wept as loud as I did as we sat next to each other inside the limousine. It wasn't until we were far down the road from the cemetery that our crying became sniffles.

Resting my head on the back of the seat, I kept thinking, "This can't be real...this just can't be real. What would happen to us now?"

We found ourselves, like we were 12 years ago, wondering who would step in and care for us.

'Why God, why!?' I wondered over and over again.

The very ones who had encouraged us and had told us life was still worth living, in spite of all we'd been through, were no longer with us. Death was ravaging our family, and I was convinced Chris and I were next on the list. In fact, though I had just turned 18, I didn't expect to live much beyond that.

For days, and even weeks, after Daddy's death, we received a constant flow of phone calls. People poured out so much compassion and sympathy, doing their best to try to keep us encouraged.

Not really having anyone to step in and take care of us, I realized that Chris and I had no choice but to begin living on our own.

Having just turned 18, I was glad that at least I was old enough to go to court and become Chris' legal guardian. Chris was only 16, and someone had to be responsible for him. No one in our extended family challenged or complained about my decision, so with Aunt Doris' help, within months, I obtained guardianship over Chris.

At the time, that was the only thing I was grateful for, that I could take care of my brother. Believing we were all each other had left and absolutely against our being separated in any kind of way, I was willing to do whatever it took to make sure that we stayed together. Many expressed their admiration at our courage to stay on our own, but we, not trying to impress anyone, felt like we didn't have any other option or choice.

My college plans changed because there was no way I was leaving Chris to go away to school. That really was okay with me anyway because the way things were going, I didn't think I'd see college through to the end.

For weeks, my brother and I were emotional wrecks. Unable to sleep alone in our twin beds, we made a bed, a pallet of blankets and pillows on the floor of the living room, and for the next year, that is where we slept side by side.

Sleep for me was anything but peaceful because for that entire year, I'd have recurring dreams about Daddy leaving us and would wake up around the same time every morning, that same time being around the hour that I'd gone in and found Daddy dead.

Sleep-deprived and emotionally spent, I pushed myself to get up every morning and get myself and Chris off to school. Though our lives had been rough, and I did want to give up so many times, I knew that going to school was still something we were obligated to do. That's what Daddy and our grandparents had instilled in us.

Knowing that Chris and I would be on our own, I started looking for a job right away to help support us financially. It would be a while before we'd begin receiving social security benefits on behalf of Daddy. We couldn't wait months or even weeks; we needed money right then to live.

So many folks were very generous, helping us make it, buy food, and pay bills. Because I knew absolutely nothing about paying bills, our neighbors taught me what I needed to know, walking with me as I became the grown-up in the house.

As lost as I was, I welcomed every bit of assistance and guidance I was offered so that I could take care of Chris and me. I'd never be able to fill Daddy's shoes, but I was determined to make sure we were safe, had a place to stay, and food to eat.

Thankfully, our home, which was our grandparents' home, was fully paid for, so we had no mortgage to meet.

Two weeks after we'd buried Daddy, I was hired on at Kroger Grocery Store, sacking groceries to start. Having no problem with sacking groceries or even going out and rounding up basket carts, I was happy to just have a job.

Initially, I was one of only three female sackers, and that in itself worked in my favor because I was always tipped very well. Sometimes, I'd even get a decent tip just for placing groceries in bags. If I'd learned anything from Daddy, it was how to work hard.

Not long after sacking groceries, I was promoted to work in the Delicatessen. Learning the ins and outs of the hot foods area, I stayed in that position for a few months. My managers seemed to really like me, and they, along with my co-workers, made me feel like part of an extended family.

Along with working and trying to finish up my senior year in high school, I was also busy making sure Chris was doing fine in school. Understandably, in the beginning, school was challenging for Chris with all of the changes that were taking place in our lives, but after a short while, he was back on track and doing better. I was proud of him.

Chris' teachers, like mine, were well aware of our family and living situation. I made it a point, as Daddy would have done, to attend Chris' parent-teacher conferences. Always taken seriously, I was treated courteously and with respect by the teachers as they conversed with me about Chris. Chris was a junior and had only one more year before graduating, and I was hoping at least we'd see that happen.

Working a decent amount of hours after school and on the weekends but making minimum wage, I still didn't bring home a lot of money, especially after deductions were taken out. For that reason, we were very grateful for our neighbors, who became sort of like 'surrogate' parents for us, making sure we had enough food to eat. They, like close family, always kept a watchful eye on us, and they'd remember us when they went shopping. Just as they did Grandmother when she was living, they'd call for us, either on the phone or over the fence, and would then pass bags of groceries to us. Our neighbor across the street, Mr. Wilson, would pay me and Chris to cut and clean up his yard for him, which we gladly did to earn more money to live off of.

As much as I hated to, because we'd never been on public assistance, I applied for food stamps, for which we were approved for six months. Daddy didn't rely on the government for assistance, and I didn't want to either.

However, because of our situation, I swallowed my pride and looked into as many resources as I could to get help for me and Chris. From the Red Cross' Food Bank, we were able to get staple food items like cheese, butter, beans, rice, and some canned goods. When I could find them on sale, I would buy leg quarters. We'd have fried chicken, baked chicken, boiled chicken, and oven-barbequed chicken all throughout the week, usually with a side of white rice and some sort of canned vegetable.

Coming to the point one evening when all we had to eat was bread and cheese, we made grilled cheese sandwiches, along with water to drink, for dinner. We accepted the food when it came, and whenever it didn't, we made do with what we had. Not always having the kinds of food we wanted, we never went to bed hungry. We always had something to eat.

Sitting on the sofa together, so many nights we'd cry ourselves to sleep. Life hurt so much, and no one could take away the pain. At times, I couldn't console him any more than he could console me, but because we were both going through the same thing together, we strengthened each other.

Chris tried to get a job working for a local newspaper. That job didn't work out and led to his quitting shortly after being hired. It was fine with me that he didn't work while in high school because I wanted him to just stay focused on school, which he did. I was so proud of him because he was really working harder at doing well in school, and his hard work was paying off.

We continued to live as we had when Daddy was alive. Daddy didn't throw wild parties or have strange folk in and out of our lives, and of course, our grandparents didn't either, so neither did we. We had a curfew, and most nights would be home, and when we weren't, it was because Chris and I were out somewhere together, more than likely just driving through town. That was one thing that brought me peace. It still does.

When I was a little girl, I would tell Daddy that for my birthday, he could just drive us through Downtown at night. There was something so peaceful and beautiful about seeing the streetlights and the building lights shining through the darkness. Daddy, of course, didn't make that my birthday gift, but he did begin taking us for long drives after nightfall, up and down the streets of Downtown Houston.

Chris and I continued doing that, just driving the streets, not talking, and not always listening to the radio, but just riding. We didn't have many friends over our house either. I seldom hung out with my math club buddies because of my weekend work schedule, so I spent most of my free time alone with Chris.

Though my friends also became Chris' friends, just like when we were kids, Chris and I enjoyed just hanging out with each other. We'd always been close. I was both a sister and now like a mother to Chris, and he respected that.

For quite a while on most Friday nights, our neighbors would look out their windows or front door and find me and Chris sitting on top of the hood of our car, listening to the music playing on our radio, as we'd done with Daddy as kids. We didn't drink, like Daddy did, but we did sit there and just listen to the music.

Sometimes, we'd even lie down near the edge of the driveway and just stare into the night-time sky and count the stars. There weren't many streetlights, and we could see the night sky lighting up so beautifully on clear nights. Just staring into the Heavens made us feel protected and safe, as though Daddy, Grandmother, Granddaddy, and even George were watching over us.

Life was what it was, and we tried to make the best of it. We stayed busy with school and also work for me.

Initially, all at home for us was peaceful—very lonely at times, but still peaceful. Aunt Della still stayed just around the corner from us and would drop by and check on me and Chris. However, not many weeks after we buried Daddy, she became distant again, and we didn't see much of her. Our neighbors talked very negatively about her and would shake their heads in disgust.

Grandmother's church members, who were also our church family, continued to be a source of emotional and financial support. After Daddy passed, the choir of our church decided that every third Sunday, they would take up a special offering for Chris and me, and others in the congregation could donate as well if they wanted to. Our church really exemplified 'love' and 'compassion.' We were grateful because the money they took up for us was always right on time to help us pay a bill, buy groceries, or meet some other need.

Feeling hopeless and very depressed, especially during the holidays, we would find ourselves clinging to fond memories of the past, not knowing if we'd ever experience that kind of happiness again.

A new year was approaching, but we faced it with fear, not knowing what was in store for us.

CHAPTER FOURTEEN

WHERE IS GOD???

JANUARY 1985

When the New Year rang in, I found myself in a lot of pain. I'd been quietly suffering with an ache in my belly for some weeks. Finally making a doctor's appointment, I went to a family physician who then sent me to a gastroenterologist for further examination.

Because money was so tight, and the medical benefits on my job hadn't kicked in yet, I had to find a doctor I could afford. Although the specialist I was referred to was well outside of what I could afford, he was very gracious and worked out a payment arrangement with me for my first visit, charging me much less than I would have ordinarily had to pay. His wife worked as his office manager, and she was so kind and wonderful to me as well, allowing me to come in and see the doctor, even when I couldn't pay a single cent.

Filling out some basic information on the medical forms, I sat anxiously waiting to see the doctor. After a short wait, I was taken into an examination room by a nurse, who prepped me. The gastroenterologist came in shortly thereafter, introducing himself and letting me know what my visit that day would entail.

He was as nice as his wife, and after examining me, he said, "You have an umbilical hernia, young lady."

"I have *a what?*" I asked him, having never heard of that diagnosis before.

He explained to me that it was something I'd had since birth and that it involved a problem around my belly button area. The pain was excruciating at times, and the doctor told me the only way to correct the issue was by having surgery.

I couldn't afford the surgery!

Again, being a very compassionate doctor, the specialist told me to pay whatever I could pay, and he would still perform the procedure to repair the hernia. Wow, that was really nice of him, but I was scared to follow through with it. He tried to put my fears to rest by telling me that he didn't anticipate a complex surgery at all. He didn't know that my entire life had been challenging, and the thought of going under anesthesia and being put to sleep caused me great anxiety.

Even though I was in as much pain as I was, I was just so afraid that something would go wrong and that I'd die, leaving Chris all alone. I was too afraid to have the surgery but also in far too much pain to continue dealing with the hernia.

My thoughts were all over the place. Remembering how Grandmother had called telling us to come and pick her up and then finding out that she'd died once we made it to the hospital haunted me. I didn't want that to happen to Chris because I didn't know if it was now my turn.

When I told Chris about the surgery, he wanted me to have it so I wouldn't be in pain anymore. Being the sweet brother he was, Chris wanted me to do something to stop the suffering, and he, *unlike me*, wasn't expecting something bad to happen. Anyway, if he did think about it, he didn't express it to me.

The one thing I didn't have to worry about was getting Chris back and forth if I decided to have the surgery because he was now driving himself the short distance back and forth to school. We had two cars, the one I drove and the one Daddy had, and so Chris drove my car while I chose to drive Daddy's long, green and white old model, two-door Cadillac.

Facing what felt like the decision of a lifetime, I called to schedule the surgery a week later because the pain intensified, and I couldn't take it anymore. Not necessarily good news to me, there was a time slot still available within the week to have the operation. All I could do was trust that all would be okay.

The day of the surgery came, and Ms. Bettye was there with me. She, like a few others, continued to stay in contact with us. Offering to take me, she wanted to be there with me, and I wanted her there.

The morning of the procedure came, and I was terrified. My doctor came in, met Ms. Bettye, and briefly explained what was getting ready to take place. When it was time for me to go into the operating room, I was breathing very heavily.

Chris was not there because the surgery was scheduled on a school day, and I wouldn't allow him to miss school. Anyway, I was a bottle of nerves, and I didn't want him to see that and start worrying himself. Even more than all of that, I didn't want him there just in case something did go wrong.

My only desire in life at that point was for me to make it through the surgery and wake back up. For Chris' sake, I wanted to live. I had to live.

I prayed for the first time in quite a while, "God, please let me wake up."

Once pushed into the surgery room on the gurney, I was prepped for the procedure and then administered the anesthesia. A mask was placed over my mouth, and I was told to count backward from 10. I remember saying how the air in the mask tasted like 'pot roast,' at which the people in the operating room laughed, and then soon after beginning to count, "10, 9, 8..." I was out.

Waking up a couple of hours later in the recovery room, I was told by the doctor that the surgery had gone well.

Yes, I was alive!

Though a little sore from the surgery, I was so very relieved and happy that I made it through! Excited to get home before Chris got out of school, I was ready to leave the hospital. The doctor and his wife gave me all of my discharge papers and recovery instructions. I would have to take it easy for the next couple of weeks. I couldn't walk long distances and would have to be pushed around in a wheelchair at school until I healed enough to take the stairs.

Ms. Bettye drove me home from the hospital and planned to stay there until Chris made it home from school. I lay on the sofa while she went into the kitchen to prepare some food for me and Chris. She'd brought a couple of bags of groceries with her so that she could fix enough food for us to last the week.

Mama was just as concerned about my surgery, but because she didn't travel far distances or drive on freeways, she wasn't sure how she would be able to come to our house. The people she generally could depend on for rides were all tied up with their own affairs.

I called Mama after being released from the hospital and let her know that I was fine and that she didn't have to worry about trying to come. Disappointed that she hadn't been able to be with me at the hospital, Mama apologized and said somehow she would get a ride out to our home, which was clear across town from her house.

Shortly after Daddy passed, Mama moved back into our family home on the north side of town. It was paid off, and no one was living there, so she decided to move back in. Chris and I were fine with that and were glad she felt comfortable enough to stay there and take care of the house, given all of the memories in the house, including those of George. She was obviously able to deal with it.

I was okay with Mama not coming because I knew Ms. Bettye was there, and Mama didn't particularly like Ms. Bettye. To her, Ms. Bettye was the 'other woman,' though it wasn't really fair to label her that way.

Mama had been out of the picture for some time before Daddy began seeing Ms. Bettye. Ms. Bettye had been a blessing to our Daddy and our family, but to Mama, she was an 'intruder.'

We'd been home from the hospital for just a couple of hours when there was a knock at the door. Ms. Bettye walked over to the door and opened it. To her surprise, and certainly mine, there Mama stood. She'd taken the city bus all the way across town to come and check on me.

While being moved by her concern for me, I instantly became nervous. Mama seemed to also be surprised to see Ms. Bettye. I guess she'd expected her to be gone by the time she got there, not thinking that someone would have to be there to take care of me until Chris made it home from school.

Honestly, I'd never been alone with Mama. Either Chris or someone else was always around, so right then, I was so grateful that Ms. Bettye was still there.

The two of them 'coldly' greeted each other, making more eye contact than saying words, as Ms. Bettye stepped aside, allowing Mama to come in. Ms. Bettye stood there for a moment watching Mama, and then she walked back into the kitchen and resumed cooking.

Mama, seeing me lying on the sofa, came over, sat next to me, and began talking.

"Hey baby," she said, rubbing me on the leg.

"Hi, Mama," I said, smiling.

"How do you feel? Are you in much pain?" she asked.

"I feel okay, just a little sore. The anesthesia hasn't worn completely off. I do have pain medicine that the doctor gave me, so I…"

'Clank! Clank!' The sound of a pan hitting the floor caused me to jump a little, stop mid-sentence, and then look off into the kitchen.

Ms. Bettye had accidentally dropped a pan on the floor. Mama, with a frown on her face, looked at Ms. Bettye, hard at work cooking in the kitchen.

I prayed that Mama would stay sitting on the sofa with me, but that prayer failed as, without warning, she got up and went into the kitchen where Ms. Bettye was. Right away, they began to argue, and I began to panic, feeling my rapid heartbeat. It was obvious that from the moment Mama saw Ms. Bettye, she was irritated.

I'd just had surgery and couldn't move very much and couldn't walk at all without some assistance. So nervous that the two of them were going to fight, I tried to figure out what I should do. Not able to easily lift my head up from the pillow, I did my best to look into the kitchen. I was thinking to myself that if they got into a physical altercation, maybe I'd be able to holler loud enough to make them stop.

Wanting to call for Ms. Mandy to come over, I was too afraid to try to get up and leave them alone together, even for a minute.

"I was going to cook for my babies. They don't need you cooking for them!" Mama said angrily, looking around at the food and the pots and pans strewn on top of the counter.

"Well, I wanted to come and cook for them. They are my babies too." Ms. Bettye said, stopping what she was doing and staring at Mama.

'Oh no!' I thought, 'I wish Ms. Bettye hadn't gone there.'

While it was true that she had treated us just like her own kids, Mama wouldn't understand or even appreciate that bold statement. To her, Ms. Bettye was trying to take her kids, even if only emotionally, away from her.

"They are not your kids, Bettye! They are mine! I gave birth to them! I'm their Mother!" Mama said, getting louder and louder, with a trembling in her voice.

Mama was visibly upset because of Ms. Bettye's statement, and I was afraid for Ms. Bettye.

"Listen," Ms. Bettye said, trying to remain calm, "I'm not doing anything wrong by fixing Cheryl and Chris some dinner. I'm just trying to help out so they won't have to worry about cooking anything the rest of the week. Cheryl doesn't need to be doing a lot of moving around, and Chris will have enough to do."

"Well, I could have did whatever needed to be done, you didn't have to cook for them!" Mama shot back, still angry, moving closer to Ms. Bettye. My babies know I love them, and I'll do whatever they need me to do! I'll do just like I did today and ride the bus to get to them if I have to. That's how much I love my babies."

"I know I didn't have to do it; I wanted to do it. And I know you love them, Alice, and I love them too. All I'm trying to do is help." Ms. Bettye responded, turning away from Mama and reaching for some meat to season and place in the oven.

Ms. Bettye awkwardly began cooking again, doing her best to ignore Mama's ranting and keep the situation from escalating. One of them had to be levelheaded enough to extinguish the argument, and I was glad Ms. Bettye was levelheaded.

Placing my hand over my face, I prayed Mama would just come out of the kitchen and leave Ms. Bettye alone.

Mama didn't say anything else but did stare at Ms. Bettye for about five minutes, standing there with her arms folded. She watched Ms. Bettye's every move. It was the most intense five minutes. Any wrong or sudden move and things could have gone downhill quickly!

Surely Ms. Bettye, not trusting Mama and not knowing what was going through her mind, was watching Mama's every move as well.

Laying on the sofa, sweating, I watched both of them. There were way too many knives and sharp objects in the kitchen, and I couldn't help but think about the horrible thing that could take place.

Finally, and thankfully, after a few minutes, Mama came out of the kitchen and sat back on the sofa with me.

What a sigh of relief I breathed!

I'd stretched my neck so, trying to keep an eye on them in the kitchen, that it felt almost strained. Mama sat there on the sofa with me and watched TV, trying to ignore Ms. Bettye's presence.

After almost an hour, Mama got up to leave.

"Okay baby, well I'm going to leave now. Cheryl, you know if you need anything, you let me know. If I can't do it, you know I'll ask your Aunt Doris or Uncle Charles," she said, leaning over to hug me.

"Yes ma'am, I know. Thank you, Mama." I said, hugging her back.

Not saying one word or even glancing her way, Mama ignored Ms. Bettye, who was now sitting at the dining room table, waiting for the food to finish cooking.

After saying "Goodbye," Mama left and disappeared out of my sight as she went out the doorway, closing the door behind her. She headed back down the block to the bus stop.

Once Mama had left, Ms. Bettye got up from her seat and walked over to me.

"My goodness," she said, smiling at me, "I'm sorry your mama and I had words, Cheryl."

"I just want her to know that I love you and Chris too, and I just want to help."

"Oh yes ma'am, we know. It's okay. Mama will be alright," I said.

"Thank you for coming with me this morning to my surgery, and thank you for cooking for us," I said, smiling at Ms. Bettye.

"Anything for you and Chris. Your daddy would want me to make sure y'all are okay," Ms. Bettye said, tearing up, thinking about Daddy.

I nodded and smiled. It had already been such an emotional day. I didn't feel like crying because thinking about Daddy would make me do just that. Instead, I turned my attention back to the television. Ms. Bettye got up from sitting and returned to the kitchen.

In spite of the spat between Mama and Ms. Bettye, I was touched that Ms. Bettye would set her entire day aside to be with me and that Mama would spend more than an hour riding the city bus across town to come and check on me. Having someone taking care of me felt good.

Being able to finally rest, I closed my eyes after taking the pain meds my doctor had prescribed for me and fell sound asleep. No nightmares this time, no painful dreams, just sweet rest. That's what I needed—*peaceful* sleep.

Still knocked out when Chris made it home, I didn't see him until early the next morning when I woke up with him sleeping next to me on the floor, on a pile of blankets.

Ms. Bettye, staying for a little while even after he'd made it home from school, had cooked up a bunch of food for us. For at least a week, we wouldn't have to worry about cooking anything.

After a couple of days of rest at home, I returned to school, having to be pushed around in a wheelchair for about a week as I continued to recover. My best friends, Micheala and Wanda, were happy to volunteer as my personal escorts. I had to do my best not to laugh around the two of them because it hurt so much to do so.

Within weeks, I'd healed up nicely and was back on my feet once again. Chris and I continued on, still adjusting to Daddy's absence. It had been only a little over a couple of months since his death, but it still seemed like yesterday, remaining fresh in our minds.

After I stopped the pain meds for my surgery, the dreams started again, and I was again waking up every morning around 4 a.m. Unlike before, I at least now was able to fall back to sleep.

Fighting for our Home

Towards the end of the same month as my surgery, January 1985, I answered a knock at the door. Looking through the peephole, I saw a man I didn't recognize standing there and asked who he was. He only gave me his name and said he had a package for me. Curious, I cautiously opened the door. The screen door in front of our wooden door was locked.

As I looked at the man, he said, "Hi, I'm looking for Cheryl Battle. I have a package for her," he said, displaying a brown envelope.

"I'm Cheryl," I said, unhooking the screen door while trying to see the sender's name on the envelope.

"Ok, ma'am," he said nicely. "I have something here for you then, and I need you to sign for it."

"Uh, okay," I said, wondering who'd sent me a package.

As the man passed the package, I took it and signed the paper he held out for me to sign. He left, and I closed and locked the door, staring at the envelope.

Opening the big brown envelope, I read the first few lines of the letter inserted inside. My eyes bulged from shock!

Aunt Della was taking me and Chris to court, suing us for our home, and the letter was a summons for us to appear in court!

I had to read the first page several times to make sure I was reading it right because I couldn't believe my own eyes. Our aunt, our relative by blood, was actually taking us to court to have our home sold so that she could get half the proceeds from the sale.

Hurrying next door, I showed the paperwork to Ms. Mandy. She gasped.

"What?! I can't even believe this!" she said, looking at me and then looking down at the papers again.

She, like me, had to read the letter again a couple of times. Telling me to come inside her house, Ms. Mandy went directly to her phone and made a phone call. Hearing the person on the other end, I realized she'd called Ms. Bettye. The two of them had become good friends, and Ms. Mandy thought she was the best person to contact.

We would need some help. The situation between Daddy and Aunt Della had now spilled over onto us. No longer on the sidelines of the fight, Chris and I were directly involved in the fight. It was us against Aunt Della.

We'd talked about how she'd begun acting cold towards us again shortly after we buried Daddy and how we hadn't seen much of her in the days following. She'd stopped coming by and had also stopped calling. Now we understood what she was up to. Uncle Irving had also kept his distance, but then again, that was not unusual for him.

Word about what Aunt Della was doing spread quickly amongst our neighbors, and from that moment on, it wasn't just Chris and me against Aunt Della; it was our neighbors, Chris, and me against Aunt Della. So disgusted and enraged about her suing us, our neighbors immediately came to our aid, supporting us once again and ready to help us fight.

Aunt Della soon became one of the most despised and detested people in our neighborhood because not only did our neighbors know what she was doing, but she'd also told her neighbors and apparently didn't receive the response she sought from them, as they too, thought what she was doing was wrong.

Mama and our other family members were also upset about how she was treating us. How in the world could someone be so cold? Why was she lashing out at us like this?

We didn't know what to do or how to handle the situation. One thing for sure was we needed to hire an attorney right away. With Aunt Doris' help, we consulted with the attorney who helped me get guardianship over Chris.

Because she and Aunt Doris were good friends, she sat down and talked with us right away to see how she could help. After she was briefed about our case, it became apparent that she wouldn't be able to represent us because of the specific area of law our case involved. However, she did immediately refer us to an attorney who dealt specifically with cases like ours in probate court.

Bettye and Ms. Mandy contacted the attorney on our behalf, and we had our first consultation with her. Here we were again, needing help but unable to afford it. No one around us had the kind of money it would take for us to pay for the type of legal representation we needed in court.

However, the attorney, Mrs. Daniels, hearing the exceptional circumstances surrounding our case, graciously offered to represent us for close to nothing, only requiring that we pay court filing fees, to which we agreed. Eventually, our attorney was even covering those fees for us, as she was busy filing different papers in response to the lawsuit.

Another stranger, just like the doctor who operated on me, selflessly moved to help. Wow!

Chris and I were happy to have someone on our side who was qualified and willing to stand up for us in court. Attorney Daniels was sharp in her intellect and her dress sense! I really admired our attorney because not only was she female, but she was also African American, with caring ways like Grandmother.

At a point in my life when I had so many doubts about my future, her presence, in a huge way, really encouraged me. Moving forward with our defense, we understood that Aunt Della absolutely had a stake in our home since there, unfortunately, was no will. However, we believed she was being unreasonable in trying to force us to sell the place we'd called home for ten years, all so she could get money.

The biggest concern for those involved in helping us with our case was our age. I had just barely turned 18, and Chris was still a minor.

Motivated to even forsake family relationship, Aunt Della did all she could to put us out, especially now that Daddy was gone. Uncle Irving worked, supported her financially, and paid all of the bills, so what else was behind her actions? It had to have been greater than greed.

She had not anticipated the fight that would result. Though we were but kids, we realized we had not been left alone to defend ourselves. It was as if Daddy and our grandparents in Heaven were watching over us and sending us the help we needed. Aunt Della became the most evil woman we knew. Mama had done a terrible thing, killing George, but she had a mental illness. To us, what Aunt Della was doing was harsh, hateful, and inexcusable. What she was doing was unforgivable.

For the first time in my life, I knew what it felt like to hate someone. Chris and I hadn't harmed her in any way, yet she was determined to do whatever she could to see us put out of our home. The betrayal we felt was sharp and deep. I wrestled with trying to understand how the heart of man could be so wicked.

Though plenty of folks let Aunt Della know just how 'evil' they thought she was, she didn't care about being labeled as such. Even though Aunt Della's action caused a rift between her and her own neighbors, she didn't let up one bit, proceeding forward with taking us to court.

Our first court date came, and we were introduced to the 'receiver' of the court. Her name was Ms. Runger, and she, from the outset, was a very nice lady. Her job was to act as a 'mediator' between us and Aunt Della. Ms. Runger wanted an amicable resolution, at least so that we could remain in the house until we were older and better able to support ourselves.

Devastated at the possibility that we'd have to move out of our home, Chris and I became more depressed than angry. Where could we go?

Moved by our case, even the receiver, along with her husband, made an unscheduled visit to our home late the next evening, bringing us food and clothing. Very surprised to see her standing outside our door, we let her in, and she and her husband, whom she introduced to us, also greeted us. The bags full of clothes and food left us just about speechless.

Ms. Runger had to do what was fair in the courtroom, which she did, and outside the courtroom, she showed us compassion that went above and beyond her call of duty.

Managing to utter the words "Thank You," it was obvious to Ms. Runger and her husband that we were both very touched and grateful.

They didn't stay long, and she never said one word about our court case. Walking them out, we thanked them again and watched as they got into their very nice vehicle and drove away.

We were stunned, but this time for a good reason. We'd just about lost faith in family, but a stranger helped us not lose hope about our situation or people in general.

Our schedules became even busier, now including meetings with Attorney Daniels. We were in school, Chris had band practice, I worked at least 20 hours a week, and we still attended church most Sundays. Life was moving at a fast pace.

In addition to all of that going on, it was my senior year, and I was preparing for my senior prom and senior graduation day. Altering my college plans, I applied to the University of Houston-Central Campus in town. Through reputation, it was a very good college. After being accepted, I decided to pursue a degree in Biology.

No longer seeing myself going to medical school and with the responsibility of taking care of Chris, living from one day to the next was my focus. Thinking too far into the future stressed me out. From time to time, I'd get terrible migraine headaches, so I tried not to stress so much. Stress, I'm sure, contributed to Daddy's untimely death, and I was doing my best to stick around, if for no other reason than to still be here for Chris.

Prom weekend arrived, and I was ready. My date was just a friend, though he'd always wanted to be more. Still, he was a nice guy, and I was happy to go to prom with him after my heart had been broken by my football boyfriend.

Graham and I had already talked about the plans for that night. We would wear white and pink. Aunt Greta was excited for me and offered to buy me a beautiful prom gown. If it hadn't been for her, I wouldn't have had a gown to wear to my prom. I was so excited about the gown. It fits perfectly!

My closest friends were going to meet up with us at the hotel where the prom was being held. Graham arrived on time, looking very handsome in his white tuxedo and light pink tuxedo shirt. His coat was very long, hanging down beyond his knees. Graham pinned a pink corsage on my left lapel, which made me smile.

We were ready to go have fun! Graham told me he was going to rent us a limousine to ride to prom, but instead, his uncle ended up taking us. I didn't have a problem with that at all since his uncle drove a very clean, shiny, two-door car.

The only issue we did have was that the hoop of my dress was very wide, making it difficult for me to climb into the back seat of the car. In fact, both Graham and his uncle had to help me get in.

Standing outside the car door, they pushed the bottom part of my dress down as I climbed into the car, with my rear end going in first. We all had a good laugh.

Finally making it to the prom, we found my friends and stood there as we all chatted away. Graham, excusing himself, left me for a moment and walked up to the DJ booth. He requested a song in my honor. It was a very bold and slightly embarrassing thing to do, but it made my night even more special. We, along with my friends, left the prom just as it was ending and decided to drive down to Galveston. Graham and I rode along with Micheala and her boyfriend, Trenton.

Not being much of a night owl, I slept most of the way there. Once we made it to Galveston, we all headed straight for the beach. The night was so beautiful, as the light from the moon shone on the bay waters. Playing in the sand, my friends and I ran up and down the beach, kicking sand at each other.

After a little while, a few of my friends who were coupled up with actual boyfriends walked away to go make out on the beach—no sex, just a lot of smooching.

Graham was not my boyfriend, and I'd already made my mind up that there would be no touchy-feely stuff going on between us. He did try but respectfully backed off when he saw how uncomfortable I was. He was a gentleman and didn't press the issue. I appreciated that. One thing that wouldn't be happening that night was my losing my virginity. I didn't even want to do anything that might lead to that happening, including kissing and smooching.

Sitting together on the pier, we just talked and watched as the waves beat against the rocks. An hour or so passed, and thinking about Chris being at home alone, I was ready to go. Anyway, I, from the beginning, never had any intention of staying out all night, and Graham, though disappointed, knew that.

Loading back into the vehicles, my friends and I headed back to Houston, and I was dropped off at home. After taking a bath and getting all of the sand off of me, I laid down on the floor in the living room and fell asleep next to Chris. He was already asleep, with the blanket covering him from his toes to over his head.

I think maybe he'd become afraid of being at home by himself, so he covered completely up with the blanket. That was the first night I'd stayed out beyond my 12 am curfew. Seeing Chris like that, I vowed to myself never to leave him alone like that again unless I knew for sure he wouldn't be afraid.

I scooted right up under Chris. I wanted him to know I was there; I was home.

Our graduation and promotion days were quickly approaching. Maintaining the course, Chris made it through the school year and was promoted to the 12th grade! Grateful that we'd actually made it through the tough school year without Daddy, I was very emotional during my graduation exercise. Chris and I made it! Chris was headed for his final year of high school, and I was headed for my first year of college!

Daddy, Grandmother, and Granddaddy weren't physically there at our ceremonies, but they were certainly in our hearts.

On Graduation Day, Mama and one of her sisters from the church came to both of our ceremonies. Mama, however, missed some of my graduation because she'd accidentally put on mixed-matched shoes. I believe she'd been in such a hurry to get there on time that she grabbed the wrong shoe. At any rate, she thought she would embarrass me, so she insisted on going back home and changing her shoes. She did come back before the program ended, and everything was fine.

That day meant far more to me than anybody's attire, and I wouldn't have at all felt embarrassed about my mom having on two different shoes. Chris and I had gone through so much that mix-matched shoes weren't even 'attention-worthy,' though I did appreciate Mama's concern for my feelings.

Senior Graduation/Awards Day turned out to be one of the best days, besides prom, I'd had in a long time. Receiving unexpected scholarship funds, I was ecstatic to be able to pay for college. One of my scholarships would stretch across four years of college! Though I wasn't going where my heart was initially set on going, I was content being able to enter college and hopefully pursue a career of some type, still in the medical field. My passion to still work in the medical field, in some capacity, hadn't changed.

Even after graduation, I continued to stay in contact with a few of my high school friends, and we hung out whenever we could. Soon, that would change because we would all be going different ways, going to different colleges, or taking different paths in life. Knowing our time together was short, we made the most of our 'hanging' out. We acted silly and had good, clean fun, not that we didn't know how to be 'naughty' kids, because we did; we just chose not to do so because of how disappointed those around us, like our neighbors, would be. They constantly praised us for doing well despite all that was going on, and that inspired us to stay on track.

Besides that, the one thing always at the forefront of my mind was, "If we get into trouble, *who would come and bail us out?*"

We literally couldn't afford to get into trouble.

Though there were positive things finally happening again for Chris and me, the drama with Aunt Della continued to unfold as she did all she could to try to make life for us a living hell as if it hadn't already been that.

Uncle Irving was so upset about what she was doing to us that he left her, divorcing her after many years of marriage. Following the divorce, Aunt Della became an even more vengeful, scorned woman. About a year after severing his relationship with Aunt Della, Uncle Irving began communicating with us again, eventually remarrying and introducing us to his new wife, whom we absolutely adored. It didn't take him long to move on.

To say Aunt Della seemed to be mad at the world would be an understatement. She did, however, fall to a new level of low amid so many people turning against her because of her actions.

A few days after a court hearing, I walked outside and saw a utility worker in our yard. I knew he was a utility worker because of his uniform and because of the utility truck parked on the outside of our ditch in the front. I approached him to see what he was doing. Surely, he wasn't turning off our water because we'd paid the bill.

There were a couple of times when our lights were turned off for non-payment, but within a day, we would have the money to get them turned back on. During those couple of times, Chris and I would just pull out some candles and light them until we had lights again. Not falling apart, we just did what we had to do.

This day, however, our utilities, *all of them*, had been paid, and there was no reason why they should have been turned off.

"Uh, excuse me," I said, approaching the utility worker.

The man in a blue uniform looked up and said, "Yes, ma'am, good morning."

"Uh, I live here. Is there a problem?" I asked.

"You do? Well, I have a notice to turn off the services. It says here the occupants are moving," the man said, reaching into his top pocket and pulling out and reading some paperwork.

"No sir, we are not moving. You can't turn off our water. We didn't call that in." I said, confused about the notice.

"Yep," he continued on looking down and scanning over his work order, "Uh, let's see here, okay… an 'Idella Rogers' called it in yesterday. Who is she? Do you know her?" He said, with a puzzled look on his face.

"Oh," I said, getting a deep pain in the pit of my stomach and sighing.

"Yes, I know her. She's my aunt, but we stay here, and she has no right to call and have our water turned off," I said, very irritated that she would stoop so low and do such a thing.

Without going into too much detail, I explained to the worker about the court battle we were involved in with her. He'd apparently heard of such family disputes and apologized. Leaving our water on, he told me that he would call his supervisor and tell him what was going on. He then advised me to get the water utility put in my name. Daddy hadn't changed any of the utility accounts after Grandmother passed, so all the utilities were still in her name. Putting the utilities in my name would avoid any such future disruptions.

Taking his advice, I immediately called in to have the services placed in my name. Of course, there was the additional cost of a deposit for doing so. I'd never had any utility in my name, but I paid the deposit as required to protect our water service.

Less than a week later, an electric utility man was in our backyard, there also to turn off another utility—our lights. Unbelievable! I was fuming mad. Why wouldn't she just leave us alone?!

Just like with the water utility, I had to also place the lights and the gas in my name. Neighbors and our church gave us money to help us with the deposits for each. I found it somewhat amazing and a relief that on both occasions, in the process of our utility services being disconnected, I caught the person just in time!

Cruel, heartless, mean, wicked, hateful, and evil were just some of the words that came to mind whenever we thought of Aunt Della.

Unfortunately, she wasn't finished yet.

A couple of weeks later, shortly after arriving home in the evening from school, Chris and I discovered that our air conditioner had been removed from the back bedroom window! There was nothing there but a big gaping hole! It had hung just outside of the room which had belonged to Grandmother.

At first, we thought that maybe we'd been random victims of a crime, which was so hard to believe because crime was almost unheard of in our tight-knit, for the most part, peaceful community. The people in our community looked out for each other, and rarely were there public fights or disputes.

Ms. Mandy made a phone call to Aunt Della's neighbor and found out that Aunt Della was indeed the culprit behind the theft.

We, along with Ms. Mandy and other neighbors, were standing in Ms. Mandy's driveway. As soon as Ms. Mandy hung up the phone, she told us to also check the garage to make sure Granddaddy's antique car was still in there.

Walking with Ms. Mandy over to our garage, as the others looked on, we could tell right away that the lock had been tampered with. It was no longer locked. Raising the garage door up, we discovered that Granddaddy's 1962 mint condition black and silver New York Chrysler was gone too!

How could she?!

She stole Granddaddy's car and stole the air conditioner, leaving a huge hole in the rear of our home! Crying, even wailing, we were just sick and tired of life, so sick and tired of all the problems! Our neighbors, just as furious as we were, tried to console both Chris and me.

I wondered, "God, *where are you?*"

I wondered why He was allowing this woman to wreak such havoc in our lives. Why is He allowing all of these awful things to continue to happen to us!? If God loves us, why didn't He prevent our home from being broken into and our stuff from being stolen? If He really loves us, why did He allow Grandmother and Daddy to die when He knew we needed them? If God is with us like Grandmother believed and said on so many occasions, why didn't He stop Mama from killing George? He could have stopped all of it from happening, but He didn't!

I remember how Grandmother had such faith in God, how she even insisted we go to church so that we too could learn about Him. But it was hard for me now to believe that God even cared. Grandmother believed He was real. She taught us that He was real. Daddy taught us how to pray to Him when we were mere babies, but I started tracing all the things that had happened and wondered, 'If God loved us, why was He allowing so many bad things to happen to us?'

Where is God?

He couldn't be with us because if He was, that meant He didn't care about all the suffering we were going through. My conclusion, based on the evidence around us, was that God wasn't with us. He couldn't be. From that moment on, my faith, as small as it already was, took a downward turn. I was angry, but beyond that, I just didn't care anymore. Whatever was going to happen was going to happen. I was convinced that God didn't care.

We called the police, and they did come out. However, they informed us that because the matter was a court matter, there was nothing they could do. They couldn't intervene, even though there were witnesses.

From our point of view, a crime had been committed. It was enough for me. That day, I almost reached my breaking point. I felt like God had failed us by not protecting us, and the police failed us too. I lost hope in God and in the justice system the same day.

Not only had our air conditioner been ripped out of the wall and the antique car my grandfather treasured stolen out of our garage, but upon going from room to room, we discovered that pictures and other mementos had been taken.

Later on that evening, after seeing a few folk congregating near our home, our neighbors from across the street walked over to us. They were a retired couple who stayed at home most days.

Telling us that they'd actually seen Aunt Della and two guys at our home earlier in the day around 3 pm, they said they felt bad about what happened. They said that they didn't think to call the police when they saw Aunt Della break the lock off the garage door and, with the help of the men with her, drive the car out of the garage and on down the street.

The next evening, a handful of those close to us gathered together and actually came up with a plan to have someone throw combustible cocktails through Aunt Della's house windows! They were so angry that they plotted to burn her house down, with her potentially inside it! It took them no time to put it together, and they even had someone already in place to carry it out. One of the people involved mentioned it to me and Chris, and we were shocked that such a plan had been devised!

As much as we did hate her and hate her with a passion, we could not do that or allow that to happen without trying to stop it.

Did we think she deserved something bad to happen to her because she'd taken so much from us, including our peace? *ABSOLUTELY!* But was it worth causing her to lose her home and possibly her life? *Absolutely not.*

I remember that day that she and Daddy had an altercation, and I called her a name and how quickly Daddy rebuked me and stressed that she was 'still our aunt,' and we were still to respect her. He did more than just chastise us that day; he perhaps helped spare Aunt Della's life. Daddy, of course, wasn't with us to see her sink to a new level of hatred, but he knew his sister and what she was capable of, and I believe his instructions regarding how we should treat her would still be the same.

We told the group of folk how we felt about what they were about to do, and thankfully, they called everything off even though a couple of them weren't too happy to do so.

Aunt Della never knew how close she actually came to death that night.

The nasty and bitter court proceedings continued on, and though there wasn't much left for her to do to us outside the courtroom, Aunt Della still, from time to time, would do very intimidating things to us, like throw rocks at our house late at night. She did that a couple of times, one of which we actually witnessed ourselves.

On most court days, we'd be accompanied by Attorney Daniels, Ms. Bettye, and a few of our neighbors who'd come along as a show of support for us.

We'd watch as Aunt Della would smugly strut down the hallway, walking in between her two high-powered attorneys. We were so surprised that she had two attorneys, both of whom were tall, White, middle-aged-looking men. Her attorneys had such a serious demeanor, and though this was a serious matter, you'd think the case involved some kind of heinous crime.

Over the course of the four years, we were in and out of court, and there was the occasional showdown between Aunt Della and one or more of those who'd come with us.

During one such court day, Aunt Della was alone in the lobby just outside the courtroom doors. It was strange to see her without her attorneys alongside her.

Arriving with Attorney Daniels, Chris and I sat down a couple of benches away from her. Ms. Bettye, Ms. Mandy, and a few of our neighbors sat down beside us. Seeing Aunt Della sitting alone and waiting by herself, I immediately felt my heart beginning to race. I was nervous. Our aunt had become our enemy. It wasn't time for us to go in yet because the court was running behind.

Attorney Daniels went inside the courtroom to check on our hearing time. All of a sudden, Ms. Mandy, glancing at Aunt Della, got up from her seat and began walking down the hallway toward her. The others immediately jumped up from their seats and followed Ms. Mandy, looking worried, not knowing what Ms. Mandy was about to do. Intentionally stopping in front of her bench, Ms. Mandy began to go in on Aunt Della.

"You ought to be ashamed of yourself, Idella! I bet your mother and father are turning over in their graves!" Ms. Mandy said, squinting her eyes at Aunt Della.

Aunt Della didn't say anything back but just looked at her, rolled her eyes, and turned her head.

"They are just kids! How could you do this to them?!" Ms. Mandy said, tearing up, trying to appeal to Aunt Della.

However, Aunt Della wasn't moved.

"They've already been through enough, Idella!" Ms. Mandy continued on, raising her voice and looking as if she wanted to punch Aunt Della in the face.

Her eyes were fiery red, and droplets of sweat began to build up on her forehead.

"Think about what you are doing," Ms. Bettye said, also trying to get through to Aunt Della while the others with them nodded their heads.

Aunt Della then finally speaks, spouting out, "I'm only getting what's rightfully mine! Rudy and those kids stayed in that house and didn't bother about asking if it was okay with me!"

"It's my house too!" she said, raising her voice loud enough to get the attention of those passing by.

"You have a house, Idella!" Ms. Mandy fired back. "These kids don't have anything. Instead of you trying to hurt them, you ought to be trying to help them. For God's sake, Idella, they are your niece and nephew! Your flesh and blood! Who does that to family?!"

"Mandy, I don't care what you or anyone else says. It's my house too!" Aunt Della said, rolling her eyes at Ms. Mandy and then looking down at us and rolling her eyes again.

Grabbing her purse, Aunt Della stood up angrily and began walking the opposite way down the hallway, away from all of us.

"It's not right. It's just not right, and you'll get yours one day, Idella! You better believe that!" said Ms. Mandy, pointing her finger at Aunt Della as Aunt Della hurried away.

"Come on, Mandy, don't worry, it's like you said, her day is coming. Leave her to the Lord. He'll get her," Ms. Bettye said, trying to calm Ms. Mandy down.

"You're going to HELL you big time, Christian!" someone else shouted at Aunt Della.

By that time, our attorney came out and saw what was going on. She stood in front of us and told those with us to calm down and leave Aunt Della alone. She stated that the one thing we didn't want was to make matters worse by having an altercation in the courthouse.

We weren't in the courtroom long.

Attorney Daniels, approaching the judge with Aunt Della's attorneys, asked the judge for more time with our case. Although Aunt Della's lawyers contested, the judge agreed to give us more time.

Attorney Daniels was succeeding in what she originally set out to do, and that was to stall as long as possible and hold off the sale of our home, at least until Chris and I were older and in a better position to move out if need be. Other than selling the house, our only other option was to somehow get enough money to pay her portion out of our home. That was unlikely because Aunt Della was asking for no less than $14,000 to buy her out. No one we knew had that kind of money on hand to lend to us. We just had to wait and see what the outcome would be.

The summer of '88 was near, and I'd just finished up another year at the university. As a freshman and sophomore in college, I'd been able to maintain a very good grade point average, hovering around 3.5, but the past year had been so tough and stressful that my grades began to drop, but I continued to work and go to school.

Thankfully, my first two years of college had been paid for with grant and scholarship funds. That was a tremendous help because, at one point, we hit rock bottom financially, compounded by Chris' car being stolen from his school's parking lot and my car breaking down due to transmission problems. Money was so tight that we barely had money to ride the bus back and forth to school and work. Many days, I rode my ten-speed bike back and forth to college when I didn't have bus fare. Not really being concerned about that; I was just glad to still be able to get to class.

One of the scholarships I'd received for school was a four-year scholarship, and as part of my eligibility requirements, I had to attend school full-time. Working full-time, going to school full-time, and taking care of Chris and myself took its toll, not to mention the stress of our ongoing court battle with Aunt Della. Being so emotionally drained and overwhelmed, I dropped my course load to below the scholarship-required minimum of 15 hours, and in doing so, I forfeited those scholarship funds.

Feeling caught between a rock and a hard place and having to decide between losing my sanity and losing my scholarship, I opted for the latter. Somehow, I'd have to make up for the now-lost funds.

The Fall and Spring Semesters of my junior year came, and I was just barely able to cover my tuition and book expenses, but somehow it worked out.

When the summer of '88 hit, I was more than ready for a break from school. I spent even more time at work. Going to my job, as usual, I clocked in and headed for my department. I'd been promoted twice and was now working in the over-the-drug counter department, which was called the 'Drug Department'.

I was feeling strange, even nervous. My heart was racing, beating abnormally fast, for no apparent reason. Wanting to cry, I had nothing to cry about because nothing beyond the usual had occurred.

Shortly after I made it to work, I suddenly heard my name being called over the loudspeaker, "Cheryl Battle, please report to the manager's office."

"Hmm, I wonder what this is about," I said to myself.

I was called again moments later before I could even stand to my feet. Putting down the items I had in my hands, I stood up and became very lightheaded. Maybe that's why I'd experienced the rapid heartbeat all morning.

After standing in place for a few seconds to gather myself, I began to walk towards the front of the store to go up the stairs to the manager's office. By the time I made it to the stairs, to my surprise, Ms. Mandy was standing near the entrance to the stairs. Something must be wrong, and I immediately thought about Chris!

We'd listed Ms. Mandy as an emergency contact on all of our important documents. Panicking, I quickly looked around and breathed a sigh of relief when I noticed Chris approaching from the right. My thought then was maybe they were just coming to visit me at work. Our weeks and months had been so trying; perhaps they were surprising me with lunch.

Ms. Mandy reached out to hug me as I smiled and spoke, "Hey, Ms. Mandy, what are you all doing here?"

She looked at me and tried to hide a look of sadness behind her smile.

"Cheryl, baby…your mother passed today," she said.

"What?" I said, in shock.

I didn't know what to say after that and began to feel very lightheaded again, as I had earlier. As I began to cry, Ms. Sanders, my manager, and another male coworker standing nearby helped me up the stairs.

Ms. Mandy said, "I'm so sorry, baby. I'm so sorry," while continuing to hug me once we made it upstairs.

"She died this morning. They think maybe she had a heart attack or stroke. I'm very sorry, Cheryl," Ms. Mandy said, trying to comfort me.

It was hard for it to register in my head because Mama, like Daddy, hadn't even been sick. She had health issues, of course, but there had been no red flags that things would progress to this point so quickly.

We didn't stay with Mama, but she and I had become close to the point that we talked on the phone just about every day. Many times, Chris and I would travel to the north side of town to take her to a doctor's appointment or even to the grocery store. Mama's nerves were getting worse, and she drove as little as possible.

Now feeling a lot of self-pity, I looked at Ms. Mandy and asked, "Why does this keep happening to us? Why does God keep taking people from us?"

Honestly, it would have been okay if he'd taken Aunt Della at that point; I was just tired of Him taking the people that we loved.

Ms. Mandy had no answer, stumped herself by all of the events of the past few years: the tragedies, the previous deaths, the lawsuit, and now this. I wouldn't have blamed anyone for believing that there was obviously something bad going on in our family. It just wasn't normal for so much tragedy to be constantly plaguing one family.

That was it for our immediate family. Mama was the last adult left, and now she was gone, just like all the others. Though our relationship with Mama was different from the 'norm' given our history, we still loved her, and she loved us. We had a sense of family with her because she was still our mother. I was numb—again.

We weren't kids anymore. I was almost 22, and Chris 21. As young adults, we were much better able to process Mama's death than all the others. Though death hurt, it was almost as if we were becoming used to our loved ones dying.

Leaving my job en route to Mama's house with Ms. Mandy driving us, we arrived at Mama's house and found others waiting inside. The coroner hadn't too long since left with Mama's body. I appreciated that Aunt Doris and others at the house wanted to spare us additional grief and did their best to make sure Mama's body had been removed before we got there.

Aunt Doris, still Mama's closest sister, met us outside as we got out of the car. She hugged us, as did our cousin Bridgette.

"What happened?" I asked Aunt Doris, starting to cry again.

Aunt Doris, placing her hand on my shoulder, looked me in my eyes and said very honestly, "We don't know yet. Mae found her this morning in the bed."

Mama's oldest sister, Aunt Fannie Mae, had recently moved in with her to not only help with the bills but also to be company for her.

"She didn't respond after she called her name several times. When she went into her room to see what was going on, she found her dead in the bed, and then she called me hysterical. I'm so sorry, Cheryl and Chris. Your mama probably had a heart attack or stroke. We'll know after they do an autopsy," Aunt Doris lamented, then gave us another hug.

Turns out Aunt Doris was right. The autopsy indicated that Mama had suffered a stroke. She, only 47 years old, was young like Daddy when she died.

Soon after we buried Mama, the feelings I'd put on the 'back burner,' even as far back as the day she took George's life, resurfaced again, but now with a vengeance. Feeling like I was on the verge of having a nervous breakdown, I knew I needed to talk to someone, a counselor or therapist, somebody, soon. Free counseling services were provided for students on campus, but that was a closed door for me because I would have to, for the first time ever, sit out the upcoming semester. I simply didn't have the money for school.

I was not only concerned about not being able to attend the upcoming semester to see a counselor, but I was also even more worried about not being able to return to school at all. Something had to happen because I'd come too far and through too much to quit now. I needed help—a plan to get the money to pay for school. I needed a miracle.

I'd been so angry at God that I thought praying to Him would be useless. However, Grandmother came to mind at that very moment, and I remembered what she said about God 'hearing us when we prayed to Him.'

It was like a sign, a message from Grandmother herself, telling me what to do.

Obviously, God hadn't heard any of my shouting and ranting because He didn't intervene, but maybe He would hear a desperate cry for help. Down to nothing, I was at least willing to give it a try. My prayers seemed awkward at first, as I stuttered, trying to get the words out. Knowing how forsaken I'd felt by God, I wasn't sure He would hear or even care to hear me. Having no other way to continue my education, I prayed for God to make a way for me to be able to go to school.

Friends of mine had already stopped going to school for various reasons, including due to a lack of finances, but Chris and school were all I had left that made me want to live on.

Stunned to the point of almost disbelief, I experienced God work a miracle! In the mail, just prior to the start of the Fall Semester of 88, I received a package from the university. Inside the envelope was paperwork detailing a scholarship I'd just been awarded! So much had happened, but for a moment, it seemed like God was paying attention! I didn't understand why He couldn't just put a stop to all of the madness Chris and I were still enduring at the hands of Aunt Della, but I was so glad that He at least answered my prayer about money for school!

I had what I needed for the upcoming semester! The most baffling thing of all is the fact that I hadn't even applied for the scholarship! I'd filled out no application, no paperwork, and yet, out of the blue, I was awarded it! I couldn't explain why or how I was given the scholarship other than to chalk it up to what Grandmother would always say, **"God does work in mysterious ways."**

There was no way this was luck or happenstance.

My hope in God had almost become bankrupt, but receiving the scholarship not only helped me continue pursuing my degree, but it also began to slowly grow my faith, even if just a little.

The money did more than pay for my classes for the semester; it also enabled me to seek counseling immediately, made only available to currently enrolled students. Thanks to that scholarship, that included me!

Walking onto campus, I registered for my classes and, following that, headed straight for the counseling center to make my appointment. Relieved that I was given an appointment within the week, I couldn't wait to sit down and talk with a counselor.

The day of my session, I felt so overwhelmed, almost like I was going to burst. Signing in, I took a seat and waited to be called.

Soon, the counselor, a young White lady looking to still be in her 20s, came out, got me, and led me back to her office. After we introduced ourselves to each other, I began telling her why I was there.

I think I unloaded years of disappointment, anguish, and feelings of hopelessness in about 30 minutes, talking non-stop, going from one major life event to the next. She had to have been overwhelmed because I was giving it all to her at one time. Experiencing it over a span of time almost did me in, but here I was, sharing my entire life in one session.

By the time I was done, the counselor was in tears and simply passed the box of Kleenex to me. She listened, she empathized, and she cried with me. I'm not sure who used the most tissue, me or her. She was overwhelmed.

Without addressing any one particular thing that had gone on in my life, the therapist, after pulling herself together, leaned over and, grabbing my hands, simply said, "Cheryl, you are a survivor."

Placing her hands on my knees, she looked intently into my eyes and repeated it again, only with more emphasis, *"Cheryl, you are a survivor."*

She said five words, and what a difference that made in how I viewed all of my years of loss, suffering, agony, and pain. That was about as deep and as intense as the therapy session got that afternoon, and it was exactly what I needed!

"I'm a survivor. Huh," I said to myself.

That young lady helped me see that what I'd gone through hadn't taken me out. As tough as things had been, I was still alive; I was still here. That in itself was an accomplishment!

She pointed out that some good things had happened in my life and that *something* had been 'keeping' me. Something indeed had been 'keeping' me—me and Chris. I hadn't really thought about my life from the counselor's perspective before. All I could see was death, loss, hurt, pain, and suffering, but my session with her helped me see so much more.

After all, I was 22 at the time of our session and had already lived beyond my own personal life expectancy. That was a definite positive!

Referring to the day of the tragedy, she said I could have lost my life then, yet I was still here. She was right. If I'd walked through the door first, it would have been me instead of George, who would have died that day.

While it was very sad that my brother died, his life being so unfairly taken, at that very moment, I had a revelation of sorts: my life had been intentionally saved. It could have easily been me. Even when I came face to face with Mama after she'd killed George, she still had the opportunity to kill me, but my life was spared.

I didn't understand *what*, but for sure, *'something'* protected me and Chris from the fate Mama had planned for us.

Although life seemed to be so out of control, beyond my ability to steer or navigate, the most invaluable thing to me, my sanity, was still with me. Yes, through it all, I had been kept, and just the counselor pointing that out to me made me feel stronger, able, and willing to continue dealing with life, even as tough as it had become.

That one day was my only session with the counselor. That fall semester, I was back on track at college. It was a good thing that I was able to remain focused and determined because the very next semester, in the Spring of '89, our court fight with Aunt Della ended with our house being ordered by the judge to be sold at a public auction.

Though very sad, we weren't shocked because for months we'd been expecting the news. Attorney Daniels had done a phenomenal job holding back the sale of our home of 14 years to give us time to grow up. If there's anything the court battle with Aunt Della had done, it had definitely matured us. Chris and I were not the same young boy and girl we had been just four years earlier. A greater form of resiliency had developed within us. I could see it in Chris, and he could see it in me.

We'd lost our battle, lost our home, and were given 30 days by the court order to vacate the premises.

The afternoon of the auction, I missed my classes so that I could go downtown and sit in on the auction. My professors understood and sympathetically gave me the okay to miss class that day. Being more curious than anything because we certainly didn't have the money to purchase our home ourselves, I just wanted to see what would become of it and who would buy it.

Wandering around the Family Law Center, I finally found the listing of homes slated to be sold at public auction for the day. Looking over the list, I discovered that our home had actually already been sold during the morning auction for the sum of $3,000! That was it. For a total of three thousand dollars, the home we'd been raised in now belonged to an investor from California! Our home was emotionally worth way more than that to us!

Attempting to bolt out of the court building before the tears began, I quickly headed for the exit door but didn't make it before the tears started to fall. All of the heartache and the hell Aunt Della had put us through reaped $3,000, none of which she or we would receive because every last cent of it went towards court fees! For her evil and vindictive ways, Aunt Della didn't get a brown penny!

Of course, we didn't get any money either from the sale of our home; though we never wanted the money, we just wanted to remain in our home.

Our fight with Aunt Della was finally over. At least now we looked forward to having peace, lives void of her presence. The matter was over, and so was, as far as we were concerned, our relationship with her.

Several of our friends came with trucks and willing hands to help us pack up and relocate. It took a week for us to move out.

Since Mama's death almost a year earlier, our home on the north side of town had been vacant. Chris and I really didn't want to move back there because of all of the memories, especially the bad ones. However, we did not really have any other option, so we decided to move back. Like our grandparents' home, it was also paid off.

Already knowing the neighbors and the area well did make our return easier, but our return also uncovered some wounds that had not healed. Soon, we were in a home we didn't want to be in and away from the people, even the neighbors, who'd helped keep us on course. Now, it was solely up to us to keep our lives together.

Giving Mama's clothing away, we rearranged and changed the house to our liking, with furniture and paint, so that it wouldn't resemble so much the home we'd grown up in. This time in our lives, we were initiating change and looking forward to things being different.

CHAPTER FIFTEEN

EMPTY PLACES

WINTER 1989

Continuing to work at the grocery store, I now had to travel across town because of our move. Just in time to handle the additional gas expense, I received a promotion at work, becoming an over-the-counter assistant drug manager. A little more income coming into the house was very much needed.

In her will, Mama left her car to Chris, which we shared until I was able to eventually get another vehicle after my last vehicle bit the dust. Sometimes, Chris would have to pick me up, or if I had the car, I'd have to pick him up. Whatever we had to do, we made it work.

Having very understanding managers who allowed me to work split shifts enabled me to schedule my college classes around work. Generally, I'd go to work in the morning for about four to five hours. Depending upon the day of the week, I'd usually then leave to attend class. Returning to work after my classes were over, I'd then work until about 9 p.m. Most days, that was my schedule.

The year we lost our home, I was so physically and emotionally drained that I took a break from school for a year. As much as I'd been afraid to do so in the past, I was at a point where I'd either take a break from school or quit school altogether. It was tougher than I thought it would be sitting out for a couple of semesters, but I promised myself that I would finish. I had to finish.

"Don't give up!" the words of so many who'd touched our lives echoed throughout my head and kept me focused on completing college and getting my degree. A desire to succeed had been planted and nurtured on the inside of me, and that caused me to continue to strive to make something of myself. Though many times I became tired, physically and mentally, I didn't want to give up. The struggle so often was on the inside of me, but I kept thinking about Daddy and my grandparents, and that continued to give me strength.

My past, however, was also a constant presence in my mind as it hovered over me. I didn't want it to guide my life, but it was hard to shake free from it. It absolutely affected me. Mama thought no good would come out of our lives, and proving her wrong became my purpose.

I remember reading a quote by W.E.B. Dubois that said, "Nothing is as powerful as the determination of a man or woman to rise."

I wanted my life to have meaning and purpose—*good* purpose. I wanted to be happy. But could I ever find the kind of happiness I desired? If so, in whom or *from* what?

There were so many empty places in my life—voids left by the deaths of those I loved. For a couple of years following moving back to the north side of town, Chris and I traveled a distance to still attend our same church because that's just what we'd been raised and taught to do.

It's honest to say that we went out of tradition. Many of Grandmother's friends had passed away, including the Pastor who'd been there for our family. Church just wasn't the same. Still, because of Grandmother's example, I wanted to go to Sunday services, believing that somehow that would make me a better person.

SEARCHING FOR LOVE IN ALL THE WRONG PLACES

Longing for 'true' love and lacking a close family connection led me to seek what I thought I needed through a relationship with a man.

Shortly before moving back to the north side, I met a guy who was a few years older than me, eleven to be exact. I was twenty-one, getting ready to turn twenty-two, and he was thirty-two. Our meeting was by chance one late evening. His car had veered onto the grassy side of the outside of our ditch. It had recently rained, and his car was good and stuck in about two inches of thick mud.

Chris and I were inside when we heard his tires spinning, burrowing the car even deeper into the mud. Going outside to see if we could help, we saw a man walking around the car, trying to figure out how to get unstuck.

Seeing us walking his way, he met us at the end of our driveway. He said he was trying to avoid hitting a dog in the street and swerved, ending up in the mud in front of our house.

Chris and I, trying to help him out, grabbed some boards from our garage and helped place them as far as we could between his tires and the mud. After gunning his engine and his car, of course, slinging mud all over, he finally got his vehicle out.

The man, Jonathan, was very grateful that we'd helped him. After the car was on the street again, the three of us remained outside and talked for a while.

To me, Jonathan was very attractive. With a very contagious smile, he was physically fit, having a nice, solid build. Being so much older than me was appealing. But he wasn't too much older than me because then that would just be gross.

We exchanged phone numbers, and after talking to Jonathan on the phone every day for a number of days, I began to fall for him, which led to our dating. The 'perfect' relationship is what I thought I'd have with him because we seemed to have so much in common.

Could he be the one for me? I wanted love, I needed love, and I really wanted Jonathan to be exactly what I was looking for and for me to be what he was looking for. We soon became intimate, and I thought, *surely our relationship will be long-lasting, leading to marriage,* because I've given him what I hadn't given anyone else, something I'd guarded for years. Even my friends thought I'd probably be the only one amongst us who'd actually remain pure until marriage.

Though I didn't have a lot of experience with boys or men, I hadn't felt about anyone else the way I felt about Jonathan. It didn't take long for me to learn that what we had was not a 'perfect relationship,' as Jonathan would soon break my heart.

Being that he was 11 years older than me, after a while, it became obvious that he and I had *less* in common than I previously thought and were going in different directions. He was 'comfortable' in his job working for a retirement home. Having to only take care of himself, he wasn't looking for a committed relationship or a lot of responsibility.

No doubt sensing my deepening feelings for him, he severed our 'boyfriend-girlfriend' relationship within just a few months of dating, saying he just wanted to be 'friends.' I was hurt and mad. How could he break up with me?! I'd maintained my virginity for 21 years, and *he knew that.* Why couldn't he have said in the beginning, "We should just be friends"?

My purity had been so special to me, and I wanted the one that I gave myself to, to be '*the one,*' the one I'd marry and stay with until death would we part.

Becoming upset with myself, I realized that I'd *moved too soon* with Jonathan. It was my fault, not his, because he didn't force me to do anything. Remembering the words of Grandmother, "Hindsight is 20/20", I knew that I should have waited for that special someone who wanted to share the rest of his life with me.

Living and learning from my mistakes is what I continued to do. As devastated as I was, there was nothing for me to do but get over Jonathan, learn from that experience, and move forward. Nothing could give me my virginity back.

Thinking back, just as Chris and I were entering puberty, those closest to us were leaving us, and so no one ever sat down with us and had a conversation about 'the birds and the bees'.

Certainly, we learned a lot from our friends, and whenever my high school teachers would get wind of some trouble going on with the students having to do with a relationship, they'd lecture us in the form of 'life stories.' They'd talk about the danger of losing our focus in school. They would also stress the pitfalls of promiscuity, including unwanted pregnancy and even the possibility of catching a sexually transmitted disease.

Certainly not wanting a baby at that point in life, especially not without being married, and never at all wanting a sexually transmitted disease of any kind, fear helped me take my mind off of Jonathan and get my focus back.

Refocusing on school also helped. At the university, I received a scholarship from a sorority, of which one of my Grandmother's friends was the Graduate Chapter President. The $1,000 scholarship really came in handy! Almost immediately I joined the sorority, impressed not only with their kindness towards me but also with their outreach work in the city.

Being particularly known as a sorority that is very community-oriented, it did a tremendous job of helping people in the community, especially mothers with small children. Enjoying doing anything connected with helping other people, I began to develop a passion for that kind of community involvement. Helping others was also kind of my way of giving back on behalf of all those, including strangers, who'd come to Chris' and my rescue.

Other than my sorority sisters, there weren't too many other people that I hung out with at the university. By pledging to a sorority, I learned the fine art of 'stepping.' My sorority sisters and I would practice at one of our houses for upcoming step competitions. I'd have to say we were pretty good.

Dancing was something I continued to enjoy, and learning to execute quick, precise dance movements involving just about every part of my body was very impressive to me. We'd sometimes step to compete with other sororities, and at other times, we'd step just to showcase our talents.

The more I hung out with my sorority sisters, the more I began to meet other people. Along with the socializing came partying and indulging in alcohol. Never partying at my own house, I chose to follow others to wherever a party was being held. That's what we did on the weekends: we danced and partied! It wasn't long before partying led to 'clubbing.' Thankfully, clubbing for me became something I ended almost as quickly as I started.

Most times, I didn't drink alcoholic beverages at the club because I was in what felt like a 'foreign' place, and I wanted to be fully sober and alert, being surrounded by so many strange men that I simply didn't trust. I'd heard too many stories about people slipping *something, a 'mickey,'* into drinks to make women *and* men vulnerable and more susceptible to being taken advantage of. Staying on my 'A' game was more important than ever when I was in a room full of more people that I didn't know than I knew.

Besides that, I'd watch some of my friends, in particular male friends, get wasted, and I wanted no part of that. Chris and I never hung out at clubs together, and I felt like a 'fish out of water' as soon as I walked through the doors. Realizing that I just didn't fit in, I no longer had a desire to go to clubs, and I was okay with that.

Still looking for love, I kept running into and dating the wrong men. I was experiencing firsthand much of what my high school teachers had talked about because I was looking for love, even my purpose in life, in all the wrong places, including in men. No one made me happy.

Soon, I began alienating myself from not only the parties but also from a lot of the people that I hung out with. Reverting to my life of going to school and work, I left the party scene altogether. By this time, Chris had formed his own friendships, and that was a good thing. Though we remained close, we spent less time together. I thought it was healthy in the beginning because all Chris knew was me, hanging with me and my friends, who also became his friends.

That was okay with me; however, after a while, I wanted him to be able to hang out with people other than me. It was important that he be able to make it on his own if something happened to me one day. After the life we'd lived, not much was off the table.

Moving on, I became somewhat of a loner, which wasn't all bad because I did know how to have fun by myself, and of course, the best part was that I didn't have to deal with drama. I did still, at times, hang out with a handful of good friends, some of whom I'd met on the job at the grocery store. One such friend became my best friend.

Ann, short for her actual name, was White and a couple of years younger than me. Ann's personality was so much like mine that, as friends, we were drawn to each other, clicking almost immediately. Though most folks didn't look twice at Ann and me when we were out in public together, on occasion, we were subjected to name-calling by complete strangers who, I guess, thought our hanging out together was the perfect cause for ridiculing, as they called us names like, "Salt and Pepper," or "Vanilla and Chocolate." Chalking it all up to ignorance, we didn't allow it to hinder our friendship at all.

I grew up in country music, went to an ethnically diverse high school, and worked with different races of people on my job. It meant nothing at all to me that Ann was White, and she didn't mind that I was Black. We were friends straight from the heart and would hang out as much as we could, sometimes just the two of us and, at other times, with other friends we'd met at work. Work brought me some of the best connections.

While still working at the grocery store, I waited on a guy who'd come in to have a key made for his mother. That was one of the many things we did in my department. 'Daniel' had the most genuine-looking smile. Nice smiles always seemed to catch my attention.

After I'd cut and given back the key to Daniel, he hung around and made small talk with me. It was obvious that he wanted to get to know me better. That afternoon, I talked and laughed with Daniel in between waiting on other customers. Hitting it off, we exchanged phone numbers, and Daniel wasted no time calling me. In fact, I'd barely made it home when my phone rang.

Daniel would call me every evening after I got off work and also visit me at my job during my lunch break. He then asked me out but wanted me to meet his family first. Though I liked him a lot, I did think that it was kind of quick to already be meeting his family.

At any rate, we were going out on a date to the movies, and he wanted me to come to his house earlier that evening so he could introduce me to everyone, and I agreed to it. Not having his own car at the time, Daniel drove his grandparents' car. He lived with them, and his mother stayed just around the block.

The night came, and I was a little nervous, not knowing what to expect. When I pulled into Daniel's driveway, he walked out.

'Gosh, he is so excited to see me. He must have been waiting at the door', I thought.

He'd been sitting in their den and saw my headlights through the patio door as I pulled into the driveway. We greeted each other with big smiles.

"You look so pretty, and girl, you sure smell good," he said, complimenting me and then taking me by the hand.

"Oh, thank you," I said, blushing a little, trying to make it seem like I really hadn't done anything out of the ordinary, though I had. I took a lot of time preparing myself for our date.

Escorting me to the front door, Daniel seemed to be the perfect gentleman. He was polite and respectful; he knew how to put a smile on my face.

After having my heart broken before, I was determined, however, not to allow Daniel to capture my heart so quickly, or at least not let him know he'd done so. Daniel would have to work for my love and my attention. My strength held up for about as long as it took me to meet his family because they immediately stole my heart!

His grandparents were in their late sixties, and his mother, who was also there, was in her forties. Tina, his cousin and his sister, because Daniel's grandparents adopted her after her mom died, had also dropped by. They all made me feel right at home. We sat around in their den, talking, laughing, and getting to know each other.

Daniel's grandparents, Mr. Daniel, Sr., after whom Daniel had been named, and Mrs. Sheila were very down-to-earth people. It was obvious from the look of their home and the nice boat parked out front that they had a little money, but thankfully, they were in no way snobbish.

Daniel's mom, Sheila, also carrying the first name of her mother, was just as nice.

Tina was a character and kept me laughing, sharing stories of Daniel when he was a little boy.

Was my search over? Had I finally found what I'd been looking for?

Daniel and I began spending more and more time together, and before long, outside of work and school, I could be found most days at his house, or he could be found at mine.

Chris took to Daniel right away but cautioned me to 'take it slow,' remembering the heartbreak I'd gone through. I was happy Chris was happy for me and wanted only the best for me. That's how we felt about each other; we only wanted the very best for each other. We'd been through so much together and felt like each other deserved to be happy one day.

Daniel's grandparents reminded me of mine, and the fact that they felt better about my life than I did and spoke good things into it gave me such an emotional boost. Hearing how their family also experienced tragedy, which led to the death of a loved one, I realized we had something in common, something that connected us.

Honestly, the one thing that worried me the most when I began dating was being accepted and not having my past, in particular, what my mother had done, held against me. Daniel's family accepted me—history and all!

All seemed well with Daniel, except for one huge issue: Daniel was unemployed. He'd been looking for a job after losing his last one but was having a hard time getting hired. Because of the obvious love and support of his family, I believed I could help Daniel get back on his feet. After all, my life had been far from perfect, and if anyone understood life setbacks, I did; and if anyone knew what it was like to need to be given a chance to succeed, I did.

Anyway, his being unemployed was about the only thing that I didn't like, and so to me, helping him was worth it, especially if we ended up marrying.

The days I was in school, Daniel assured me that he was going on interviews, or at least actually out looking for a job. He was an amazing cook, he was very sweet and respectful to me, and his family adored me, so I was hopeful, believing he would eventually become gainfully employed. After all, if we were going to get married, which after several months seemed to be the path we were heading down, he'd *have to* get a job; I wasn't compromising on that.

Daddy had been such a hard-working man and did what he needed to, and thought was best, in providing for our family up until his death. I'd already resolved in my head that I would not marry anyone who wasn't able or willing to take care of me as his wife and any children we had together.

Who couldn't see what a nice guy he was and what an asset he'd be to any company?

Well, finally, the 'truth' came out, and I discovered that Daniel had an addiction.

How did I miss that???

He was an intellectual, able to hold great conversations, a gifted artist; his work spoke for itself, a fabulous cook, making some of the best meals I'd ever eaten, a sweet, sensitive boyfriend, always willing to go the extra mile to make me smile. Daniel really did capture my heart, but what kind of life would I have with him? I was torn.

My mind said, 'Put your sneakers on and run for the hills!' but my heart said, 'You love him; you love his family. Maybe you can still help him.'

Going with my heart, I decided to stay with Daniel and work with his family to try to get him. Confessing that they didn't want me to know right away what Daniel was dealing with because they didn't want to run me away, his family said they thought I was good for him and just what he needed to get himself together.

Two of the **greatest** lessons I learned in life occurred during my relationship with Daniel, and they were:

1. 'You can't change a grown person if they have no true desire to change or help themselves,' and

2. 'You shouldn't look to other people to *complete* you or hold them responsible for making *you* happy'!

Those lessons came at a cost!

As hard as it was for me to break up with him because, by that time, we were engaged to be married, I walked away from our almost

3-year relationship because it just wasn't working or healthy. Daniel was devastated, and I was sad too, but I did what I knew was the right thing to do. I stopped selling myself short because I wanted better for my life. After everything I'd already been through, it made no sense for me to purposely choose a life I didn't want.

Although I felt as though a piece of my heart had been removed, I moved forward and didn't look back. In my darkest moment, a question came to me, and it was the answer to that question that helped me heal and move forward.

I pondered on this: 'Daniel thought I was good for him, and his family thought I was good for him, but was it also good for me?

The kind of relationship I sought was one in which both my partner and I were good for *each other*. Although there are no perfect people, including me, I believe there are people who are 'perfect for each other,' and that's what I wanted, nothing less. I wanted the person who was perfect for me and vice versa.

LOOKING FOR PURPOSE

Moving on with my life, I needed a fresh start, something that would help me realign my focus. Graduation was drawing near, and I was close to finally accomplishing my greatest goal in life up to that point!

I really wanted to get a job working in my actual field of medicine or science, and I was confident my degree would help me get my foot in the door somewhere, so I began searching the employment section of the newspaper, looking for a job.

One evening, after looking for about a month, I came across an advertisement for a job opening at a large, reputable reference laboratory in town, and immediately got excited, thinking, 'What a wonderful change this would be for me!'

After looking over the job requirements in the newspaper, I thought I had a pretty good chance until I walked into their Human Resources Department to fill out the application and realized people much more qualified than me were applying for the same position. Though there was more than one slot available, there were far more applicants than available positions.

After interviewing with one of the head guys in charge of the laboratory, I was told to come back at night for an additional interview with *four* more people. Wow, that was a lot of folks to have to interview with for a lab job. It felt like I was trying to secure some top security job with the federal government. The application was extensive, and the interviews even more so, but finally, after interviewing with the last person, I was offered the position! Ecstatic, I immediately accepted the job!

As I was introduced to those with whom I'd be working on the third shift from 12 midnight to 8 am, I realized I had the least amount of medical/science background and work experience of them all, including those who had been recently hired on. While many of them had previously worked for companies like Dow Chemical, Brown and Root, etc., I, upon being asked where I'd worked prior to coming here, would very honestly reply, "Kroger."

"Kroger? Is that an oil company?" They would ask, surprised at my answer.

"No, Kroger, the grocery store," I said, smiling.

It was surprising to all of them, and even to me that I got the job, but I took it all in with humility, just glad that it worked out in my favor.

After my initial training and three months of probation, I settled into my job, really enjoying what I was doing. Working nights did take some adjusting. In three months, I was awarded "Employee of the Month." I felt like my life was moving in the right direction!

Also, continuing to work full-time days at Kroger kept me busy, and that helped keep me disciplined and out of trouble. Grandmother's words would come echoing in from time to time, "An idle mind is the devil's workshop."

Though I wasn't an overly religious person, I did know there was absolutely some truth to that. I was grateful that though I hadn't finished my studies, the door had still been opened for me to work at the laboratory. Giving the managers my word that I would finish college, I made good on my vow. Less than a year after starting my job at the lab, I finally received my degree!

One of my greatest regrets in life is not walking across the stage during my commencement exercises. In fact, I didn't even go to my graduation. I wish I had given myself that moment.

In thinking about all that had occurred in the pursuit of my college degree and all else that I had been through, I just saw myself breaking down on stage, being overcome with emotion. I thought, 'No one would really understand my tears or my joy without really knowing my story,' and so I chose to spare everyone.

Though I did rob myself of the opportunity to celebrate publicly the hard work, sweat, tears, and sleepless nights I endured to get to that moment, I did cry alone, after which I celebrated!

Chris and I lived our own separate lives, and soon after graduating, I moved out and into an apartment that was closer to the lab.

Each night, I had to travel so far across town to get to work, and each morning, after getting off, I would struggle with being so drowsy to make it back home safely. Many mornings, for brief seconds, my eyes would close on their own. That scared me so badly because I realized that it would only take a second for me to leave my lane and crash into another car. I knew that something had to change before I hurt myself or someone else driving in the early morning hours.

Thankfully, by this time, both Chris and I were gainfully employed, and Chris would be just fine living by himself. Having attended a trade school, Chris secured a good job with a geology company and was doing very well. He made me so proud! Not once did I ever have to bail him out of jail or get him out of any kind of serious trouble. As a grown man, he went to work and was learning to support himself.

Because I was working two jobs, I was able to continue to help pay bills at home. We were both in agreement with the arrangement. One thing we'd learned from early on was that life is short and that our relationship was far more important than money or material things.

From time to time, we had our differences, but we never allowed any disagreement to break our bond of love. We would do what we needed to do to keep our bond as friction-free as possible.

Continuing to remain close even after I moved out, we purchased our first new vehicles together. I bought a 1993 Toyota Corolla, and Chris purchased a 1993 Toyota Tercel. How awesome it felt to drive out of the car dealership that same day together in our brand-new cars! We were so excited about our new rides and that things seemed to finally be looking up for us!

Because I hadn't found the love of my life and was beginning to doubt that I ever would, my attention shifted to wanting a child. Now having the finances to support one and willing to settle for one without being married, I wanted something of my own to love and to love me back.

In my mind, I thought, *'Yes, I know Grandmother would be dead set against what I wanted and would even interject God into the conversation, but I wanted what I wanted.'*

I was determined to do things my way, and I found myself continuing to *fail* time and time again. *Failing* to find a good man, *failing* to secure the kind of true love I'd sought after and had even compromised myself for. I realized how far I had deviated from the foundation my daddy and grandparents, especially my grandmother, had laid. I was ashamed.

I still had some good friends and had a new job as I acquired a position working the first shift for a government agency, which put my science degree to good use. By that time, I'd also purchased my second brand new vehicle, a 1995 2-door Toyota Sport Coupe.

Ironically, over time, the more things I obtained, the more things I *needed* to feel 'good' about life; good feelings seemed always short-lived. I had a good job, money, and possessions, but I still felt so *unsatisfied* and unfulfilled on the inside.

The few close friends I had were great, but even those friendships couldn't take away the feelings of loneliness I quietly dealt with. Though I had my physical health, on the inside, I was crumbling emotionally. Having mood swings, vacillating between happiness one day and then anger and bitterness, and being mad at the world the next only caused even more instability.

At first, I tried to justify to myself how I had been living, how it wasn't my fault, and how none of it would have happened if the people that I loved had still been around. However, in the end, I had to face the truth—I'd made bad decisions and bad choices and had drifted away, far away, from my roots.

Grandmother was a faithful woman of God and did her best to instill that faith in Chris and me, but because God took those closest to us from us, I was very bitter and not interested in doing things 'God's way.' Revisiting the lessons of Grandmother for the first time in years,

I decided to try to do things differently and stop doing everything my way. It hadn't worked for me.

Grandmother's teachings were back with me, and so was the conviction that came with my doing the wrong thing. I judged myself.

'I'll never get this right,' I thought to myself.

Though it had been a while, I prayed, feeling desperate for 'that something' I needed to complete me. I didn't know if I was calling on God to help me or just doing so because I was feeling sorry for myself.

As it turns out, that moment was the beginning of a turn-around in my life. I couldn't change my life by myself; I knew I needed help. While it looked good on the outside, my life was so messed up emotionally, and I needed the type of intervention that Grandmother talked about. I'd steered off the path, but I felt like there was still a small chance that I could make it back to my senses, back to what I'd been taught, the way I'd been raised, back to the things I'd for too long left.

It was more evident than ever before that I needed the God Grandmother had placed so much faith and hope in. Church had become an occasional event for me. Discouraged and angry at God for a long time because He'd taken people from me who meant so much and left Chris and me the one that gave us the most grief, I figured *attending* Church hadn't made a difference in how things turned out.

Now, I wasn't so sure as I looked at my life. A scarred childhood seemed to flow right over into my adult life. The only hope I had at that point was to try to do something worthy of living. George hadn't been given that opportunity, and I eventually realized how I was wasting mine.

One of my 'aha' moments came as I realized that moving on in life didn't mean burying the past and pretending that it never happened. It meant being able to come to terms with the things that had happened in my life and vowing to do whatever was necessary to make my life better.

Yes, I'm sure that's what Grandmother would say anyway.

I couldn't change my genealogy. I couldn't change my history. But I did have some control over who I would become because of it.

Grandmother taught me and Chris that God brought us into this world for a reason, a purpose. It wasn't by accident that we were still here. That had to mean that there was still some purpose for my life. Just maybe Grandmother was right in her thinking that God still had something special for Chris and me to do. If so, I hoped that it was more than what I was already doing.

CHAPTER SIXTEEN

NOT FORSAKEN

Forgiveness- 'Something we might not always want to give, but certainly something we all, at some point, will stand in need of.'

The year that we lost our home at public auction, to my great displeasure, Aunt Della began shopping at the same grocery store at which I worked.

Almost gasping the first time I saw her walk through the front entrance, I thought to myself, 'What the…!' This woman has some kind of nerve!' What was she doing at my place of employment, *knowing* that it was *my* place of employment?!

Not only was it not close to her home, but she passed up several other stores, including one store that was the same chain as the one for which I worked, getting to my store.

She started coming in so frequently, seeming to line her visits up with my workdays and times. Was she trying to provoke me to hurt her? Why wouldn't she just LEAVE US ALONE!?

Losing our home was like losing the last thing we'd been able to hold on to since Daddy and our grandparents had passed. Now that it had been taken from us, what was left for her to do to us?

Bad words began to spew out of my mouth, under my breath.

Whenever I knew she was in the store, I'd drop whatever I was doing, if possible, and head straight for the inventory area in the back of the store so that we wouldn't 'accidentally' bump into each other.

It was bad enough we had to put up with seeing her at court or even noticing her driving down the street when we were still living in our home, but to now have to tolerate seeing her at my job, where I spent so much of my time, was just too much!

Daddy had taught us to still love her, but that was something I could no longer do. I couldn't bring myself to hurt her either, so the only thing I could do to rid her out of my life was to avoid being around her or running into her.

That worked for only a little while, as she then really crossed the line, beginning to ask my coworkers about me because she'd no longer see me when she came in to shop. Why was she looking for me? I had absolutely nothing, *nothing* nice to say to her!

Eventually, I got tired of running away every time she came into the store, so I began staying out on the floor and just ignoring her whenever she passed my way. And what an effort she seemed to make to intentionally pass by me and get my attention.

After a few months of continuing to come into the store, she spoke to me one day, only saying "Hi."

Only because I remembered how Daddy said to be 'respectful,' I said 'Hi' back, without smiling, making very little eye contact. I didn't have to look up. I sensed her presence.

After a month or so of that, she then 'pushed the card' even more and began to attempt to hold short conversations with me. As painful as it was even to open my mouth and speak to her, I continued to be respectful, as Daddy taught me, but I kept the conversation to a bare minimum. It made my chest hurt just to communicate with her.

Was she trying to 'brush under the rug' everything that had happened as if what she'd done was insignificant? She still had her home, and not much had changed for her, while our lives, on the other hand, had been turned completely upside down.

I asked one of my coworkers, who also happened to attend the same church as my aunt, "Why is she coming into this store? Why can't or won't she shop somewhere else?" I was very frustrated.

My coworker then told me something that took me by surprise.

She said, "Cheryl, she's very sorry for what she did to you all, but she doesn't know how to say it. That's why she keeps coming in here. She's trying to make up with you guys and let you know how sorry she is for what she did. She wants you to forgive her."

"Huh, forgive her?" I snorted, rolling my eyes, not knowing how to respond to my coworker.

'If there was one person on the face of the earth who didn't deserve forgiveness, it was Aunt Della,' I thought to myself.

Regardless of the reasons for my aunt's behavior towards us, whether it arose out of bereavement because of Grandmother's death, or jealousy towards us because of all the attention we'd received following our family tragedy, or whether she did what she did because she was just that mean and heartless, being able to forgive her seemed to be an impossibility for me.

How in the world could I forgive someone who'd hurt me so deeply? Someone we should have been able to depend on? I hadn't even considered such a thing before my coworker told me that's what was going on. She was *seeking* forgiveness. Forgiveness*???*

Perhaps the best thing for us to do was to make a greater effort at never crossing paths again, and maybe then I could heal, without disruption from her, and move forward.

'Yeah…' I thought to myself, 'I guess it would be hard to find the right words after doing what she did.'

How can you say, 'I'm sorry for putting my foot through your face when you were already down'? How do you apologize for treating your own family, kids at that, worse than most folks treat a stranger? What words can you offer that will help mend all of the wounds you personally caused and, at times, reopened again and again?

Forgiveness???

No. There would be no forgiveness. My mind was made up. I wouldn't, just *couldn't*, let go of all that had happened over the course of time. It was too hard to do.

Every time I thought about what she put us through, anger rose within me. I couldn't let go of how 'dirty' she'd treated us, and the worst part was that we hadn't *deserved* any of it. How could a woman who helped take care of us turn so cold and callous towards us? Instead of being there for us after our dad, her own brother, died, she made our lives miserable.

Our lives became a living hell, and at the time, she really seemed to be enjoying what she was doing to us. Not one time did I see any sign of remorse or regret on her part. I remembered how she'd walk down the courthouse hallway nestled between her two attorneys most of the time, with her nose up in the air, only looking our way to send the message through facial expressions that 'she was going to win.'

Grandmother taught us that there were two ways to do anything: a right way and a wrong way. What she wanted to accomplish, making sure her part in our home was secure, may have been right to do, but she did it all the wrong way.

That night, driving home, I thought about what my co-worker had shared with me, but still, I couldn't find it in my heart to even consider forgiving my aunt.

As more and more time passed, it became a little easier to look at her without wishing she was dead. Though Chris didn't see her, just hearing my accounts of her visits to the store kept him in the loop, and initially, he was as upset about it as I was.

Aunt Della began bringing me little tokens, items like porcelain dolls, and also items to pass along to Chris. In her sixties, by this time, Aunt Della really was *trying* to make amends.

Again, out of not wanting to be disrespectful, I accepted the gifts. The fact that we now began having small conversations when she'd come in to shop led to my being able to accept the gifts.

Though I didn't hate her quite as much as I did before, I was still having such a difficult time putting the past behind me. Over the course of the next five years, Aunt Della continued coming to my job until 1994, when I retired from Kroger, deciding to work only one job, that being my job with the local county government.

We exchanged phone numbers at her insistence once she found out that I would no longer be working at the grocery store. Surprisingly, we remained in touch, talking to each other at least once a month.

During the next couple of years, my life seemed to be at a standstill. At least things weren't getting worse, for which I was thankful. My life was comprised of work, a lot of sleeping, and more drinking by myself, mostly on the weekends.

Attending church more than I had for some years, I started going to a Methodist church across town. It wasn't the same one I'd grown up in, but ironically, the pastor of the church was also a product of Grandmother's church. There were many more young people at his church than the church we'd attended with Grandmother while growing up, and it was large enough for me to go and *get lost in the crowd.*

Being at that point where I felt God tugging at my heart, but not wanting to commit myself, I thought it might be good for me to go to a large church where no one knew me or my story and where I could slip in and out easily without being noticed. I was searching for something, but I wasn't sure what.

The pastor had a reputation, which preceded him, for being a sound, engaging preacher, and the church's music department was recognized throughout Houston and beyond, being led by well-known, established gospel music recording artists.

Good preaching, good music, and a place where no one knew me. It seemed like a good fit for me.

Though the pastor and I were raised in the same church, he was quite a few years older than me, and the chance of him remembering me, *I thought,* would be slim to none.

Even though I didn't go to church every Sunday, I was no longer what many referred to as a C.E.M. Christian; that is, one who only went to church for *C*hristmas, *E*aster, and *M*other's Day. My life was still riddled with issues of the past, but the more I at least began going to church, the more hope I began to have that there was a chance that life would get better. That's one of the things Grandmother believed, and some 14 years later, I was on a path hoping that what she said, what she believed, would materialize for me and for Chris.

Towards the end of 1997, there were many advertisements and flyers inviting all to come to the church's upcoming New Year's Eve Celebration. The service would be what was known as 'Watch Night,' which would consist of a lot of preaching and singing up until the clock struck midnight, at which time we'd all welcome in the New Year together. There was nothing else for me to do, no one for me to hang out with, so I decided to go.

One thing that caught my attention was the announcement of a six-week fast and prayer the church would be going on together as a church family. I listened intently as the pastor and others talked about issues directly related to the purpose of the Fast and Prayer. The very questions I'd mulled over most of my life were posed as if Heaven was sending me a message:

'Why are you here?'

Yes, that was for me! I had no clue as to why I was *still* here and was at a point in my life where I desperately wanted and needed to know.

'Do you need to draw closer to God?'

I was pretty sure that was me too. My thinking was, 'I'm still here, and maybe if I know more about God, maybe I'll find His reasoning for allowing so many bad things to happen to my family and me.' Grandmother had always talked about how *good* God was, but I didn't understand why. He hadn't been that *good* to me and Chris over the years.

I had so many questions that I wanted answered, and the way the pastor was talking, if I went on the fast and prayer, I just might get the answers I'd been looking for.

'How very odd,' I thought.

For so long, He seemed to be silent, but that night, I was sure God was speaking to me. The details of the fast and prayer were explained. We were to receive journals to write in during the fast and prayer. All of the specifics of fasting were explained, as well as what it meant to pray and how to pray with the right attitude.

I hadn't talked to God in some time. In fact, the last time I remembered saying anything to God, other than when I would bless my food, was when I prayed, asking Him to make a way for me to continue going to school, and He *did* answer that prayer.

The congregation seemed to be very excited about the fast and prayer. Each day, we would pray for a specific area, always putting others before ourselves. I thought that might delay my prayers getting answered because I was so anxious to hear from God right away—if He had anything to say to me. Nevertheless, I was willing to be patient and was determined to follow the fast and prayer guidelines.

This would be the first time I'd ever fasted. To give up food so that I could draw closer to God was a very new principle for me, but the pastors showed us in the bible that sometimes fasting and prayer would change things that *prayer alone wouldn't*. Believing what the pastors said, I was convinced enough to try it.

The Bible was nothing new to me since Grandmother kept one in just about every room of our home and would read hers aloud often, so I knew something of substance had to be in there. However, rarely picking up the bible to read outside of church service, I honestly wasn't looking forward to studying the Word, mainly because it seemed so difficult to understand. However, again, I was willing to try it. Given the shape my life was in, I was willing to try just about anything to get my questions answered and hopefully make my life better.

Along with expecting to finally hear something from God, I was just as excited to be a part of something the church at large was doing.

It had been a while since I'd been in church on a regular basis, and the fast and prayer made me feel like I was a part of something good, though I still had my *reservations* about really getting involved in church. Unlike so many others, I wasn't there yet.

The fast and prayer began a month into the New Year. Each day, I skipped breakfast, prayed, and wrote in my prayer journal. My journal was my personal diary, for my eyes and God's eyes only; that's what we were told.

In the beginning, I didn't pray my own personal prayers. To me, the fast and prayer was like a class assignment that I needed to complete. I didn't put much sincere thought into it, though I did still want answers from God. During the first four weeks of the Fast and Prayer, I didn't feel any different and hadn't received any special message from God like I was hoping to. Of course, I wasn't sure what or how I was supposed to feel since this was my first time ever doing this.

No longer being skinny at all, I was happy I'd lost weight, but I was hoping that wouldn't be all I experienced. One more week passed, and I did notice one thing different. I started having a greater desire to be in church, and in fact, I would not allow anything to cause me to miss Sunday service. The pastors would always encourage us regarding the Fast and Prayer and would give me what I needed to continue with it. In addition to that, something just compelled me to want to be there.

Not that long ago, I was intentionally sitting in the back of the church, but now, hiding in the crowd and not being seen was no longer my agenda as I began moving closer to the front. I even began engaging in small conversations with those around me.

For me, that was a huge change! For the first time since the day I received that scholarship, out of the blue, I felt like God was looking at me, paying attention to me. It felt like God was there—that He was right there with me.

It could've had something to do with the fact that my prayers, unlike the ones at the beginning of the Fast and Prayer, became more sincere and heartfelt. I began to pray to God openly and honestly as if I was sitting in front of Him and we were having a conversation.

By the time the last week of the Fast and Prayer was just about to end, I was filled with a greater expectation than in the onset that something good really would come out of it!

The Night I Met Jesus

An 'End of the Fast Revival' had been scheduled to close out the six-week fast and prayer and to, as the pastors put it, "celebrate all that God had done and would do."

Looking forward to the service that night, I made it to the sanctuary before the services started and sat up close to the front.

A female evangelist from out of town had been selected to give the message for the night. I hadn't heard many female preachers besides my female pastor and an associate pastor at our church, and I was really looking forward to *something out of the norm* happening that night.

I never realized just how 'out of the norm' that night would be for me.

Many good things had been said about the revivalist, and I, along with the rest of the people, was excited as she finally took center stage. I had no idea what I was in for. The Evangelist delivered a sermon that not only touched my heart but *changed* my life!

I was amazed, even captivated, as she spoke very candidly about some of the very things that were still impacting my life. The Word got my undivided attention!

For so long, I'd disregarded what pleased God, thinking that God obviously wasn't concerned about me, including how I lived. He wasn't paying attention to me, my life, or what was going on in our family.

For the first time, I was sincerely sorry for not living my life God's way. Grandmother had taught us a lot about living 'good' lives for God. My goal for so long had been to please man—my daddy, my grandparents, our neighbors, and to even please myself. I was finally getting it, and it was a true BREAKTHROUGH for me!

If I had lived to please God, as Grandmother was trying to teach us to do, maybe my life wouldn't have been so difficult or at least would have been easier to bear. For the first time, I owned my mistakes, even the ones I didn't want to ever think about, *and* the consequences they brought. Likely, the deaths in my family, and maybe even the bad things, would have still occurred, but how I handled and processed it all would have been different had I had a closer relationship with God. I really believed that to be the case.

The minister helped me realize that God hadn't left me at all. I'd left Him.

I understood that my being convinced that my life had been cursed and that God had turned His back on us caused *me* to *disconnect* from Him. It was my thinking; it wasn't what God had done. The truth is I rebelled because I was angry and didn't care how God would perceive how I was living because I didn't think anything about my life mattered to Him anyway.

My emotions were so high that night; the anger, bitterness, and even resentment I'd had towards God and those at the center of my hurts, like Aunt Della and even my mother, were fading.

That night, Jesus met me exactly where I was—bruised, wounded, shattered, and He began to heal my heart and my mind!

I know God was healing me from deep within of the pain I'd carried for many years.

Already on the verge of tears after the sermon, I sat there as the Evangelist gave an altar call. She sent out a general call for all those who needed prayer. I needed prayer.

I was experiencing feelings I'd never had before about God and about my life. I'd been so bitter, so angry, so unforgiving, not just towards man but also towards God, but now my heart had softened, and the burdens I'd carried for so long were leaving. The things I'd worried so much about in life seemed of little importance now. My priorities were already changing too.

In fact, that night, my entire life changed!

Also, for the first time, feeling free from the shame of our family tragedy, I realized, from the Word given, that all I'd been through was allowed to happen 'on purpose' because it was all a part of who God was making, molding, and shaping me to become! That counselor some years earlier told me that I was a survivor and that 'something' had been keeping me all those years.

That night, I met Jesus in a very real sense and realized that He, all along, had been keeping me and Chris.

Tears rolled down my face as I stood up to go up front for prayer. I *wasn't* afraid. I *wasn't* ashamed. I knew I needed to surrender and give my life to Jesus, and I was ready. What I'd been doing since Daddy and the rest of my family had died hadn't given me freedom. However, that night, my life was coming full circle.

The peace, joy, and fulfillment I'd enjoyed as a very young girl before the tragedy were coming back, but in a much greater way.

Earlier in my life, before life changed for us all, I was surrounded by people that I knew loved me, and I was excited just to wake up every day.

That night in March of 1998, though I was 31, I felt like a kid again, free from the emotions that had plagued me for so long, and now looking forward to waking up every morning, having newfound joy just to still be alive!

Though the church was full, I walked up front, feeling as though it was just me, the preacher, and God.

Slowly climbing the steps leading up to the stage where the minister was waiting for me, I felt an overwhelming Presence I'd never experienced before. I felt God all over me, and it was the most beautiful, calming, peaceful, yet joyful feeling I'd ever had!

After the minister touched me and laid her hands on my head, and prayed for me, I walked away dazed, as I heard someone quoting a scripture: "If any man be in Christ, he is a new creature; old things have passed away, behold, all things become new."

That's exactly how I felt, NEW…BRAND NEW, as if my life was starting all over again! A miracle happened for me that night, as Jesus was making me whole again.

I'd hear others talk about how God had changed their lives, but I thought it really had no relevance to my life, and I could only listen but not relate until that night. Finally, my life was starting to make sense, and I was so glad about it! God had been working on me all those years. I just didn't know it. He'd been preparing me for a new life in Him!

I had little knowledge about salvation or about God's Spirit. That night, I received the message that Christ had died for every sin I'd already or ever would commit, and my acknowledgment of that and acceptance of what He did for me changed who I was!

Almost simultaneously, while emptying me of all those things that had held me captive for so many years, God was filling me with the love, kindness, forgiveness, grace, mercy, joy, and peace I needed. That night, I forgave my mother, I forgave my aunt, and I forgave myself for the things I'd done, for the mistakes I'd made, and the pain that I'd brought upon myself. That night, I was delivered from the very 'wrong' way I viewed God.

For nearly half of my lifetime, I'd believed God didn't love me and that He'd abandoned me, but on the night of my salvation, Jesus took me back over my life, almost as though He was showing me a movie of my life, and HE showed me that He had been with me, with Chris, the entire time! God had been there all along. HE'D NEVER LEFT.

Because of faith, I could now look back and see His Footprints all over my life. God had NOT forsaken us—not my mother, not my family, and not me. Not once had He stopped loving us, providing for us, protecting us, keeping us. Those times when we could have been harmed physically, even going back to the day Mama broke down and killed George, it was God who protected Chris, Daddy, and me.

Looking back, I could see that we never went hungry, without clothes or a place to stay because God always provided, even sending complete strangers our way to help us. What I couldn't see before, I could see now. I remembered how my managers did for me what many others weren't aware of, flexing my schedule so that I could both work and go to school. That was God working things out for me!

When I didn't want to live after Daddy died, God gave me a reason to live; He gave me Chris to look after. Though I did not know the full details regarding my purpose in life, for sure that night, I knew that I *did* have a purpose and that my life had meaning.

Except for Chris, up to that point, nothing in life made me feel like life had been worth living. I just survived to take care of Chris and be there for him, but God wanted me to do more than survive; it was time for me to 'Live with Purpose on Purpose,' as He had created me to do.

I was expecting to just have a few questions answered, but God did so much more! In that one night, His embrace loved my hurt away, and I felt the forgiveness of God at the center of my heart, and that brought a peace I hadn't been able to experience.

After walking towards the other end of the stage and down the stairs, I made it back to my seat, where I lay down, unable to sit upright. God filled me with His Spirit; I'd never experienced anything like that before.

Jesus waited for me, and I was ever so grateful for that!

I no longer saw myself as the girl whose mother wanted to kill her, but rather as a grown woman who was overcoming, filled with purpose, and destined to do great things in life!

Not having much physical strength, I just lay there on the pew, not caring who may have been watching or staring at me. The glory of the Lord was so intense, deeply intimate, and absolutely liberating. God was with me, working on me, healing and restoring me!

I felt His Spirit, His Presence, and I understood at that moment why Grandmother had the depth of faith and love for God that she'd had all those years.

That night, I met and accepted Jesus as my Lord and Savior, and it turned out to be the best night of my life!

Christ was restoring me to wholeness again, and I made the decision to stop allowing my past to negatively define who I was and who I would become.

My life, the days, weeks, months, and even years to follow would be a sheer 'work in progress' as I learned to surrender more and more control of my life to the One who created it and gave it Purpose and Meaning.

BEAUTY FOR ASHES

MENDING HEARTS

It seems that *one* of the first things on God's agenda was reconciling me and Chris with Aunt Della.

Overwhelming evidence that God had truly touched my heart was the fact that, for the first time since the entire saga with our aunt began, I had more than just tolerance for her. I had love for her again. For me to feel that way after so much had gone on was nothing less than amazing, nothing less than God's intervention!

A little shy of 10 years after losing our home, I wanted Aunt Della to be a part of my life, and so I began personally reaching out to her more, now readily accepting her efforts to make amends. I believe the sudden, dramatic change of heart on my part had to have even taken her by surprise. Chris and I had remained respectful towards her, but it was obvious that we still held what she put us through against her. Now, however, I wanted us to start over and have a much better relationship this time. I'd shared with Chris my newfound life in Christ and told him how I wanted to make peace with Aunt Della.

Chris had always been a caring and compassionate young man despite all the ordeals we'd suffered, and he agreed with me that we should just forgive Aunt Della and move forward. After all, she was old, and we weren't getting any younger ourselves, and the best thing for all of us was to put it all behind us.

GOD AT WORK

Chris and I began dropping by Aunt Della's house for brief visits, which seemed to make her very happy. Aunt Della owned two dogs and a cat, and whenever we'd stop by, she'd talk to her pets in a baby voice, telling them how glad she was that we'd come to see her and them. We, of course, thought it was a bit hilarious, but it was a good way to really break the ice.

A little more time passed, and Chris and I began picking Aunt Della up on Sundays after church and taking her out to eat. She enjoyed soul food, so we would take her to a family soul food restaurant near the edge of downtown. Sometimes, we'd go there for lunch and, at other times, for dinner. The times we shared out and about with her were, for the most part, good times.

On occasion, we would see a side of her, however, that we didn't care for. One such time occurred while eating out at a restaurant: Aunt Della was very dissatisfied with her meal. The food was generally very tasty, though the service wasn't always fast, with there being too many customers for the few staff.

Aunt Della began complaining about the taste of her dinner, and I was a little taken back by how rude she turned in an instant. After all, we were paying for the meal, and all she had to do was alert the management that there was a problem. Instead, she made a scene and complained more than she expressed her thanks to us for taking her to dinner.

That was the last dinner we took her to for a little while, and I was close to abandoning my mission, but because the Lord had given me a forgiving heart, I continued to call and check on Aunt Della. Within a couple of weeks, we were back to visiting her.

One late evening, we drove across town to check on her. Pulling into the driveway, we found her meandering around her front yard. The grass was badly overgrown, and she said she'd had a hard time finding someone to cut it.

Believing it was the right thing to do, we volunteered to cut both her back and front yards. This time, she showed Chris and me her deep gratitude. We could tell that she was appreciative and thrilled that we were willing to take care of her yard for her.

Aunt Della's neighbors were very curious the first time they saw us at our aunt's house visiting. It was surprising to them to see us together again in a friendly and amicable way. The court battle had been so nasty, and I don't think Aunt Della even shared with them that we were talking again.

I certainly understood their bewilderment and would only say, "It's God," whenever they asked why we would have anything to do with her—and they did ask.

Unable to really explain my restored love and compassion for her, I put it all on God for having changed my heart. **God was rebuilding our love and our relationship.**

The more we visited Aunt Della, the more at ease she became with us because I'm sure in the beginning, she probably questioned our motives, maybe believing we were up to 'no good.' Nonetheless, time showed her our intentions were genuine and that we had no hidden motive or agenda. If I'd done someone the way she did us, and that person *wanted* to be around me, I'd have my suspicions too.

Eventually, the occasional visits and dinner outings made Aunt Della comfortable enough to ask us if we would, from time to time, take her grocery shopping. Aunt Della didn't have a car anymore and would either have to catch the bus or get someone to take her to the store. We didn't have a problem with her request, so we immediately arranged to make it happen.

From the outset, we quickly realized that going shopping with Aunt Della required a whole lot of **patience**! Right away, I understood why she never seemed to get anywhere on time and even why when Grandmother was living, she would complain about how long Aunt Della would stay in the store. My goodness!

I had to say a prayer or two while shopping with her because we'd spend close to two hours picking up just a few items.

Initially, I found it amusing that she would do things like shake the jars of jelly and vegetables and listen to them to try to determine how much liquid was inside. Our aunt was like some food inspector or detective. At the Dairy department, she'd have to examine *every* egg in the carton very closely. She'd pick up each egg, one at a time, and carefully look it over before placing it back into its spot very carefully, and then proceed to the next one.

I thought to myself, 'You've got to be kidding! Is there a hidden camera somewhere?'

Trying to remember that Aunt Della, with declining health, was getting up in age, close to 65 years of age, I did my best not to become agitated. Some days, I succeeded. On other days, I failed miserably. Because I would keep my feelings bottled up, I would many times leave her house after having dropped her back off with a splitting headache. Remembering the goal was to reconcile with Aunt Della, I just bit my tongue and kept my feelings to myself.

We'd sometimes stay with her for a little while after shopping. Ironically, the inside of her house looked nothing like what I would expect from someone who was so attentive to how eggs looked. While her home was by no means nasty, it was cluttered from floor to ceiling! Aunt Della was a hoarder.

In fact, her problem was so severe that she had to sleep in her living room in a recliner because her beds were piled high, literally from the bed to close to the ceiling fan, with all kinds of stuff! Her bed looked like a huge garage sale! Anything from curtains, underwear, shoes, bed linens, shower rods, boxes of crystal glasses, and so much more in between littered her entire bed. Most of the items still had tags on them, and her other two beds were piled high with the same kind of stuff.

Not much better, the floors were covered with still more items, including canned goods of vegetables stacked high in what used to be a dining room. A trail literally ran from the kitchen through the living room, then divided off into each of the three bedrooms and the bathroom. **I'd never seen anything like it.** I didn't know how she even managed to get to the bathtub to bathe because cleaning supplies, many different kinds, were lined up three rows deep in front of the bathtub.

It took my breath away, and not in a good way, the first time I saw the inside of her home following our reuniting.

Aunt Della was a shopaholic, and she had no room for any of the 'overflow' of stuff. She'd always been a 'packrat,' but what we saw wasn't just someone who liked to collect things or who didn't like to throw anything away. Oh no, what we saw was evidence of a woman with a problem, a shopping addiction.

One of the first things that came to my mind was that if there was ever a fire in her home, there was no way she'd be able to make it out. Thank God the plan to start a fire in her home years back was squashed because, if her house looked like this back then, she would have surely perished in the fire. I really felt sorry for her. She really was sick and didn't realize it.

Daddy was right. Grandmother's death had taken a toll on Aunt Della. She obviously hadn't been able to deal with it appropriately, trying to cope by shopping.

From 1998 to 1999, our relationship grew stronger and closer than it had been in many years. Early one Thursday evening in May of 1999, I called Aunt Della, and we talked for a few minutes on the phone. She was preparing to go to a banquet being held at her church that evening, and we spent the majority of our conversation discussing what she should wear.

"Cheryl, I have a blue suit and a red dress, and I can't decide which one to wear. The colors for the banquet are red and blue," I remember her saying.

"Well, describe them to me, and I'll see if I can help you decide," I replied, listening to the details as she described her outfits.

We decided that she should wear the red dress. Though Aunt Della kept an extremely untidy house, whenever she had to go to a special event, she'd leave her home looking like a million bucks. It was so puzzling to me, but that's just the way she was. She'd be dressed from head to toe, with a nice fancy hat, coordinating outfit, and shoes and purse to match. Looking a lot like Grandmother, Aunt Della was a very attractive lady and could have even been a model in her younger days.

We ended our conversation so she could finish getting ready for the banquet.

Friday came, and then Saturday, and I hadn't yet heard from Aunt Della. I just knew she'd call me and tell me all about the banquet. Our relationship had grown to the point that we would hold conversations like 'girlfriends.'

Late Sunday evening, I received a phone call from a hospital. Aunt Della had suffered a massive stroke sometime during the very evening she and I last talked!

Her neighbors, accustomed to seeing her outside moving about in the yard, messing with her plants, hadn't seen her for a couple of days and became concerned. They called the police to do a welfare check. The police, after not getting a response but seeing no signs of trouble, left. They were called back out on Sunday. This time, after the police arrived, they made their way into her home by breaking down the front door.

They found Aunt Della lying in the hallway, on the floor next to the bathroom. She'd been there since Thursday evening and was only wearing part of the outfit we had discussed she should wear to the banquet. Never making it to the banquet, she lay in her waste on the floor for more than three days.

I was told that, at first, the police thought she was dead because she wasn't moving. She was, in fact, still breathing, though very near death. Paramedics were immediately called. Arriving within minutes, they, upon examining Aunt Della, detected a weak pulse and immediately transported her to a nearby hospital.

Stunned, I was speechless as the person on the other end of the phone told me what had happened. Aunt Della's neighbors had gone through her purse and wallet to find my phone number, aware that we were communicating again. Thankfully, both Chris and I were at home when the call came, and we hurried to the hospital to be with her. So many thoughts ran across my mind as we drove across town to the hospital. We were her only next of kin.

Walking at a fast pace, Chris and I made our way to the Intensive Care Unit, where she was being cared for. As soon as we entered the room, Aunt Della's eyes lit up. We rushed over to her bedside. We talked to her as each of us leaned over and gave her a kiss on the forehead. The stroke had left her unable to talk. The only thing she could still do was move her left arm and smile a little.

Chris and I took and held onto her hand as she lifted it up to us. Tears began to well up in her eyes at the sight of us, and I assured her that we would be there for her and that everything would be alright.

Seeing her condition, I wasn't sure how things would turn out, but I did my best to encourage her not to give up. What an overwhelming moment it was.

We really didn't know what to say, so we just kind of stroked her hand as we stood at her bedside. How very sorry we felt for her, but we were still hoping and praying that with extensive rehabilitation, she'd be able to regain some, if not most, of the faculties and abilities she'd lost. We could only hope because the stroke had, for now, left her bedridden.

Visiting hours were over, and we had to leave for the evening, but we reassured Aunt Della that we'd be back the next day. With her only functioning arm and hand, she gripped my hand even tighter as we were beginning to leave. She didn't want us to leave.

Honestly, I probably should have stayed, but I had to go to work the next day. I planned to at least inform my supervisor the next day about what was going on and then make plans to take time off to be with Aunt Della.

"We'll be back tomorrow," we told her, kissing her again on the forehead just before leaving.

Though the stroke left Aunt Della unable to talk, we could still see her countenance fall. I believe she was afraid. Who wouldn't be after suffering a stroke and not knowing what the future would hold?

Before leaving the hospital, we did see and talk to her doctor, who gave us a grim report about Aunt Della's condition. Very candidly, he let us know that the prognosis wasn't good at all because the stroke, being as extensive as it was, did considerable brain damage and would cause Aunt Della to more than likely be bedridden for the remainder of her life.

Trying to process what the doctor was saying, we were crushed and didn't know what questions to ask. We needed time to process it all.

In the course of just a few days, things had dramatically changed since our last conversation. Despite what we'd been through with her, our hearts really ached for Aunt Della. Feeling so much pity for her, I hated to see her like that. I guess that was evidence that we had forgiven her because it hurt to see her suffer.

After speaking with her doctor and being asked legal questions regarding who would be responsible for making decisions on her behalf, it was suggested by the doctor that we pursue a Power of Attorney on her behalf.

Chris and I decided that I would do that. Since I was the oldest, I would carry the brunt of the responsibility, though I knew I could depend on Chris whenever I needed to.

The words of my grandmother resonated in my mind once again, "God sure does work in mysterious ways."

Just to think about all we'd been through with Aunt Della and to now experience such a turn of events was mind-boggling.

While driving home, Chris and I talked about what our next step would be. We agreed that the next day, I would call Aunt Doris and get Attorney Dansby's number. She was the same attorney who helped me get guardianship over Chris.

Early the next morning, before I could even make that phone call to Aunt Doris and before I could get back up to the hospital to see Aunt Della, the hospital called again. During the night, Aunt Della had suffered *another* massive stroke, and she was now on life support.

"Oh my God!" I said to the doctor, feeling my heartbeat so rapidly as I began to cry.

The doctor offered his sympathy and his medical opinion about her condition, which had gone from 'not good' to 'hopeless' in less than a day.

Hurrying again to the hospital, I tried to prepare myself to see her in an even worse condition, and as I walked into her room, my heart sank seeing her now hooked up to all kinds of tubes, hoses, and machines. She couldn't breathe on her own, and the sight of her stomach and chest rising and falling in response to the oxygen being pumped into her body was almost too much for me. It just didn't seem real. She couldn't do anything anymore, not even raise her arm or hand. Aunt Della lay there like a vegetable, and the only thing she was still able to do was open and close her eyes.

Her doctors said she wouldn't be able to survive without life support, that she was essentially a vegetable, brain dead, and that I, now the person responsible for her, needed to seriously consider removing her from life support.

"No! I don't want to be in charge of making that decision!" I screamed on the inside to myself.

Her deteriorating condition was already a huge blow to us, but now having to decide to remove her from the system that was sustaining her life was such a heavyweight. The anxiety and overwhelming stress I felt was indescribable. To think, we'd just begun getting much closer, and then this happens. I was as baffled as I was scared.

Though my faith was now far greater than it ever had been, I didn't feel anywhere near strong enough to make such a tough decision. Aunt Della's life was in my hands, and I absolutely did not want it to be! Why had I been put in the position of deciding whether my aunt would live or die?

Following the prayer and fast, I drew closer to God and learned to pray to Him and believe with faith that He heard me. With a lot of faith and emotions, I prayed to God, explaining to Him how big this situation was for me, and I asked Him to help me make all the right decisions on behalf of Aunt Della. I trusted that He knew more than me and knew exactly what I was facing. I just needed His guidance because it all was just so overwhelming.

He let me know that the first order of business was for me to take care of the legal matter of becoming Aunt Della's Power of Attorney, which I did with Aunt Doris' assistance.

Secondly, I met and talked with all of Aunt Della's doctors and specialists about her condition to better understand what was going on. Because I was her Power of Attorney, the doctors fully disclosed her condition to me. Writing down questions to ask, I asked my questions one by one, not moving on to the next one until I was satisfied with the doctors' responses and answers.

Before coming to Christ, I endured through some tough times and hadn't realized how God was still present. Now, I was facing another tough situation, but this time, I knew for sure that God was with me. What a difference that made in how I approached and dealt with this situation!

For the next week, I called and went each day to the hospital to check on Aunt Della. Chris also checked on her.

The report was always the same, 'There has been no change in her condition.'

After a few days, the doctors really began putting pressure on me to remove Aunt Della from life support. To move me to act, I was asked, "Would your aunt want to live this way?"

The pressure was mounting with each passing day.

I prayed and cried, realizing that taking Aunt Della off life support was probably inevitable. It was not a question of 'if' but 'when.' If she didn't show some sign of improvement soon, I'd have no other choice. Even the slightest improvement would have been enough for me to refuse to take her off life support.

Though I was grown, I didn't feel grown enough or that I had the authority to make that decision. The bottom line is I didn't want to make that call. That was God's call, not mine. I wrestled with the issue, doing my best, towards the end of the next week, to avoid her doctors when I went to see her. So much pressure was being applied, and I was trying to buy time, hoping something would happen so that I wouldn't have to make the decision.

My prayer literally was, as I pleaded with Him, "Lord, if she is going to pass, please just take her before she's taken off of life support."

Well, that didn't happen, and it was still in my hands to make the decision.

I told God, "Lord, I can't do this."

God, in His perfect way, reassured me that I could and that everything would be alright. Finally, after much agonizing, I decided that taking Aunt Della off life support was the right and the best thing to do, given the circumstances. Chris and I talked about it, and we agreed.

As I came to grips with what was about to take place, a calming sense of peace came over me, and I said to God, "Lord, this is in your hands."

I remembered *Isaiah 26:3,* which says, 'He'll keep his mind in perfect peace whose mind is stayed on Him.'

After a couple of more days passed, I went to the hospital to talk with Aunt Della's doctors to let them know my decision. The doctors, of course, were pleased that I'd decided to remove her from life support to allow her to die "in peace," in their words.

Initially, I thought they seemed to be in too much of a hurry to disconnect her from the machines, but then I thought about the fact that they were professionals and they were giving me the best recommendation possible based on *what they knew.* My conscience was clear since I'd prayed and received what I believed to be an answer from the Lord.

Trying to prepare ourselves for burying Aunt Della once she'd passed, Chris and I visited a couple of funeral homes to get an idea of how much we'd need for burial expenses. Prior to going to the funeral home, I looked for insurance policies Aunt Della might have had, only to discover that she'd lost them due to non-payment of the premiums.

Aunt Della had no insurance policy and no money in the bank, so the burden of burying her fell on us. Having to cover all her funeral expenses, as well as purchase a burial plot for her, Chris and I began discussing what we'd need to do to get the money together. Although it was a difficult time, it was perfect timing because Chris and I had the money on hand to bury her.

We learned from the past and were determined not to allow anything, including money, to get in the way of our relationship. The greed for money had contributed to our family being torn apart, and Chris and I would not allow money to come in between us.

Because both he and I owned our family home on the north side of town, and because I wanted to get my own home and not return to leasing another apartment, Chris agreed to buy out my portion of the house. Obtaining a loan, he paid me the amount we both agreed to.

Prior to Aunt Della getting sick, in fact, within just a few days, I'd found a house that I thought was perfect for me. The house was very spacious and had the most beautiful *purple flowers* growing in the front yard. The purple flowers were the final thing that made me want to sign on the dotted line. Purple has always been my favorite color.

After checking the house out, I thought, 'How wonderful it would be to live here.'

Ready to move forward by putting down earnest money and proceeding with purchasing the property, I'd asked my Uncle Earnest, Aunt Doris' husband, to go with me and check it out one more time to make sure I was getting a good deal. Thankfully, my Uncle Earnest did a little more investigating than I had, and upon asking questions, he discovered that the home had been flooded and had possible mold damage! Uncle Earnest saved me a lot of heartache, time, *and* money!

Though I was disappointed, it turned out to be a good thing that the deal fell through because now I had money to bury Aunt Della.

God's perfect timing again? Yes indeed!

After learning about Aunt Della and the attention we'd now have to give her, I immediately put my home-buying plans on hold. Chris also had funds available from the loan he'd taken out to pay me, and we agreed to equally share the cost of burying Aunt Della. Of course, that meant I wouldn't be able to buy a home just yet, but I was just glad that with all the issues we were facing, money wouldn't be one of them.

Our next move involved deciding on a funeral home to handle all the arrangements. Chris and I went together and met with the funeral director and made tentative plans for Aunt Della's services.

Aunt Della hadn't yet passed, but basing our actions on the doctors' prognosis for 'no recovery,' we wanted to be ready for whenever she passed on.

The funeral home director was so gracious and helpful and really encouraged us because we were still young, in our early 30s, and had to be responsible for burying someone close to us. That director had no idea what Chris and I had already been through, including with Aunt Della. He was correct, however, in that this was such a heart-wrenching task to have to do.

We didn't have to personally handle burying our grandparents or parents because someone else took the lead.

The day Aunt Della was scheduled to be removed from the ventilator, I went up to the hospital that morning to sign the final papers, crying from the parking lot all the way up to her hospital floor. Chris wasn't with me, and I really didn't want him there. It was too much for me, and I knew it would be too much for him, so I didn't press the issue with him. We agreed that I would go alone, and I was okay with that.

After signing the last of the consent forms, I entered the room to say 'Goodbye' to Aunt Della. It had been some years since we'd lost someone close to us.

Walking over to Aunt Della lying in her hospital bed, I noticed that her eyes were closed, and I wasn't sure if she had been aware of anything going on since the second stroke. She didn't open her eyes. After reaching down to kiss her on the cheek, I completely broke down and started sobbing. I told her that we loved her, as I cried, and said, "You rest now, Aunt Della. God has you".

The doctors and technicians were standing near, just outside the door, remaining there to give me a moment of privacy with Aunt Della. The doctor informed me that it would only take a few minutes at the most for her to stop breathing.

As they began unhooking the machines and tubes, Aunt Della actually began to fight, moving her upper torso, though not her arms or hands. To me, that was shocking because I didn't think she could move any part of her body!

Was that spontaneous movement? I thought she was completely brain-dead.

Initially thinking that I would be able to stay in the room as they disconnected the machine, I was overcome with emotion and found myself running out of the room while crying.

'What was that?' I continued to think to myself, 'Was that supposed to happen when patients are removed from life support?'

I was so grieved because I didn't want my aunt to die, but I had been convinced by the doctors that she was no longer living, just merely existing with the help of machines.

As I exited the door very distraught, the doctor placed his hand on my shoulder and told me that she wouldn't suffer long. Reassuring me that I had done the right thing, he said that within an hour, or even less, she would pass, and the hospital would then notify me so that I could make the necessary arrangements to have her body picked up.

Unable to rest, I went from one thing to another at home, trying to get my mind off what had happened. There were things that still needed to be taken care of in preparation for her service.

What should the program say?

Who should I contact to sing at the service?

What would be the best day to have the service?

I needed to contact Aunt Della's pastor and church and proceed from there in finalizing the plans.

Chris and I were both trying to come to grips with Aunt Della's impending death.

Several hours passed, and I hadn't heard from the hospital, so I called to see what the next step would be. One of the doctors spoke with me over the phone and informed me that Aunt Della hadn't passed yet.

"Really?" I responded, very surprised and somewhat relieved.

The doctor, detecting that in my voice, told me that *for sure,* if she didn't pass during the night, she'd pass sometime the next day. He said sometimes patients live a little longer than they might have originally been expected to, but not too much longer.

To their surprise, Aunt Della began breathing on her own, but given the extensive damage she suffered from the stroke, they still expected her to die within the day as her body shut down.

Well, that caused a small change of plans.

Though the doctor didn't seem too thrown off by Aunt Della's persistence to live, I was completely floored! To go from being declared 'brain dead,' 'a vegetable,' and 'only able to live on a ventilator' to being able to breathe on her own, Aunt Della proved to be stronger than we all thought!

Hanging up with the doctor, I told Chris that Aunt Della was still living but that the doctor said she'd be gone by tomorrow sometime. We called the funeral home and put them on standby notice.

The next day, I still hadn't heard from the hospital, so again, I called. Aunt Della was still hanging on! In fact, not only did she not die the following day, but she also continued to live the day after that, and the day after that, and the day after that, confounding the doctors!

I was shocked but ecstatic! Everyone else was shocked too, but none more than her doctors! The fact that Aunt Della was still living was nothing short of a miracle!

I was happy because, to me, that meant that I *hadn't* caused her death! She didn't die right away despite being taken off life support! What a load off my conscience that was! I thanked God over and over and over again because He gave her the ability to breathe on her own! God had heard and *answered* my prayers!

Through it all, I found out for myself how God really is in control and how He, *not man,* will always have the last say!

Of course, Aunt Della's immediate death *wouldn't have signaled in any way* that God wasn't still in control, but the fact that she was still alive really got all our attention! I continued to visit her in the days that followed, and she was still with us! Each time I walked into the room, she'd open her eyes. Unable to talk or move, however, I'm sure Aunt Della knew that I was there.

I began to, each time I visited her, read a few bible verses and pray with her. Unsure if she could hear me, in my spirit, I believed that she could. I'd heard it said that *when facing death, the hearing is usually the last sense to go.*

The fact that our aunt was still alive continued to perplex the professionals, and they couldn't explain why she hadn't died. It was kind of funny to me that by day four, the doctors weren't willing to accept what I already knew, and that was that God was in control and my aunt was allowed to *still* be here for a reason. The Lord obviously still had something to accomplish in her life.

I certainly understand that God gives us professionals like doctors and specialists to help us to the best of their ability with our health needs and concerns, but the only One who knows with certainty when someone's time on this earth will be up is God.

That week, I saw the sovereignty of God at work as Aunt Della continued to defy even the doctor's report and expectations and live on.

Now that Aunt Della had outlived the doctors' expectations, after a week, the pressure was on me again, but this time to move Aunt Della to a nursing home. Obliging their requests because I was really just sick of them hounding me, and because I knew they wouldn't allow my aunt to stay there in the hospital much longer, I began the search for a nursing facility that could take care of Aunt Della the way she needed to be tended to.

At that point, none of us knew how long she'd continue to live, but it was certain that she'd be around longer than first projected, so I needed to find a place that could provide long-term care for her. After checking out several nursing homes, I soon realized what a chore it was just to find a decent one.

On more than a few occasions, I walked out of a facility as quickly as I'd walked into it because of the smell of urine. There was no way we could put her in such a place.

There were other nursing homes that were very nice, but unfortunately, they were out of the price range Aunt Della's disability income would cover.

Chris was helping with the search and investigated facilities closer to Aunt Della's home, to no avail. Finally, after a few more searches, I found a place on the far north side of town that I was not only pleased with but one that would be covered by Aunt Della's benefits. After looking for almost a week straight, I breathed a sigh of relief as everything with the facility checked out. It was in a good area, easily accessible from the highway, and it was affordable. All of those were check marks to us.

We made all the necessary arrangements to have Aunt Della transferred by ambulance to the nursing home.

This was the first time I'd dealt with a nursing facility, and I learned early on that the more you go to see a loved one in a nursing home, the better they are cared for because, unfortunately, there always seems to be a shortage of workers in such facilities.

Because I worked in the mornings, I would only be able to go see Aunt Della in the evenings after work. Upon visiting her for the first time, which was two days after we'd transferred her to the nursing home, I noticed an odor coming from her, signaling that she hadn't had a bath or even a sponge off since the previous day. That was completely unacceptable.

Aunt Della couldn't speak for herself, so it was my and Chris' job as her family to make sure she was taken care of properly. She was completely bedridden, but the home had a special transportation chair that was to be used to take her to the shower. The chair would support her weight while she was being cleaned off. That's what I was told would happen, but it obviously hadn't happened because Aunt Della smelled very bad.

After I got the attendant and complained about my aunt's condition, Aunt Della was immediately scheduled to be taken to the shower area and cleaned.

I thought, 'How pitiful that I had to bring something like that to their attention, something that should have been taken care of as part of her daily care.'

My visits of only three times a week, or every other day, increased to five times a week or more, as my schedule permitted. It was so sad that Aunt Della was in the condition she was in, but at least we could do whatever we could to keep her comfortable. One thing was for sure: the staff would soon learn that they'd be seeing a lot of us, so they'd better do the right thing by Aunt Della.

Thankfully, things did improve after we initially brought some of the issues to their attention.

Whenever I couldn't make it to the nursing home for whatever reason, Chris would either drop by or call, so we had it covered.

In the beginning, an adrenaline rush seemed to keep me on my feet and help me adapt to my new schedule, and I was just happy Aunt Della was still with us.

Each time I walked through her door, my heart sank, though, seeing her lying in the bed, motionless and completely dependent on others for her every need. Like the deaths of George, Daddy, and Grandmother, Aunt Della's grave condition was so unexpected and seemed so surreal.

The one thing that put my heart at ease a little was that just about every time Chris or I walked through the door, Aunt Della would open her eyes if they'd been closed. That's why I knew in my spirit she was aware of our presence. She seemed to look forward to our visits.

After kissing her on the forehead or cheek, I'd take my seat in the chair at her bedside. Always starting our visit off with a small prayer,

I would take her hand and hold it tightly while I prayed. She couldn't respond, but her eyes were wide open, and I knew she knew I was there. Our aunt, at one time, sang in the Gospel Choir at her church and loved Gospel music, so I would bring along her gospel cassettes and play them softly.

Sitting there next to her, I'd read the bible aloud and then turn the cassette on and let it play until it was time for me to leave.

Thinking about how the fast and prayer prepared me to be able to minister to my aunt in that way, as bad as our situation was, I stood in awe of God because I knew He already knew this was going to happen. It hadn't taken Him by surprise.

The plan and move of God continued to be so evident. The way God brought us closer together during those times further demonstrated His Sovereignty. Aunt Della needed us, and we were there for her. He also continued to give Chris and me strength during the days and weeks that followed.

Wearing on us physically and emotionally, the frequent trips to the facility were starting to take a toll, but we were determined to stick it out. Aunt Della had no one else but us.

On occasion, a church member would drop by, and it would be such a wonderful boost of encouragement for us and, I'm sure, for Aunt Della as well.

JUNE 1999.

Each time I'd arrive at the nursing home, I'd talk with one of the staffers to see what kind of day Aunt Della was having, making sure things were okay with her. After that, we'd move along as usual with prayer, bible reading, and music. Towards the end of each visit, I'd just sit there with her and hold her hand. I wanted her to know that we meant what we said when we told her that we were there for her.

Though praise came, we weren't seeking any kind of applause from anyone regarding how we took care of Aunt Della. We did what we did because it was simply the right thing to do. One thing Daddy and Grandmother especially taught us was to 'Treat people the way we wanted to be treated.' What I was doing was from the heart, a heart that had been healed by God.

I thought about how awesome it was that God tugged at my heart when He did, and I responded. My entire attitude towards our aunt had changed. Grateful for a relationship with Christ, I'm convinced that doing the right thing, even when others do the wrong thing, will, in the end, always work out in our favor. That huge step, the best thing I've ever done in life, more than prepared me for this time with my aunt.

After being in the nursing home for a couple of weeks, Aunt Della's condition remained unchanged. She was neither getting any better nor getting any worse. Though she was in a miserable state, nearly three weeks had passed, and she was yet holding on.

Around week four, her condition, however, did begin to deteriorate, with the development of bed sores. I understood that her immobility, unfortunately, made her susceptible to getting them, but it was still hard to accept the fact that she now had these unsightly, no doubt painful, open wounds on her backside.

Aunt Della couldn't communicate in any way how she was feeling. She was only able to somewhat control the opening and closing of her eyes, but not enough to respond to questions.

I wondered why she wouldn't just let go and be with the Lord. Still, I remembered and understood that it wasn't up to her as to when she'd pass; that time had already been appointed by God. The entire situation was in the Lord's hands. She and we would have to wait on Him.

Aunt Della had been in the nursing home for about a month when I received word that Daniel's grandfather had passed. I made time to attend the services. Even though I was no longer involved with Daniel, I did continue to stay in contact with his family. Daniel's grandmother, especially, asked me to keep coming by to see her and calling her, and I knew she was sincere because she would still call me and stay in touch with me.

After the funeral, I followed the motorcade to the cemetery, which happened to be near Aunt Della's nursing home.

Generally, I went to see Aunt Della after I got off work. However, because I'd taken the day off to attend the funeral, I had an overwhelming urge to see her that afternoon, though Chris was supposed to go in my place that evening.

When I arrived and spoke with a staff nurse, she told me that Aunt Della seemed to be taking a turn for the worse. Leading me to the room, the nurse walked in first. Noticing Aunt Della opening her eyes, the nurse said that was the first time that day she'd noticed my aunt's eyes opened. She had them closed all the other times others walked in. I guess she heard my voice, and so she opened them for me. I knew she noticed when I walked into the room.

Her kidneys were failing, and the nurse showed me her very dark urine collected in a bag alongside her bed. I thanked the nurse for her attention, and then she left us alone.

We would have no music today. I always kept her cassettes together in a case. As soon as I would get home after visiting Aunt Della, I would place it back in the case with the others. Because my early visit was unplanned, I hadn't brought a cassette with me. As usual, I kissed Aunt Della and then sat next to her, prayed, and then began reading the bible to her for a few minutes.

This visit was not one of our usual visits. Of course, the music was missing, but there was *something* else that just felt different. After reading the bible, I closed it and just held her hand. What happened next was nothing short of God's Amazing Grace as He *orchestrated* the moment.

Standing up and looking into my aunt's eyes, which by now had turned pale yellow because her body was indeed shutting down, I grabbed her hand, and being prompted by the Spirit of God, I began talking to Aunt Della, saying, "Aunt Della, I just want you to know that we forgive you for everything that you did to us, *everything* that happened. And I pray that you forgive us for anything we did. We love you. I want you to know that."

Choking back the tears, I bowed my head as my tears began to flow. Without a doubt, I knew God had placed those words in my heart to say to my aunt. Aunt Della needed to hear that. She knew she had done some awful things to us, and she had sought forgiveness dating almost ten years back but had never actually come out and said the words, "I'm sorry."

I believe in my heart that she was holding out for forgiveness. Our aunt needed peace. Forgiveness can *bring* peace to the giver and the recipient. My brother and I hadn't, to our knowledge, done anything to Aunt Della, but *if* she felt that we had, I *wanted* her forgiveness as well. Expressing *for her* what she couldn't say for herself, I believe at that moment, Aunt Della was set free, free to die in peace.

Forgiveness may not be something we believe a person deserves, but it is absolutely something every one of us will stand in need of at some point because no one is perfect, and we all will fall.

No longer hindered by human emotion, I was able to forgive Aunt Della as an act of obedience to God, and upon giving it, I felt the peace of God, too. I prayed again before I left, and unlike the other times when I visited my aunt, this time, she closed her eyes before I left. In my spirit, I knew that this would be the last time I would see her alive.

Walking out of the door, I looked back at Aunt Della. She still had her eyes closed.

Early the next morning, around 1:00 a.m., I received a call from the nursing home. Aunt Della had passed.

Weeping, I was sad that Aunt Della was gone, but I was also relieved for her because she was no longer suffering. For almost five weeks, she'd been bedridden, likely in a lot of pain, but unable to tell us since the second stroke left her only able to open and close her eyes. That last day with her let me know that she could *still* hear and understand. Aunt Della was free and finally at rest with the Lord. I had no doubt about that.

I discovered early in life that one of the hardest things to do sometimes is to forgive someone who has caused us hurt and pain, especially when it's emotional pain and especially when it's someone close to us. Having been healed of the hurt that strife and contention in relationships can bring, I also understand that forgiveness is one of the most essential and gracious gifts we can give to not only free others but also ourselves.

We worked with the funeral director, Aunt Della's Pastor and the church staff to arrange a very nice funeral service for her. Because we'd already been preparing for this day, the only thing that we needed to do was finalize the plans.

Aunt Della had always been known as a 'dresser,' so I chose a very nice baby blue outfit for her. Looking for a matching hat to go along with her ensemble, I searched resale shops an entire day before finally finding a beautiful light blue, perfectly adorned hat to go with her suit. She looked so lovely, and the service was beautiful.

The Pastor preached, and several people sang. A few others made remarks as quite a number of people came to pay their respects.

Chris and I were beyond pleased with the way everything turned out. Securing a plot at a nice cemetery not far from her house, we laid Aunt Della's body to rest.

Her death seemed to, in more than one way, close a major chapter in our lives. The life that I'd known seemed long gone now.

A new season, a new beginning, was dawning, and I was very happy about being able to look forward to change—good change. God brought us back together, just in time, before He took her home.

There's no way to fully explain how God did what He did, but I sum it up by saying He's *'SUPERNATURAL,'* and so *'EXTRAORDINARY.'*

With our aunt now buried, Chris and I next needed to settle the issue regarding what to do with her house. Because we were her only heirs, her home, along with her two dogs, Alphie and Bullet, and her cat, Blessing, now belonged to us.

I thought to myself, 'Now this is really *something*. We just never know how life is going to turn out.'

Even more interesting was what one of Aunt Della's church members told me. She said that Aunt Della initially had planned to leave her house to her church in the event something happened to her, but as we began to communicate and draw closer again, she *changed* her mind.

Nobody But God.

Coming to a quick agreement, we decided that I would take ownership of the house and buy Chris' portion out, just as we had done earlier with our family home. There was no fighting, no bickering.

Though I'd spent a large portion of my down payment money for my house on Aunt Della's funeral, God made it all right and provided me with a home. Things didn't happen the way I thought they would, but I was not disappointed in the least. My goal was to purchase a home for myself, and Aunt Della's home was, with a few repairs and changes, the right home for me.

Because the house was so unbelievably cluttered, it took more than a few days to clean it up and get it in decent living condition. It was so overwhelming to look at the mounds and mounds of items Aunt Della had collected over the years. Where in the world do we begin?

The yard also required some 'TLC.' We'd done our best while Aunt Della was in the hospital and nursing home to cut the grass but hadn't touched the bushes and the hedges, which had begun to wildly overgrow. Aunt Della always liked trimming her own bushes and hedges, so it was just habit for us not to touch them, but now they were badly in need of cutting. I would have to do the hedges myself since it was now my house.

Deciding not to stress myself out, I chose to, before tackling the inside of the house, get the yard together first and then focus all my energy on the inside. Yard work had always been therapeutic for me, and looking at all the work waiting for me on the inside did cause considerable anxiety.

Returning on the weekend, I started early in the morning, gathering everything together I needed to manicure the front and back yards. Equipped with my lawn mower, rakes, hedge clippers, shovel, driveway edger, garden gloves, and garbage bags, I was ready for the task at hand!

Working my way around the backyard, I cut and trimmed and then moved to the front yard. Going from one bush or hedge to another, I continued to carefully clip and trim. My aunt had plants and bushes everywhere! She did have a green thumb, though, having well-maintained her plants.

I could cut grass, but the more precision work required more attention to detail and took some time for me to accomplish. After spending a few hours in the yard, I was getting tired. Being close to finishing, I pushed myself to complete the last of the trimming. There was one bush left. It, unlike the other bushes, was located more within the perimeter of the yard rather than on the outer boundary of the front yard.

Approaching the final bush in the yard, I raised and opened the clippers, ready to start trimming, when I noticed something that caused me to stop immediately. The bush had the most beautiful 'purple' buds coming out of it! I couldn't believe it!

Some might say that it's just a *coincidence* that I loved purple flowers, and the house I almost purchased had purple flowers in the yard, and now, here in the yard of my new 'home,' there are purple flowers blooming.

Luck, coincidence, or *even* happenstance? *Absolutely not*; it was ALL God!

I had experienced so much instability and so many trials, having to uproot from here and go there, but now I was finally home, and to me, my Heavenly Father was saying, through the blooming of those purple flowers, "*This is your new beginning.*"

I thought about how Daddy had built us a playhouse that I now believe he did to give us a different space, in a playhouse, to build new memories as kids. Now, as a grown woman, my Abba had given me a new space of my own to make new memories. I was home.

Emotionally and spiritually healthy, after so many trials, I was *finally* at peace, right where I was supposed to be, realizing God had not for one moment forgotten about me or my family. He had not forsaken us.

In exchange for my ashes left from sorrow, anguish, and pain, God has given me 'His beauty'. I was finally happy, finally free, and ready for everything else God had waiting for me.

God Bless you.

A LIFE WORTH LIVING

When life changed for my family and me, it felt like the end, and in some ways, it was. It was the end of the life we knew, but God's Plan was still in effect.

As life continued to change for me and the crutches that I'd leaned on were removed, the only thing left was God. It took me some time to understand that He was still there, holding me up, keeping me.

Realizing, acknowledging, and accepting that became the hallmark of my faith walk. That's why I believe my story is worth telling.

For me, paramount to overcoming life's challenges is believing and trusting in a power higher than myself. That is, believing and trusting in Almighty God!

To those desperate or seeking a ray of hope in a bleak situation, I submit to you to have the kind of faith that extends beyond simply trusting in yourself and your own capabilities. Regardless of how difficult things in life may become, life is still worth living!

We owe it to ourselves to discover the purpose for which we were created. From that revelation, our mindset can be renewed to see how even the challenges of life work toward the fulfillment of our God-given purposes.

God knows the challenges and the issues we'll face, even the bad decisions we'll make, and yet we can be encouraged by the Word of the Lord, which says, 'For I know the plans I have for you,' declares the Lord, 'plans to prosper you and not to harm you, plans to give you hope and a future.' Jeremiah 29:11 (NIV).

His Plan for our life will help us move beyond the past, live on purpose in the here and now, and have great expectations for the future!

We can experience the abundance of God's Plan when we are walking with Him.

Trusting Him with our lives, we'll experience His Goodness, His Faithfulness, and the Assurance of His Word in reaping every blessing He has ordained for us!

It is then, especially, when we can see that life is worth living!

I arrived at a point in my life when I felt so empty, as though I had nothing left worth living for, striving for, but in pursuit of a better life, I found what I needed—God.

Looking back over my life, I can see the countless ways He was still there with Protection, Patience, Peace, Love, Perfect Timing, Favor, Counsel, Guidance, Provision, Comfort, Encouragement, Support, Purpose for each day, and Strength for my journey! With all of those blessings, He's still here today, and not just for me, but for every person who will seek Him.

Nothing happens without God's Knowledge or Permission.

Romans 8:28 says, 'God will cause ALL THINGS to work together for good for those who love Him and who are called according to His Purposes!'

Thank God, I know that includes me! I am who I am today because I finally learned to TRUST HIS PLAN!

ACKNOWLEDGMENTS

Honoring My Lord, My Redeemer, and My Keeper-
My earnest heart desire is to please You and satisfy Your Will for my life. Your Grace and Mercy have brought me through times deemed hopeless by others, deemed hopeless even by me. I am grateful for the vision to write this book for Your glory.

Thank You for the wisdom, revelation, patience, healing, and strength to press forward in bringing this vision to fruition!

I pray that 'No Ordinary Sunday' will cause the eyes of men and women to open to the reality of Your Presence, the depth of Your Love, the magnitude of Your Power and Provision, and the availability of Your Grace and Mercy, which is more than sufficient to carry anyone through even the most trying situations and seasons.

To my Beautiful Daughters-
This vision could not have become a reality without you all!! For the unconditional love, unending encouragement, sweet joy, and pure strength you continue to give me, thank you! My mother, your grandmother, had no idea the good God had in store for me, which included beautiful, blessed babies! I'm so proud of each of you and am so very grateful that God blessed me to be your mother!

To my brother -

I just can't imagine life without you! We both were spared, and I'm so grateful to God for you! God knew we needed each other! Thank you for the love, support, and encouragement! I love you more than you'll ever know!

To my village-

Bridgette, Doris and Earnest Collins, The Jacksons (MamaJ and Mo), Gail and Anthony Hawkins, Cheryl Lee and family, Helen Jones, Karla McKissack-Richardson, The Maloneys, my immediate and extended family, and so many awesome men and women of God who listened, prayed, encouraged me and kept me grounded, ministered to me, and who've, knowingly and unknowingly, been an invaluable support to me in so many ways, I say to all of you: Thank you!

I want to also extend my sincere thanks and appreciation to
Pastor Keith Strahan, First Lady Theresa Strahan, and the entire Northeast Community Church Family-
It was at your Church that I received confirmation to move forward with this book. This has been such a phenomenal journey, and I'm grateful for all of the love, support, encouragement, and certainly prayer you've given. Thank you for providing me with a platform from which to minister. You've played an important role in my spiritual growth and my ministry, and I celebrate the finished work of this book with you! God bless you tremendously for the richness you've deposited in my life.

I love you, my Brothers and Sisters in Christ!

Also, a special thank you to *the teachers/staff of Michael E. DeBakey High School for Health Professions and the class of '85* for the love and support during one of the toughest seasons of my life.

Wherever you may be, God bless you!

And finally, last but certainly not least, to every family member, neighbor, pastor, minister, church member, teacher/professor, friend, coworker, supervisor, neighbor, and even stranger, not mentioned by name, who has deposited into and blessed my life through a heartfelt, encouraging word, a kind deed, or some other demonstration of the love of Christ, to you all I say, "Thank you, and God bless you! God knows who you are!"